Seventh Edition

Author: Ray Holder

TABLE OF CONTENTS

CONTRACTORS STATE LICENSE BOARD
9821 Business Park Drive, Sacramento, CA 95827
Mailing Address: P.O. Box 26000, Sacramento, CA 95826
800.321.CSLB (2752) | www.cslb.ca.gov | CheckTheLicenseFirst.com

IMPORTANT NOTICE REGARDING CONVICTIONS PLEASE READ CAREFULLY

Failure to accurately report a conviction (except as explained below) may result in an application being denied. In this notice and on the application, the term "conviction" includes pleading guilty or nolo contendere ("no contest") or being convicted by a court of any misdemeanor or felony in this state or elsewhere.

As part of the Contractors State License Board (CSLB) application process and as required by law, you must be fingerprinted if you have not been fingerprinted by CSLB before or if your previous fingerprint record was purged by CSLB due to a voided application; disassociated, revoked, or cancelled license or registration; or for some other reason. After an application is accepted by CSLB as complete (also known as "posted"), the applicant will be sent instructions on the process for obtaining and submitting fingerprints, usually via live scan electronic transmission.

Your fingerprints will be compared to the records of the California Department of Justice and the Federal Bureau of Investigation. **If you have ever been convicted of a crime, your criminal record information will be reported to CSLB.** This includes DUIs and other Vehicle Code violations resulting in a conviction. Even if you pled "no contest," had the conviction set aside, or judgment deferred pursuant to Penal Code sections 1000 or 1203.4 (commonly understood as "expunged"), the past conviction will still be reported to CSLB and must be disclosed on the application. However, some convictions or charges **should NOT be disclosed**, including the following:

- Convictions that were adjudicated in the juvenile court;
- Convictions under California Health and Safety Code sections 11357 (b), (c), (d), or (e) or section 11360 (b) that are two years old or older; and
- Charges that were dismissed as the result of successful completion of a deferred entry of judgment program (diversion program) under California Penal Code section 1000.3.

If you have ever been convicted of a crime (except in the three circumstances outlined above), you **should** answer "Yes" to the criminal conviction question on the application and provide a detailed explanation of the circumstances resulting in your conviction. To help ensure that you provide the required information, you should complete and submit the Disclosure Statement Regarding Criminal Plea/Conviction form that is available on CSLB's website on the Forms and Applications page.

Applicants with criminal convictions are not automatically denied licensure – each application is reviewed individually based on the applicable sections of law. When reviewing criminal convictions, CSLB considers factors such as the nature and severity of the crimes, the amount of time that has passed since the convictions, and any evidence of rehabilitation submitted by the applicant.

For rehabilitation evaluation, pursuant to Title 16, California Code of Regulations section 869, CSLB is generally looking for **three (3) years** to have passed after a misdemeanor conviction and **seven**

(7) years to have passed after a felony conviction, without further violations of law. These timeframes are calculated from the applicant's date of release from incarceration or from the end of probation if no time was served and are subject to reduction or extension based on several factors, including the nature of the applicant's conviction history as a whole. In addition, any type of conviction could be considered substantially related to the qualifications or duties of a contractor when evaluated in the context of the applicant's entire conviction record.

Failure to accurately report any and all disclosable convictions may be grounds for denial of your application. If your application is denied, you will be notified of the earliest date when you may re-apply, which will vary based upon the facts of each case, from one (1) to five (5) years from the effective date of the denial. (*Business and Professions Code sections 486 and 7073*)

IMPORTANT NOTICE

Dear Applicant:

Enclosed is the application you requested from the Contractors State License Board (CSLB).

Please be aware that nearly half of all applications submitted to CSLB are inaccurate or incomplete and must be returned to the applicant for correction or completion!

Please complete your application in its entirety to help ensure that your application is accepted for processing by CSLB.

After an application has been accepted by CSLB as complete (also known as "posted"), the applicant will be sent instructions on the process for obtaining and submitting fingerprints, as required by law. (*Business and Professions Code sections 144 and 7069*)

An incomplete application can needlessly delay your license. Delays can last several weeks or even months and possibly result in the application being deemed abandoned and becoming void and the application fee being forfeited. (*Business and Professions Code sections 7074 and 7138 and Title 16, California Code of Regulations section 813*)

Spending a few extra minutes now may save you weeks or months later!

Before you submit your application, follow these simple directions.

- **Sign the form.**
- **Fill out all applicable information.**

- **Make sure you submit Certification of Work Experience forms that have been filled out completely, ensuring that you have provided four (4) years of applicable experience in the classification for which you are applying.**

Carefully read the General Information and Instructions that immediately precede the application package and follow the specific instructions that are contained throughout the application to help ensure that your application is complete and accurate.

Please be aware that there are no schools or application preparation organizations that are affiliated with or agents of CSLB, although some may have company names that are confusingly similar to CSLB. If you discover that an organization has misrepresented itself as being CSLB, you should submit a complaint to CSLB or the California Department of Consumer Affairs. Official CSLB examination study guides are available free of charge on CSLB's website and are mailed to applicants when they are scheduled for exams.

APPLICATION FOR ORIGINAL CONTRACTOR LICENSE
General Information and Instructions

GENERAL INFORMATION

Listed below is general information to assist you as you complete the attached application. Detailed instructions are also provided that address the content of the application section by section. Please refer to the Applicants page on the Contractors State License Board's (CSLB) website (www.cslb.ca.gov) for more detailed information about the licensing process.

Do not submit this General Information and Instructions portion with your completed application – the actual application begins immediately following this section on Application – Page 1 of 4 and includes the Certification of Work Experience and the Owner-Builder B-General Building Construction Project Experience form, if needed.
Before you submit your application, please review and be sure you have complied with the following items.

- **Enclose the nonrefundable $330 application fee with your completed application for licensure in a single classification.** CSLB cannot process your application without the appropriate fee made payable to the Registrar of Contractors. The $200 initial license fee should be submitted separately after you pass the examination. (*Business and Professions Code [BPC] sections 7137 and 7138*)
- **Your application may be returned to you if it is insufficient or incomplete.** You must provide any missing information, make corrections, and resubmit your completed application to CSLB within **90 days** after the date that it was returned to you or your application will be deemed abandoned and become void. You cannot reinstate an abandoned application – you must submit a new application and $330 application fee if you wish to pursue licensure. (*BPC 7074 and Title 16, California Code of Regulations [T16 CCR] section 813*)

Complete the application and all accompanying forms legibly in black or dark blue ink, with a typewriter, or on CSLB's website using the easy-fill feature. Forms completed in pencil will be returned to you. Please make sure that you and other authorized individuals sign and date the forms, where applicable.

- **Leave no space blank.** If a particular question or request for information does not apply to you, write "N/A" in the blank space to indicate that the question has received your attention but that it is not applicable.
- The "#" symbol is used interchangeably with the word "number" where space is limited on the application.
- If you need additional copies of forms (e.g., Certification of Work Experience, Section 4 – Personnel Full Legal Names and Addresses), please make copies of the blank forms before you begin or print additional copies from the CSLB website, under the Forms and Applications page.

SECTION 1 – BUSINESS NAME AND ADDRESS

Business Name Styles (Box 1)

In accordance with BPC section 7059.1, the business name for a contractor license **must not be misleading in relation to the classification(s) issued to the license and must be compatible with the type of business entity licensed** (*see Section 2 on next page*). For example, it would not be acceptable for ABC123 Tile to apply for a C-10 Electrical contractor license, but it would be acceptable for ABC123 Construction to apply for a B-General Building contractor license or for ABC123 Tile to apply for a C-54 Ceramic and Mosaic Tile contractor license. In addition, it would not be acceptable for a sole ownership or proprietorship to use the words "partners" or "incorporated" in its business name.

If your business is a corporation or limited liability company (LLC), the business name shown on your application must match exactly the business name as registered with the Secretary of State (SOS).

Business Addresses (Boxes 3a – 3c)

- You **must** provide an address of record (mailing address) for your business that will be made available to the public if you become licensed. This address will be published on CSLB's website and will also be used for service of all official correspondence, notices, and orders from CSLB, such as renewal notices. P.O. boxes and private mail boxes (PMB) are acceptable for the address of record.

- You **must also** provide a business street address that will be used only for CSLB's internal administrative purposes – it will not be published on CSLB's website. P.O. boxes and PMBs are **not** acceptable for the business street address.
- You are also asked to provide business phone and business fax numbers and a business email address. The business phone number is published on CSLB's website – the other contacts are for CSLB internal purposes and for service of official correspondence.

Classification Requested (Box 2)

Listed below are the contractor license classifications. **Only one classification may be requested on an original application when an examination is required.** For a complete description of the classifications, refer to the License Classifications link on the Applicants page of CSLB's website.

General Engineering... A
General Building.. B
Asbestos Abatement C-22
Boiler, Hot-Water Heating, and Steam Fitting........ C-4
Building Moving/Demolition C-21
Cabinet, Millwork, and Finish Carpentry C-6
Ceramic and Mosaic Tile C-54
Concrete... C-8
Construction Zone Traffic Control.......................... C-31
Drywall... C-9
Earthwork and Paving C-12
Electrical... C-10
Elevator.. C-11
Fencing.. C-13
Fire Protection C-16
Flooring and Floor Covering C-15
Framing and Rough Carpentry C-5
General Manufactured Housing............................. C-47
Glazing C-17
Insulation and Acoustical...................................... C-2
Landscaping.. C-27
Lathing and Plastering.. C-35
Limited Specialty (see below)............................... C-61

Lock and Security Equipment C-28
Low Voltage Systems C-7
Masonry.. C-29
Ornamental Metal C-23
Painting and Decorating C-33
Parking and Highway Improvement...................... C-32
Pipeline... C-34
Plumbing C-36
Refrigeration... C-38
Roofing... C-39
Sanitation System.. C-42
Sheet Metal C-43
Sign C-45
Solar.. C-46
Steel, Reinforcing C-50
Steel, Structural C-51
Swimming Pool... C-53
Warm-Air Heating, Ventilating, and Air-Conditioning.............C-20
Water Conditioning C-55
Welding C-60
Well Drilling (Water).. C-57

The C-61 Limited Specialty classification is for contractors who specialize in work not listed above (for example, C-61/D-50 Suspended Ceilings) or who perform work that is a specialized part of an existing classification (for example, C-61/D-29 Paper Hanging). The License Classifications link contains a full listing of the subcategories of the C-61 classification.

SECTION 2 – BUSINESS ENTITY (Box 4)

Applicants must designate their business entity. Below is information on the four business entity types that are covered by this application. Contractor licenses are also issued to joint ventures – such applicants must submit the separate Application for Joint Venture License, available on CSLB's website on the Forms and Applications page.

Corporations and LLCs must be registered and in good standing (not suspended or otherwise restricted) with SOS in order to be licensed and remain licensed with CSLB. SOS can be reached by calling (916) 653-6814 or by visiting their website at www.sos.ca.gov. Applicants who wish to change their business entity after the application is posted should withdraw their application and submit a new one.

Sole Ownership

Check the "Sole Ownership" box if the business is owned by only one individual person (not a corporation).

APPLICATION FOR ORIGINAL CONTRACTOR LICENSE
General Information and Instructions *(continued)*

Partnership

Check the "Partnership" box if the business is a partnership. Partnerships must be registered with the California SOS and in good standing prior to being issued a contractor license. Partnerships must provide their federal employer identification number (FEIN), which is available from the U.S. Internal Revenue Service (IRS). The IRS can be reached by calling (800) 829-1040. Personal Social Security numbers are **not** acceptable for the FEIN. (*See note on Page 8 of the General Information and Instructions regarding collection of FEINs.*)

Corporation

Check the "California Corporation" box if the business is a corporation. Corporations must be registered with the California SOS and in good standing prior to being issued a contractor license. Corporations must provide a current and active SOS registration number where indicated in Section 2 of the application.

Limited Liability Company

Check the "Limited Liability Company" box if the company is a limited liability company. LLCs must be registered with the California Secretary of State and in good standing prior to being issued a contractor license. LLCs must provide a current and active registration number where indicated in Section 2 of the application.

If your business entity is an LLC, before you submit your application, please be aware that the following additional requirements apply to LLC licenses (*please refer to CSLB's website and the Bond, Insurance, and Other Licensure Requirements section on Page 7 of the General Information and Instructions for more information*):

- $100,000 Surety Bond. LLC licenses are required to file a $100,000 surety bond (in addition to the $15,000 contractor's bond) for the issuance, reissuance, reinstatement, reactivation, and renewal of an LLC license for the benefit of any employee or worker damaged by the LLC's failure to pay wages, interest on wages, or fringe benefits, as well as other contributions. (*BPC sections 7071.6 and 7071.6.5*)
- $1 Million Liability Insurance Minimum. LLC licenses are required to carry liability insurance with the aggregate limit of $1 million for licensees with five or fewer persons and/or companies listed as personnel of record, plus an additional $100,000 required for each additional personnel, not to exceed $5 million total. (*BPC section 7071.19*)
- Personnel of Record. Every person and/or company that is an officer, responsible manager, member, or director of an LLC must be listed as personnel of record on LLC applications. All individuals who are members of the personnel of record are subject to fingerprinting. LLC managers and members must be listed on the LLC's record with SOS. LLCs may also have additional officers who are not included on the official SOS record, but who must be listed on this application and who will become part of the contractor license. CSLB staff will verify the number of managers and members listed on the SOS record for LLCs in order to ensure that the number of personnel listed on this application is correct and to accurately calculate the required amount of the LLC liability insurance, as discussed above. (*BPC section 7065*)

SECTION 3 – QUALIFYING INDIVIDUAL FULL LEGAL NAME AND ADDRESS

The terms **"qualifying individual"** and **"qualifier"** are used interchangeably. The qualifying individual is the person who meets the experience and examination requirements for the license and who is responsible for exercising that **direct supervision and control** of their employer's or principal's construction operations to secure compliance with CSLB's laws, rules, and regulations. (*BPC section 7068.1 (a)*) "Direct supervision and control" includes any one or any combination of the following activities: supervising construction, managing construction activities by making technical and administrative decisions, checking jobs for proper workmanship, or direct supervision on construction job sites. (*T16 CCR section 823 (b)*)

A qualifying individual is required for every classification on every license issued by CSLB. The qualifying individual may or may not be the owner of the business.

You must complete the personnel information requested in Sections 3 and 4 of the application for each individual

and company that will be listed on the license.

- Line 5a – **Full legal names are required.** You must provide the full legal name of all personnel. If an individual does not have a middle name, write "None" or "No Middle Name" in the space provided. If an individual has only an initial for their first or middle name, write "(Initial Only)" after the initial.
- Provide qualifier's date of birth where requested.

- **All applicants are required to provide their U.S. Social Security number (SSN) or individual taxpayer identification number (ITIN) if an individual does not have an SSN.** (*See note on Page 8 of the General Information and Instructions regarding collection of SSNs and ITINs.*)
- Box 5b – You must **also** provide a residence street address for the qualifier that will be used only for CSLB's internal administrative purposes – it will not be published on CSLB's website. P.O. boxes and PMBs are **not** acceptable for the qualifier's residence street address.
- Line 6 – Please enter any previous or current license numbers held by the qualifier in the provided box. Also enter the percentage of the new business owned/held by the qualifier (ranging between zero and 100%), the qualifier's driver license number, and the qualifier's home phone number.
- Box 7 – Check the appropriate box that identifies the title/position of the qualifying individual. The **title/position must be compatible with the business entity type**, as entered in Section 2 above. Please be sure your selected title/position complies with the following:
  - □ **Sole ownership entity** = either Owner or Responsible Managing Employee (RME) – see below
  - □ **Partnership entity** = either Qualifying Partner or RME
  - □ **Corporation entity** = either Responsible Managing Officer (RMO) or RME – California corporations must identify three corporate officers (president, secretary, and treasurer) in Sections 3 and 4; out-of- state/foreign corporations must identify their president only. The officers must match SOS records.
  - □ **LLC entity** = any one of RMO, Responsible Managing Manager, Responsible Managing Member, or RME – If an LLC has officers, the name(s) of their officer(s) must be listed on the application – president, secretary, and treasurer. Please be sure to write these titles in the space provided for the appropriate personnel in Sections 3 and 4 and be sure that they match those listed on SOS records.
- An **RME is a bona fide employee** who is permanently employed by the applicant and is

actively engaged in the operation of the applicant's contracting business for at least 32 hours or 80% of the total hours per week such business is in operation, whichever is less. (*T16 CCR section 823 (a)*)

- Box 8 – You **must** print and sign your name and indicate the date below the certification statement at the bottom of Page 1 of the application. Failure to sign your application will result in the application being returned to you for correction.

SECTION 4 – PERSONNEL FULL LEGAL NAMES AND ADDRESSES (Other than Qualifying Individual)

You must complete the personnel information requested in Section 4 of the application for each individual and company that will be listed as personnel on the license, other than the qualifier listed in Section 3. Be sure to include the applicant's business name at the top of the page where requested.

- See Section 3 above for instructions on how to complete the specific fields of this section. If more than four
(4) personnel must be reported, please make a copy of the blank form. All personnel **must** print and sign their names below the certification statement and include the date that the form was signed.
- LLC applicants must list **every responsible manager, member, and officer** on the application for licensure. Every LLC is required to have at least one manager or member. **The personnel on the application must be consistent with the number, types, and names of personnel listed on SOS records for that LLC.** For example, if SOS lists five (5) managers and members on the LLC's record, the application must list the same number and names of managers and members in order to be acceptable. In addition, LLCs can have officers who are neither managers nor members – those individuals must also be reported as officers on the application for licensure even though they are not listed on SOS records.
- LLCs can have managers or members that are corporations or other LLCs, as opposed to individual people. When an LLC has corporate or LLC managers or members, complete Section 4 for those companies, omitting the fields that do not apply (e.g., date of birth, SSN/ITIN, and driver license number). Since corporations and LLCs are incapable of signing documents (e.g., applications, renewals, etc.), you must also report at least one individual person who will be an authorized signer for that company. To do this, you must complete a portion of Section 4 using this individual person's personal information. Identify that person as the "Authorized Signer for______" (inserting the name of the corporation or LLC on behalf of which the individual person will sign). This individual person will not be part of the official license personnel of record (unless they are also an actual responsible manager, member, or officer of the applicant LLC), but their information will be maintained by CSLB for signing purposes only

SECTION 5 – REQUIRED APPLICATION QUESTIONS

Be sure to include the applicant's business name at the top of the page where requested. **All** questions must be answered, unless otherwise indicated, and all requested explanations and documentation must be provided or the application will be returned to the applicant for correction. Failure to thoroughly and accurately complete this section of the application can delay the licensure process or result in denial of the application.

Conviction Question and Fingerprint Requirement (Question 11)

Please be sure to read the Important Notice Regarding Convictions on the front of this application packet. All applicants for licensure are required to submit a full set of fingerprints for the purpose of conducting a criminal background check. Fingerprints will be compared to the records of the California Department of Justice (DOJ) and the Federal Bureau of Investigation (FBI) to determine whether a criminal history exists. Your license will not be issued until CSLB receives fingerprint results from both DOJ and FBI. Even though you may have been fingerprinted previously for an employer or another regulatory body, you will need to undergo the fingerprinting and criminal history check process again specifically for CSLB. California Penal Code section 11142 prohibits criminal history information from being released to any entity other than the requesting agency that you have authorized to receive it.

After an application has been accepted by CSLB as complete (also known as "posted"), each individual listed on the application who needs to fingerprint will be sent instructions on the process for obtaining and submitting fingerprints. Individuals in California are required to fingerprint by electronic live scan; individuals outside of California can fingerprint either by electronic live scan in California or by submitting hard card fingerprints that are completed in the applicant's location, as explained in the instructions that are sent after the application has been posted. For more information, please visit CSLB's website and view information on the Applicants page.

Translator for Examination (Question 16)

Check the "Yes" box if you have difficulty understanding or reading the English language and you would like to use a translator to read the examination to you. The translator you choose must be approved in advance by CSLB. If you check the "Yes" box, information will be sent to you regarding the translator process.

SECTION 6 – QUALIFIER EDUCATION, APPRENTICESHIP, LICENSURE, AND MILITARY

Education and Apprenticeship (Question 17)

CSLB may grant up to three years of credit toward the four-year experience requirement for completed training in an accredited school and/or apprenticeship programs in the construction trade for which the applicant is applying. (*T16 CCR section 825*) For formal education, the applicant's **educational institution must submit a certified official transcript directly to CSLB in a sealed envelope.** Degrees obtained outside of the United States must be translated, if in a language other than English, and evaluated by an accredited evaluation service in the U.S.

For apprenticeship programs, applicant must submit a copy of their apprenticeship certificate and indicate the dates of the program where requested on the application.

Reciprocity (Question 18)

Applicants who are seeking licensure in California and who are licensed in the same classification in Arizona, Nevada, and/or Utah, as recognized by CSLB, may be eligible for the waiver of the trade examination if the qualifier meets the requirements for reciprocity (*BPC section 7065.4*). A Request for Verification of License form completed by the licensing agency from the other state must be submitted with this application. The Law and Business Examination will still be required if the applicant has not passed that examination within the last five (5) years. (See *CSLB's website for more information on reciprocity on the Applicants page.*)

Military (Questions 19 and 20)

CSLB approves expedited processing and/or grants credit toward the experience requirements for current and former active duty military and their spouses or domestic partners under specific circumstances, as explained below.

Expedited Processing for Military Personnel and Their Spouses or Domestic Partners

CSLB is required to expedite the licensure process for a **sole ownership entity applicant** who:

- was honorably discharged after having served as an active duty member of the Armed Forces of the United States; **OR**

- holds a current license in another state, district, or territory of the United States in the same contractor license classification for which they are applying **and** who is married to, or in a domestic partnership or other legal union with, a current active duty member of the Armed Forces of the United States who is assigned to a duty station in California under official active duty military orders.

Please see the military questions (numbers 19 and 20) under Section 6 of the application. If you answer "Yes" to either of the questions and you would like to be considered for this expedited processing, please provide the documentation requested under the question, including evidence of your current military duty (copy of your military orders) or your previous military service (copy of your DD 214 – Certificate of Release or Discharge from Active Duty). (*BPC sections 114.5, 115.4, and 115.5*)

Credit for Military Experience and Training

CSLB may grant credit toward licensure requirements for applicable work experience and training received while the applicant was an active duty member of the Armed Forces of the United States performing duties in the classification for which they are applying. This work experience and training must be reported on a Certification of Work Experience form (*see Page 9 of the General Information and Instructions*) and must be supported by acceptable documentation, including evidence of current military duty (copy of applicant's military orders) or previous military service (copy of applicant's DD 214 – Certificate of Release or Discharge from Active Duty). If you are claiming military experience, please be sure to check the "Yes" box for Question 19 on the application, as discussed above.

MISCELLANEOUS INFORMATION

Experience and Examination Information

Applicants for licensure must meet specific experience and examination requirements, as explained below.

Waivers of the trade examination may be granted under certain circumstances, as indicated on the next page. If you qualify for exam waiver or exemption, do not use this application – please instead use the Application for Original Contractor License – Waiver (7065) (form 13A-1a).

Experience Requirements

To be eligible for licensure, the qualifying individual must have had, within the last 10 years, at least four (4) years of experience in the classification for which they are applying. The experience must be at no less than a journeyman level, or as a foreman, supervising employee, contractor, or owner-builder. A "journeyman" is defined as an experienced worker who is fully qualified (as opposed to a trainee) and is able to perform the trade without supervision, or one who has completed an apprenticeship program. **Experience is documented on the Certification of Work Experience form** (*see Page 9 of the General Information and Instructions*). (*T16 CCR section 825*)

Examination Eligibility Requirements

The qualifying individual for a contractor license is required to pass the written Law and Business Examination and a specific trade examination if required *(BPC section 7065)*, unless they meet the requirements for a waiver (*see next page for information regarding examination waivers*).

Re-Examination

If you are required to take an examination, subject to some limitations, you have 18 months after the approval of your application in which to achieve a passing score on the exam(s). During that time period, you may take the exam an unlimited number of times. A $60 fee is required each time you reschedule an exam. *(See BPC section 7074 for more detailed information on re-*

examinations.)

Reasonable Accommodation – The Americans with Disabilities Act

In compliance with the Americans with Disabilities Act (ADA), CSLB provides reasonable accommodation for applicants with disabilities that may affect their ability to take the required examinations. Applicants wishing to request reasonable accommodation pursuant to the ADA must complete the Special Accommodation Request for Examination form (available on the Forms and Applications page on CSLB's website) and submit it to CSLB with the appropriate supporting documentation. In order to make the necessary arrangements to accommodate candidate needs, the form and supporting documentation should be submitted as soon as possible.

Examination Waivers and Exemptions

The examination may be waived if the qualifying individual is currently, or has been in the last five (5) years, actively engaged in the construction business and meets specific waiver requirements as mandated by law, or has been actively licensed in good standing or has passed the required exams in the classification for which they are applying. *(See BPC sections 7065 – 7065.4 for a complete list.)* If you are applying for licensure based on waiver of or exemption from the trade and Law and Business exams, you should complete the Application for Original Contractor License – Examination Waiver (7065) instead of this application.

In addition, the trade examination may be waived if the qualifier meets the requirements for reciprocity based on licensure in the same classification in Arizona, Nevada, and/or Utah (*see CSLB's website for more information on reciprocity under the Applicants page*). The Law and Business Examination is still required for such applicants; therefore, this is the correct application to use – see Question 18 under Section 6 on the application.

Random Application and Experience Review

By law, CSLB must randomly review three percent (3%) of applications, including the experience claimed on Certifications of Work Experience forms that must be verifiable through payroll records or similar documents. In the event that your application is selected for review, please see CSLB's website for the listing of Acceptable Supporting Experience Documentation that may be submitted to CSLB to support claimed experience. In addition, CSLB staff may contact the certifier of experience or other parties to verify experience. *(BPC section 7068 and T16 CCR 824)*

Bond, Insurance, and Other Licensure Requirements

All contractors must meet specified bond, insurance, and other requirements for licensure with CSLB, as indicated below. Failure to maintain a required bond or insurance may result in the suspension of the license. For information on bonds, see *A Guide to Contractor License Bonds*, available on CSLB website's Guides and Publications page.
Bonds may be submitted to CSLB electronically by the issuing surety company.

Contractor's Bond

All contractors must have a $15,000 contractor's bond on file with CSLB. (*BPC section 7071.6*)

Bond of Qualifying Individual

An **additional** $12,500 qualifying individual's bond must be filed for **all** contractors that are qualified by an RME, or under certain other circumstances for corporate and LLC contractors when the qualifying individual (RMO, responsible managing manager, or responsible managing member) holds less than 10 percent of the voting stock of the corporation or membership interest in the LLC. (*BPC section 7071.9*)

LLC Employee/Worker Bond

All LLC licenses are required to have an **additional** $100,000 employee/worker bond on file with CSLB for the benefit of workers employed by or contracted to work for an LLC. (*See Section 2 – Business Entity on Page 3 of the General Information and Instructions for LLC information.*) (*BPC* *section 7071.6.5*)

Disciplinary Bond

A license that has been disciplined may be required to have an **additional** disciplinary bond on file with CSLB in an amount fixed by the Registrar at not less than $15,000 or more than $150,000. (*BPC section 7071.8*)

Workers' Compensation Insurance

Workers' compensation is required when a contractor has employees, including an RME and home improvement salespersons, and for all contractors applying for the C-39 Roofing classification. The Certificate of Insurance must be issued in the business name shown on this application. Contractors that have no employees and are not otherwise required to have workers' compensation insurance can complete the Exemption from Workers' Compensation form, available on CSLB website's Forms and Applications page. (*BPC section 7125*)

LLC Liability Insurance

All LLC licenses are required to have liability insurance in an amount that is not less than one million dollars ($1,000,000) or more than five million dollars ($5,000,000). The amount is determined based on the number of personnel of record on the license. For five (5) or fewer personnel, the amount is not less than $1 million. For each additional member of the personnel, the amount increases $100,000, up to a maximum of $5 million. For example, an LLC that has eight (8) personnel would be required to carry a $1,300,000 liability insurance policy. (*See Section 2 – Business Entity on Page 3 of the General Information and Instructions for LLC information.*) (*BPC section 7071.19*)

Asbestos Open Book Examination

All qualifiers who have not yet completed one must complete the Asbestos Open Book Examination on behalf of the applicant, which can be downloaded from the Applicants page on CSLB's website. (*BPC section 7058.5*)

Reissuance or Reassignment of License Number

If the qualifier has previously been licensed, it may be possible to have the previous license number reissued or reassigned under certain circumstances. Sole ownership license numbers may be reissued to corporations or LLCs, and corporate license numbers may be reissued to LLCs. To request the reissuance of a license number, the applicant must complete and submit with their application the Request for License Number Reissuance form (13A- 1h), available on the Forms and Applications page on CSLB's website. (*BPC section 7075.1*)

Construction Management Education Account

A grant program was established in 1991 to provide funds for qualified public post-secondary schools that teach construction management. Applicants may voluntarily contribute to the account when paying the application fee or the license renewal fee. If you would like to make a voluntary contribution, please mark the box on the top portion of Page 1 of the application, write in the dollar amount in the space provided, and include that dollar amount in the total amount paid with your application, or submit a separate check or money order made payable to CSLB/Construction Management Education Account. (*See BPC sections 7139.2 and 7139.4.*)

Collection of Social Security Numbers, Individual Taxpayer Identification Numbers, and Federal Employer Identification Numbers

With the exception of the driver license number, all information requested on the application is mandatory, including disclosure of U.S. Social Security numbers (SSN), individual taxpayer identification numbers (ITIN), and federal employer identification numbers (FEIN). Collection of the SSN, ITIN, and FEIN is authorized by BPC sections 30, 31, and 7145.5. SSNs, ITINs, and FEINs are used exclusively for the purpose of tax enforcement, compliance with any judgment or order for family support in accordance with Family Code section 17520, measurement of employment outcomes of students who participate in career technical education programs offered by the California Community Colleges as required by BPC section 30, and investigation of tax evasion and violations of cash-pay reporting laws as set forth in Section 329 of the Unemployment Insurance Code. If you fail to disclose your SSN, ITIN, or FEIN, your application will not be processed and you will be reported to the Franchise Tax Board; they may assess a $100 penalty against you.

Collection of Personal Information

CSLB collects the personal information requested on the following form as authorized by BPC sections 30, 31, 114.5, 115.5, 141, 480, 7066, 7069, 7072, 7073, and 7145.5 and T16 CCR section 816. CSLB uses this information to identify and evaluate applicants for licensure, issue and renew licenses, and enforce licensing standards set by law and regulation. Submission of the requested information is mandatory. CSLB cannot consider your application for licensure unless you provide all of the requested information. You may review the records maintained by CSLB that contain your personal information, unless the records are identified as confidential information and exempted from disclosure by the Information Practices Act, including Civil Code section 1798.40. CSLB makes every effort to protect the personal information you provide us; however, it may be disclosed in response to a Public Records Act request as allowed by the Information Practices Act; to another government agency as required by state or federal law or as provided in Civil Code section 1798.24; or in response to a court or administrative order, a subpoena, or a search warrant. The Custodian of Records is responsible for maintaining the information on this form and may be contacted at the address and telephone number listed in the letterhead at the top of this General Information and Instructions portion for questions about this notice or access to records.

Resources on the Licensing Process

CSLB has a variety of publications available to help you become a licensed contractor and to maintain your license. You can order free publications from or view documents on CSLB's website (www.cslb.ca.gov), by writing to CSLB at the address listed below, or by calling the 24-hour automated phone system at (800) 321-CSLB (2752). Please visit CSLB's website or call the toll-free phone number to find out how to order the current edition of the *California Contractors License Law & Reference Book* or other publications.

Application Processing – Follow Your Application Status Online

When CSLB receives your application, an acknowledgement letter will be sent to you that explains how to check the status of your application online at www.cslb.ca.gov or by calling (800) 321-CSLB (2752) using the Application Fee Number and Personal Identification Number (PIN) provided in the acknowledgement letter.

Please include your Application Fee Number in any correspondence. All correspondence

should be sent to: Contractors State License Board
9821 Business Park Drive
Sacramento, CA 95827-1703
Mailing Address: P.O. Box 26000, Sacramento, CA 95826-0026

CERTIFICATION OF WORK EXPERIENCE FORM

Following the application in this packet, you will find the Certification of Work Experience form that must be completed by the qualifying individual on the application and certified by a **qualified and responsible person** who has **direct knowledge of the experience and time period listed**. The experience must be verifiable through payroll records or similar documents.

Corrections on the certification forms must be initialed by the certifier. Forms containing strikeouts or modifications that may compromise the validity of the work experience certification may not be accepted.

To assist the certifier in completing Part 2 of the Certification of Work Experience form, a listing of the License Classifications is available through a link on the Applicants page of CSLB's website. This document may be used as a reference when listing the specific trade duties that the qualifier has performed or supervised in the classification for which they are applying.

The Certification of Work Experience form may not be required if the qualifier has ever served as the qualifier on a license in the same classification for which they are currently applying.

OWNER-BUILDER B-GENERAL BUILDING CONSTRUCTION PROJECT EXPERIENCE FORM

Pursuant to BPC section 7044, owners who build or improve structures on their own property are exempt from the licensure laws for contractors under certain circumstances. The Owner-Builder B-General Building Construction Project Experience form **must** be completed by the qualifier on the application if they are claiming experience as an owner-builder working on projects on their own property. The experience must be verifiable through building permits, final inspections, or similar documents. Please see CSLB's website for the listing of Acceptable Supporting Experience Documentation that may be submitted to CSLB to support claimed experience. *(BPC section 7068 and T16 CCR section 824)* A separate form is required for each project on the owner-builder's property.

SECTION 5 – REQUIRED APPLICATION QUESTIONS

All questions in this section must be answered. Questions 10 - 13 pertain to **all** individuals listed on this application (qualifying individual and **all** personnel listed in Section 4), and Questions 14 – 16 pertain to the qualifying individual only. If you checked "Yes" in response to any question, the person involved must attach a separate sheet with a detailed explanation for each situation.

10. To the best of your knowledge, is anyone listed on this application (or any company the person is or was a part of) named in or responsible for any unsatisfied final judgments, liens, and/or claims against any bond or cash deposit pertaining to a construction project?

- ☐ Yes
- ☐ No

If you checked "Yes" for this question, you are required to attach a statement identifying all judgments (pending or on record), liens, past due unpaid bills, claims, or suits and a detailed explanation of the situation. Include the names and addresses of the parties involved. If the obligation was or is being discharged in bankruptcy, attach a copy of the bankruptcy filing and a copy of the creditors list.

11. Has anyone listed on this application EVER been convicted of or entered a plea of guilty or nolo contendere to ANY misdemeanor or felony in the United States or a foreign country? NOTE: Convictions that were later expunged from the records of the court or set aside pursuant to California Penal Code sections 1203.4, 1203.4a, or 1203.41 or an equivalent non-California law **MUST be disclosed**. However, some convictions **should NOT be disclosed**, including the following:

- Convictions that were adjudicated in the juvenile court;
- Convictions under California Health and Safety Code sections 11357 (b), (c), (d), or (e) or section 11360 (b) that are two years old or older; and
- Charges that were dismissed as the result of successful completion of a deferred entry of judgment program (diversion program) under California Penal Code section 1000.3.

- ☐ Yes
- ☐ No

If you checked "Yes" for this question, please attach a statement disclosing **all** pleas/convictions, including violated law sections, and thoroughly explain the acts or circumstances that resulted in the plea/conviction. In addition, the following information must be included for **each** plea/conviction: date of the plea/conviction, level of the plea/conviction (i.e., misdemeanor or felony), county and state where the violation took place, name of the court, court case number, sentence imposed, jail/prison term served, terms and conditions of parole or probation, parole or probation completion dates, and parole agent/probation officer names and phone numbers. If you have obtained a dismissal of your conviction(s) pursuant to Penal Code sections 1203.4, 1203.4a, or 1203.41, please submit a certified copy of the court order dismissing the conviction(s) with your application. **You may submit the required information using the Disclosure Statement Regarding Criminal Plea/Conviction form that is available on the Forms and Applications page on CSLB's website.**

The information provided will be verified through CSLB's fingerprinting requirement. Failure to report a disclosable plea/conviction may be grounds for denial of your application.

12. To the best of your knowledge, has anyone on this application (or any company the person is or was a part of) ever received a citation from CSLB or had a contractor license or other professional or vocational license or registration denied, suspended, revoked, or otherwise disciplined by this state or elsewhere (i.e., other U.S. state, U.S. territory, agency of the federal government, or other country)?

For the purposes of responding to this question, "disciplined" is an administrative action that resulted in a restriction or penalty being placed on any license you have or have possessed, such as a revocation, suspension, probation, or reprimand.

- ☐ Yes
- ☐ No

(Check "No" if the license or registration was suspended due to lack of a bond, workers' compensation or other required insurance, a qualifier, or family support.)

If you checked "Yes" for this question, you are required to attach a statement detailing the events leading to this action.

13. **To the best of your knowledge, has anyone on this application failed to resolve any outstanding final liabilities, which include taxes, additions to tax, penalties, interest, and any fees that may be assessed by CSLB, the Department of Industrial Relations, the Employment Development Department, the Franchise Tax Board, or the State Board of Equalization (BOE)?**

❑ Yes

❑ No

If you checked "Yes" for this question, you are required to attach a statement regarding the outstanding liabilities. In relation to BOE liabilities, you must indicate if you have entered into an installment payment agreement for that liability with the BOE and provide verification that you are in compliance with the terms of that agreement, if applicable.

14. ***(This question must be answered by the qualifying individual.)*** Direct supervision and control over construction operations includes any one or a combination of the following activities: supervising construction, managing construction activities by making technical and administrative decisions, checking jobs for proper workmanship, or direct supervision on construction job sites. **Will you, as the qualifying individual, perform one or more of these duties?**

❑ Yes

❑ No

15. ***(This question must be answered only if the qualifying individual is a responsible managing employee [RME].)*** Title 16, California Code of Regulations (T16 CCR) section 823 states that an RME must be permanently employed by the applicant and actively engaged in the operation of the business for at least 32 hours per week or 80% of the total hours per week that the business is in operation. **Will you, as the responsible managing employee, meet the requirement of T16 CCR section 823 cited above?**

❑ Yes

❑ No

16. **The examinations are administered in English.** Will you require the use of a CSLB-approved translator?

❑ Yes

❑ No

SECTION 6 – QUALIFIER EDUCATION, APPRENTICESHIP, LICENSURE, AND MILITARY

Applicants must answer the following questions and may be granted credit toward licensure requirements or receive expedited processing as noted below. Question 20 pertains only to individuals applying for sole ownership business entity licenses. Please refer to Pages 5 and 6 of the General Information and Instructions for more information. If you checked "Yes" in response to any question, please provide the requested documentation.

17. **Have you completed an educational or apprenticeship program?**

If you checked "Yes" for this question, you may be granted credit for **completed training in an accredited school** if you:

- Submit transcripts for a four-year degree, two-year degree (or less), technical training (must include course hours and descriptions), and all other degrees in a business or construction-related field.

Transcripts must be certified official and received directly from the educational institution in a sealed envelope. *(If you received your degree outside the United States, your transcripts must be translated, if in a language other than English, and evaluated by an accredited evaluation service that does business within the United States.)*

❑ Yes

❑ No

You may be granted credit for a **completed apprenticeship program** if you:

- Submit a copy of your apprenticeship certificate; **AND**
- Enter the beginning and ending dates of your completed apprenticeship program:

From ______________________________ to ______________________________

Month/Day/Year Month/Day/Year

(The apprenticeship period cannot overlap the journeyman-level experience period being certified on the Certification of Work Experience.)

18. Are you licensed in another state in the same classification for which you are seeking licensure? If you checked "Yes" for this question, you must provide a Request for Verification of License form that is completed by the licensing agency from the other state (Arizona, Nevada, or Utah only, depending on the classification).

- ❑ Yes
- ❑ No

19. Are you serving in, or have you previously served in, the United States military?

If you checked "Yes" for this question, please provide the following documentation:

- ❑ Yes
- ❑ No

- Evidence of your current military duty (copy of your military orders) or your previous military service (copy of your DD 214 – Certificate of Release or Discharge from Active Duty).

20. *(This question must be answered only if the applicant is an individual applying for a sole ownership business entity license.)* Are you married to, or in a domestic partnership or other legal union with, an active duty member of the Armed Forces of the United States who is assigned to a duty station in California under official active duty military orders AND do you hold a current license in another state, district, or territory of the United States as a contractor in the same classification for which you are seeking licensure?

If you checked "Yes" for this question, please provide the following documentation to be considered for expedited processing:

- ❑ Yes
- ❑ No

- Evidence of your legal union **and** your spouse's or partner's military duty. For example, attach a copy of the marriage certificate or certified declaration/registration of domestic partnership filed with the Secretary of State **AND** military orders establishing a duty station in California. For other forms of "legal union" not recognized by California, you may submit other documentary evidence of legal union issued by the state that recognizes your legal union for consideration by CSLB in meeting this requirement; **AND**
- Copy of your current license from the other state, district, or territory of the United States documenting a contractor license, registration, permit, or certificate in the same classification for which you are seeking licensure.

STATE TAX AND OTHER OBLIGATIONS NOTICE

The State Board of Equalization and Franchise Tax Board may share taxpayer information with CSLB. You are obligated to pay your state tax obligation. CSLB may suspend or refuse to issue, reactivate, reinstate, or renew a license if your state tax obligation, child support obligation, or any outstanding final liability to CSLB, the Department of Industrial Relations, or the Employment Development Department is not paid. (BPC sections 30, 31, and 7145.5)

FOR CSLUB USE ONLY

CERTIFICATION OF WORK EXPERIENCE
General Information

- **This form must be filled in completely in order to document applicant's work experience, or the application will be returned for correction or completion. The qualifying individual on the application (as listed on Page 1 of the application) and certifier (a qualified and responsible person who verifies the experience in the classification for which the applicant is seeking licensure) must type or print neatly and legibly in black or dark blue ink – pencil is not acceptable.**
- FORMS CONTAINING STRIKEOUTS OR MODIFICATIONS MAY NOT BE ACCEPTED.
- Corrections on the Certification of Work Experience forms must be initialed by the certifier.
- Original signatures are required – faxed, photocopied, or stamped signatures are not acceptable.
- All qualifying individuals and certifiers must be at least 18 years old.
- All Certification of Work Experience forms must be submitted with the application.
- The Certification of Work Experience form, when filed with an application, becomes the property of CSLB and is kept as a matter of record. **Keep a copy of the completed and signed form for your records** – you may be asked to provide further documentation or testimony to verify your experience. A random three percent (3%) of applications are subject to review, and experience must be verifiable through payroll records and similar documents. CSLB staff may contact the certifier or other parties to verify experience.
- If you have ever served as a qualifier on a license in the classification for which you are now applying, you may not need to complete this form. However, if you are applying for a waiver of the examination pursuant to Business and Professions Code (BPC) sections 7065.1(b) or 7065.1(c), you do need to complete this form. *(Please refer to CSLB's website for more information on exam waivers.)* **NOTE: If you had a previous application that was denied on the basis of a lack of qualifying work experience, you must complete this form, regardless of whether or not you passed the examination.**
- Anyone who knowingly procures or offers false or forged documents to be filed, registered, or recorded in any public office in California is guilty of a felony. *(Penal Code section 115)*

PART 1 – QUALIFYING INDIVIDUAL (APPLICANT) INFORMATION

- The qualifying individual (qualifier) must complete Part 1 in its entirety before the certifier completes Part 2.
- Lines 2 and 3 request the business name of company, license number of company, and company's business street address of the place where your experience was gained, which may or may not have been your employer.

PART 2 – WORK EXPERIENCE AND CERTIFICATION STATEMENT

- The certifier must complete Part 2 in its entirety after the qualifying individual has completed Part 1.
- **The qualifying individual must document at least four (4) years of journeyman-level or higher experience in the classification for which they are applying. The experience must have been obtained within the last 10 years.**
- **The qualifying individual's work experience must have been completed at the level of journeyman, foreman, supervising employee, or contractor**, as defined below *(Title 16, California Code of Regulations [T16 CCR] section 825).* Also defined below are "owner-builder" and "self-employed individual."
  - A **"journeyman"** is an experienced worker who is fully qualified (as opposed to a trainee) and is able to perform the trade without supervision, or a person who has completed an apprenticeship program. *(T16 CCR section 825)*
  - A **"foreman"** or **"supervising employee"** is a person who has the knowledge and skills of a journeyman and directly supervises construction projects.
  - A **"contractor"** is an individual who is currently a licensed California contractor, a former licensed California contractor, or an out-of-state licensed contractor. A contractor has the skills necessary to manage the daily activities of a construction business, including field supervision.
  - An **"owner-builder"** (a person who performs B-General Building classification work solely on their own property, pursuant to BPC section 7044) or a **"self-employed individual"** must have the knowledge and skills of a journeyman as listed above and the skills necessary to manage the daily activities of a construction business, including field observation. Owner-builders must complete and submit an Owner-Builder B-General Building Construction Project Experience form for each owner-builder project on their own property.
- The Description of Classifications document may be used as a reference only and is available through a link on the Applicants page of CSLB's website.

- **The certifier (a qualified, responsible person who is able to verify the work experience of the qualifier) must complete and date and sign under the certification statement on line 9 at the bottom of the form.** The certifier can be an employer, fellow employee, journeyman, union representative, contractor, business associate, or a client if the applicant is/was self-employed. This form will help CSLB determine whether the qualifier has the experience necessary to become a qualified contractor.
- The certifier must have direct knowledge of the qualifier's experience during the time period listed. "Direct knowledge" means personal knowledge of the experience that does not depend on outside information or hearsay. The certifier must be able to certify that the qualifier demonstrated a level of knowledge and skills expected of a journeyman or higher in the classification for which they are applying.
- Any licensee whose signature appears on a falsified Certification of Work Experience form, or who otherwise certifies false or misleading experience claims submitted by an applicant to obtain a contractor license, will be subject to disciplinary action. *(BPC section 7114.1)*

FOR EXAMINATIONS SCHEDULED ON OR AFTER AUGUST 28, 2019

CONTRACTORS STATE LICENSE BOARD
LICENSE EXAMINATION STUDY GUIDE
ELECTRICAL (C-10)

Content of the Examination

The Electrical (C-10) Examination is divided into five major sections:

1. Planning and Estimating (24%)

- Existing system evaluation
- Plan and specification interpretation
- Electrical calculations
- Code requirements
- Material selection
- Energy production and storage project planning (photovoltaic, wind, generators, batteries, capacitors)

2. Rough Wiring (26%)

- System layout
- Clearance and accessibility requirements
- Raceway and panel installation
- Wire and equipment installation
- Grounding and bonding
- Energy production and storage system performance (photovoltaic, wind, generators, batteries, capacitors)

3. Finish Wiring and Trim (9%)

- Finish device placement and installation
- Motor and equipment installation
- Wire and equipment labeling
- Trims and sealants
- Energy production and storage finish wiring (photovoltaic, wind, generators, batteries, capacitors)

4. Startup, Troubleshooting, and Maintenance (21%)

- System energizing and testing
- Common electrical problems
- Location, repair, and replacement of inoperable electrical wires/components

- Selection and use of electrical testing equipment.
- Energy production and storage rough wiring (photovoltaic, wind, generators, batteries, capacitors)

5. Safety (20%)

- Lockout/tagout procedures
- Personal protective equipment (PPE)
- Tools/equipment
- Hazardous materials and job site environments

Percentages are approximate

Test Site Policy

This is a closed-book examination. No reference materials may be used during the examination. All materials brought to the examination site must be left in an unmonitored area at your own risk.

Test Strategy

This is a multiple-choice examination with four choices per question. Examination questions are written to provide only one BEST answer. Some questions require mathematical computation. A calculator will be provided.

There is no penalty for guessing. If you are unsure about a particular question, it is better to try to answer the question than to leave the question blank.

Plenty of time is provided to answer all examination questions, so be sure to read each question and its four choices completely and carefully before selecting the BEST possible answer to the question.

Sample Questions

Below are three typical examination questions. The correct answer is <u>underlined.</u>

1. Which of the following applies to solar panels, metal frames, and metal mounting equipment on a roof-mounted PV system?

a. They must be weatherproof.
b. They must be wind resistant.
c. They must be anodized aluminum.
d. <u>They must be bonded and grounded.</u>

2. Which of the following regulations applies to service-entrance conductors that are supplying service to a building or structure?

a. The conductors may not pass through the interior of another building or structure.
b. The conductors are permitted if the buildings or structures are close together.
c. The conductors are only permitted when approved construction drawings show the conductor routing.
d. The conductors are only permitted when service cannot be installed in any other way.

3. A contractor needs 13 receptacles that cost $3.56 each plus sales tax of 7.25%. The supplier states that for every 10 receptacles that are purchased, the contractor will get one free of charge. What is the total cost of the receptacles?

a. $42.02
b. $42.72
c. $45.82
d. $49.66

All questions are written and reviewed by licensed contractors who are actively working in the trade

Resources

Publisher information for reference books and code is provided below. Other sources for reference books may be found online. ***California code books can be viewed online: www.dgs.ca.gov/bsc***

2019 California Building Code. California Code of Regulations, Title 24. International Code Council. PHONE: (800) 786-4452
INTERNET: www.iccsafe.org

2019 California Electrical Code. California Code of Regulations, Title 24. BNI Publications, Inc.
PHONE: (888) 264-2665
INTERNET: www.bnibooks.com

2019 California Energy Code. California Code of Regulations, Title 24. International Code Council. PHONE: (800) 786-4452
INTERNET: www.iccsafe.org

2019 California Fire Code. California Code of Regulations, Title 24. International Code Council. PHONE: (800) 786-4452
INTERNET: www.iccsafe.org

American Electricians' Handbook. McGraw-Hill Professional.
PHONE: (877) 833-5524
INTERNET: www.mhprofessional.com

State of California General Industry & Electrical Safety Orders (Cal/OSHA) and ***State of California Construction & Electrical Safety Orders (Cal/OSHA). 2019.***
California Code of Regulations, Title 8. Mancomm.
PHONE: (877) 626-2666
INTERNET: www.mancomm.com VIEW ONLINE:
www.dir.ca.gov/dosh/LawsAndRegulations.htm

Publisher information is current as of 10/19

INTRODUCTION

HOW TO PREPARE FOR THE EXAM

Congratulations on purchasing this book! You have taken the first step towards successfully passing your Journeyman Electrician's Licensing Exam. You have in your hands the best self-study guide available for journeyman electrician's exam preparation. This book will not make you a competent electrician, nor teach you the electrical trade, but it will give you an idea of the type of questions asked on most electrician's licensing exams and how to answer them correctly. This book covers practically all the subjects you will likely be tested on, including: branch circuits and feeders, motors and motor controls, transformers, hazardous locations, special occupancies, conductors, box and raceway fill, services, and the ever present electrical calculations, plus much more.

Most electrician's licensing exams consists of multiple-choice questions therefore, these are the types of questions shown in this exam preparation guide. The exam questions you may encounter may be, fill in the blank, complete a sentence, select a correct choice, or complete a math calculation. In this self-study guide you will find simulated exams, with questions much like the actual test questions. These questions are an example of the many questions the author and his students come upon when taking numerous licensing exams in recent years.

Begin your exam preparation with two important points in mind.

* Opportunities in life will arise - be prepared for them.
* The more you LEARN - the more you EARN.

Attempting to take an exam without preparation is a complete waste of time. Don't make that mistake. Attend classes at your local community college. Attend seminars, electrical code updates, and company sponsored programs. Many major electrical suppliers and local unions sponsor classes of this type at no cost. Take advantage of them.

Become familiar with the National Electrical Code®; the Code has a LANGUAGE all its own. Understanding this language will help you to better interpret the NEC®. Do not become intimidated by its length. Become thoroughly familiar with the definitions in Chapter One; if you don't, the remainder of the NEC® will be difficult to comprehend. Remember, on the job we use different "lingo" and phrases compared to the way the NEC® is written and to the way many test questions are expressed.

HOW TO STUDY

Before beginning to study, get into the right frame of mind, and relax. Study in a quiet place that is conducive to learning. If such a place is not available, go to your local library. It is important that you have the right atmosphere in which to study.

It is much better to study many short lengths of time than attempt to study fewer, longer lengths of time. Try to study a little while, say about an hour, every evening. You will need the support and understanding of your family to set aside this much needed time.

As you study this exam preparation book, the NEC® and other references, always highlight the important points. This makes it easier to locate Code references when taking the exam.

Use a straight edge, such as a six-inch ruler when using the NEC® tables and charts. A very common mistake is to get on the wrong line when using these tables; when that happens, the result is an incorrect answer.

Use tabs on the major sections of your NEC®, so they are faster and easier to locate when taking the exam. The national average allowed per question is less than three minutes, you cannot waste time.

WHAT TO STUDY

A common reason for one to be unsuccessful when attempting to pass electrical exams is not knowing what to study. Approximately forty percent of most exams are known as "core" questions. These types of questions are reflected in this exam preparation book.

The subject matter covered in most electrical license examinations is:

* Grounding and bonding
* Overcurrent protection
* Wiring methods and installation
* Boxes and fittings
* Services and equipment
* Motors
* Special occupancies
* Load calculations
* Lighting
* Appliances
* Box and raceway fill
* Hazardous locations

Become very familiar with questions on the above. Knowing what to study is a major step toward passing your exam.

HELPFUL HINTS ON TAKING THE EXAM

* **Complete the easy questions first.** On most tests, all questions are valued the same. If you become too frustrated on any one question, it may reflect upon your entire test.

* **Keep track of time.** Do not spend too much time on one question. If a question is difficult for you, mark the answer sheet the answer you think is correct and place a check (✓) by that question in the examination booklet. Then go on to the next question; if you have time after finishing the rest of the exam, you can go back to the questions you have checked. If you simply do not know the answer to a question, take a guess. Choose the answer that is most familiar to you. In most cases, the answer is B or C.

* **Only change answers if you know you are right.** - Usually, your first answer is your best answer.

* **Relax** - Do not get uptight and stressed out when testing.

* **Tab your Code Book.** - References are easier and faster to find.

* **Use a straightedge.** - Prevent getting on the wrong line when referring to the tables in the NEC®.

* **Get a good night's rest before the exam.** - Do not attempt to drive several hours to an exam site; be rested and alert.

* **Understand the question.** - One key word in a question can make a difference in what the question is asking. Underlining key words will help you to understand the meaning of the question.

* **Use a dependable calculator.** - Use a solar-powered calculator that has a battery back-up. Since many test sites are not well lighted, this type of calculator will prepare you for such a situation. If possible, bring along a spare calculator.

* **Show up at least 30 minutes prior to your exam time.** – Be sure to allow yourself time for traffic, etc. when planning your route to the exam location.

TYPICAL REGULATIONS AT THE PLACE OF EXAMINATION

Most licensing agencies outsource their examinations to a testing agency that is a separate entity from the licensing agency. After you get approval from the licensing agency to take the exam, contact the testing agency for their regulations. To ensure that all examinees are examined under equally favorable conditions, the following regulations and procedures are observed at most examination sites:

* Each examinee must present proper photo identification, preferably your driver's license before you will be permitted to take the examination.

* No cameras, notes, tape recorders, pagers, or cellular phones are allowed in the examination room.

* No one will be permitted to work beyond the established time limits.

* Examinees are not permitted any reference material EXCEPT the National Electrical Code®.

* Examinees will be permitted to use noiseless calculators during the examination. Calculators which provide programmable ability or pre-programmed calculators are prohibited.

* Permission of an examination proctor must be obtained before leaving the room while the examination is in progress.

* Each examinee is assigned to a seat specifically designated by name and/or number when admitted to the examination room.

TYPICAL EXAMINATION QUESTIONS

EXAMPLE 1

As a general rule, an insulated equipment grounding conductor of a branch circuit shall be identified by which of the following colors?

A. gray
B. white
C. black
D. green

Here you are asked to select from the listed colors the one that is to be used to identify the equipment grounding conductor of a branch circuit. Since Section 250.119 of the NEC® requires that green or green with yellow stripes be the color of insulation used on a grounding conductor (when it is not bare), therefore, the answer is ***D*** when exceptions are not applicable.

EXAMPLE 2

An emergency electrical disconnect provided for a gasoline motor fuel dispensing pump must be located NOT more than _____ from the fuel dispensing device it serves.

A. 20 feet
B. 50 feet
C. 75 feet
D. 100 feet

Here the "question" is in the form of a fill-in-the-blank statement. Your task is to select the choice that best completes the statement. In this case, you should have selected ***D*** since Section 514.11(A) of the NEC® specifies that emergency disconnects shall be within not less than 20 ft. and NOT more than 100 ft. from the fuel dispensing devices they serve.

EXAMPLE 3

A building or other structure served shall be supplied by only one service EXCEPT. one where the capacity requirements are in excess of _____.

A. 800 amperes at a supply voltage of 1000 volts or less
B. 1000 amperes at a supply voltage of 1000 volts or less
C. 1500 amperes at a supply voltage of 1000 volts or less
D. 2000 amperes at a supply voltage of 1000 volts or less

Again, the "question" is in the form of an incomplete statement and your task is to select the choice that best completes the statement. In this case, you are to find an exception. You have to select the condition that has to be met when supplying a building or structure by more than one service. You should have selected ***D*** because Section 230.2(C)(1) requires the conditions listed in ***D*** but does not require or permit the conditions listed in A, B, or C.

EXAMPLE 4

Disregarding exceptions, the MINIMUM size overhead service-drop conductors shall be _____ AWG copper.

A. 6
B. 8
C. 12
D. 14

Here the "question" is in the form of fill in the blank and your task is to select the choice that best completes the statement. In this case, exceptions are not applicable. You have to select the minimum size conductor required for overhead service-drop conductors. You should have selected ***B*** because Section 230.23(B) specifies that the conductors shall not be smaller than 8 AWG copper.

HOW TO USE THIS BOOK

Practice exams numbers 1-12 contained in this book consists of 25 questions each. The time allotted for each of these practice exams is 75 minutes or 3 minutes per question. After taking the first 12 exams try the final exams. The two final exams are 80 questions in length; the allotted time for each final exam is 4 hours. Using this time limit as a standard, you should be able to complete an actual examination in the allotted time.

You will seldom find trick questions in this exam prep guide, but many will require careful reading. Certain words such as, shall, shall not, should and should not can make a difference in the correct answer. When a question contains verbiage such as, in general, generally, the general rule is, disregarding exceptions, etc., this means exceptions are not to be taken into consideration.

To get the most out of this book you should answer every question and highlight your NEC® for future reference. If you have difficulty with a question and cannot come up with the answer that is familiar to you, put a check mark next to the question and come back to it after completing the remainder of the questions. Review your answers with the **ANSWER KEY** located in the back of this book. This will help you identify your strengths and weaknesses. When you discover you are weaker in some areas than others, you will know that further study is necessary in those areas.

Do only one practice exam contained in this book during an allotted study period. This way you do not get burned out and fatigued trying to study for too long a period of time. This also helps you develop good study habits. **GOOD LUCK!**

ABOUT THE AUTHOR

H. Ray Holder has worked in the electrical industry for over fifty years as an apprentice, journeyman, master, field engineer, estimator, business manager, contractor, inspector, consultant, and instructor.

Mr. Holder is a graduate of Texas State University and holds a Bachelor of Science Degree in Occupational Education. He also holds a lifetime teaching certificate from the Texas Education Agency, in the field of Vocational Education.

He is a certified instructor of electrical trades. His classes are presented in a simplified, easy-to-understand format for electricians.

He has taught over 100,000 students by way of textbooks, online, and in the classrooms at Austin Community College, the University of Texas at Austin, Texas, Odessa College, at Odessa, Texas, Howard College at San Angelo, Texas, Technical-Vocational Institute of Albuquerque, New Mexico, and in the public school systems in Ft. Worth and San Antonio, Texas. He is currently the Director of Education for Electrical Seminars, Inc.

Mr. Holder is a former member of the National Fire Protection Association, International Association of Electrical Inspectors, and retired member of the International Brotherhood of Electrical Workers.

Power – "Pie" Circle Formulas

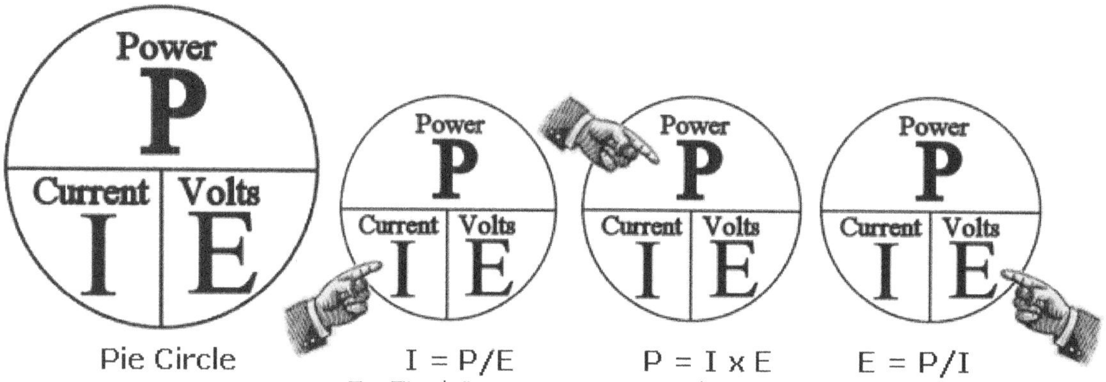

Pie Circle — I = P/E To Find Current — P = I x E To Find Power — E = P/I To Find Voltage

Ohms Law Circle Formulas

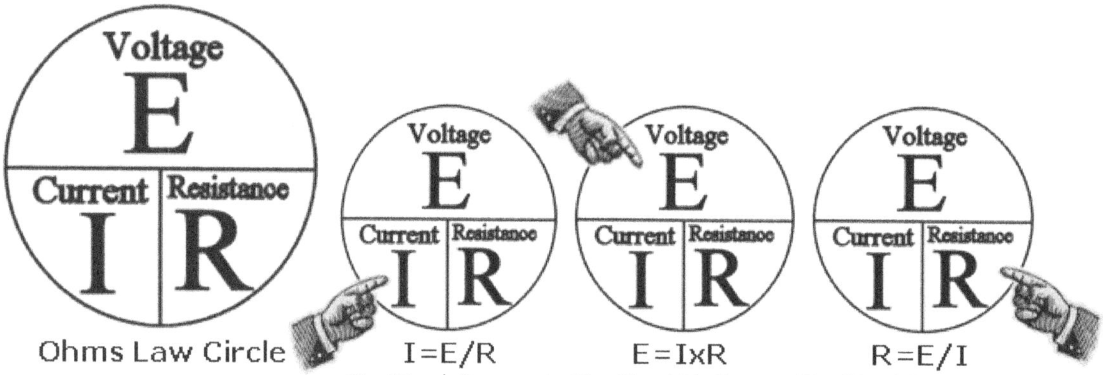

Ohms Law Circle — I=E/R To Find Current — E=IxR To Find Voltage — R=E/I To Find Resistance

Power Factor Triangle Formulas

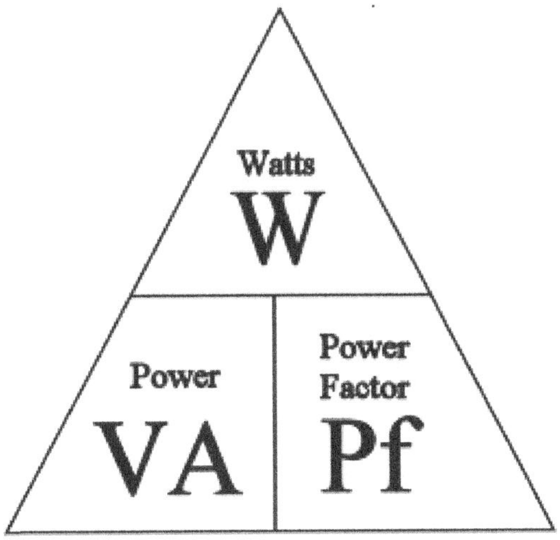

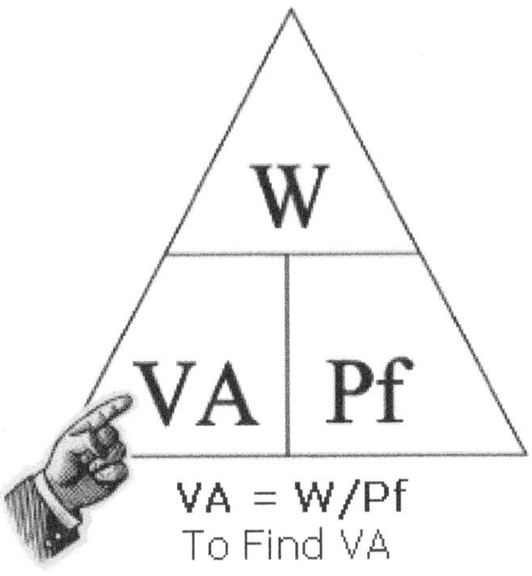

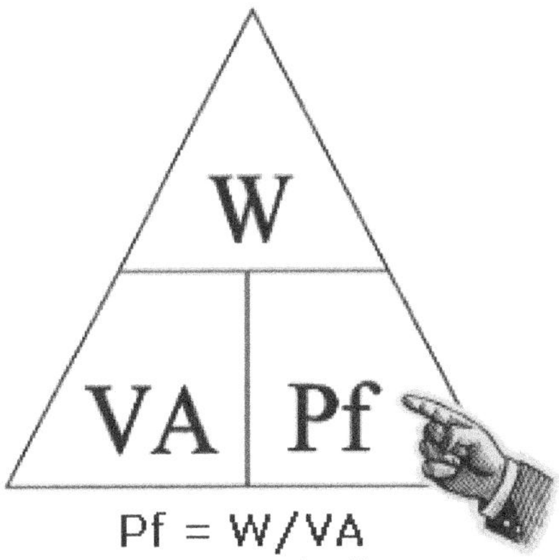

USEFUL FORMULAS

To Find	Single Phase	Three Phase	Direct Current
Amperes when kVA is known	$\frac{kVA \times 1{,}000}{E}$	$\frac{kVA \times 1{,}000}{E \times 1.732}$	not applicable
Amperes when horsepower is known	$\frac{HP \times 746}{E \times \%Eff. \times PF.}$	$\frac{HP \times 746}{E \times 1.732 \times \%Eff. \times PF.}$	$\frac{HP \times 746}{E \times \%Eff.}$
Amperes when Kilowatts are known	$\frac{kW \times 1{,}000}{E \times PF.}$	$\frac{kW \times 1{,}000}{E \times 1.732 \times PF.}$	$\frac{kW \times 1{,}000}{E}$
Kilowatts	$\frac{I \times E \times PF.}{1{,}000}$	$\frac{I \times E \times 1.732 \times PF.}{1{,}000}$	$\frac{I \times E}{1{,}000}$
Kilovolt Amperes	$\frac{I \times E}{1{,}000}$	$\frac{I \times E \times 1.732}{1{,}000}$	not applicable
Horsepower	$\frac{I \times E \times \%Eff. \times PF.}{746}$	$\frac{I \times E \times 1.732 \times \%Eff. \times PF.}{746}$	$\frac{I \times E \times \%Eff.}{746}$
Watts	E x I x PF.	E x I x 1.732 x PF.	E x I

I = Amperes

E = Volt

kW = Kilowatts

kVA = Kilovolt-Amper

HP = Horsepower

%Eff. = Percent Efficiency

PF. = Power Factor

VOLTAGE DROP FORMULAS

Formula Definitions:

VD = Volts dropped from a circuit.

2 = Multiplying factor for single-phase circuits. The 2 represents the conductor length in a single-phase circuit.

1.732 = Multiplying factor for three-phase circuits. The square root of 3 represents the conductor length in a three-phase circuit. The only difference between the single-phase and three-phase formulas is that "1.732" has replaced "2".

K = Approximate resistivity of the conductor per mil foot. A mil foot is a wire 1 foot long and one mil in diameter. The approximate K value for copper wire is **12.9** ohms and for aluminum wire is **21.2** ohms per mil foot.

I = Current or amperage draw of the load.

D = The distance from the source voltage to the load.

CM = Circular mil area of the conductor. (Chapter 9, Table 8)

*NOTE – When determining wire size, distance or current, VD is the actual volts that can be dropped from the circuit. The recommended percentage for a branch-circuit is 3%. Example: 3% of 120 volts is 3.6 volts. DO NOT enter 3% in the VD position.

To find voltage drop in a single-phase circuit.

$$VD = \frac{2 \times K \times I \times D}{CM}$$

To find wire size in a single-phase circuit.

$$CM = \frac{2 \times K \times I \times D}{VD}$$

To find distance in a single-phase circuit.

$$D = \frac{CM \times VD}{2 \times K \times I}$$

To find MAXIMUM current in amperes in a single-phase circuit.

$$I = \frac{CM \times VD}{2 \times K \times D}$$

UNIT 1

BASIC ELECTRICAL FORMULAS

Upon successfully completing this unit of study, the student will be familiar with the concepts and application of Ohm's Law, power and current formulas plus power factor.

2020

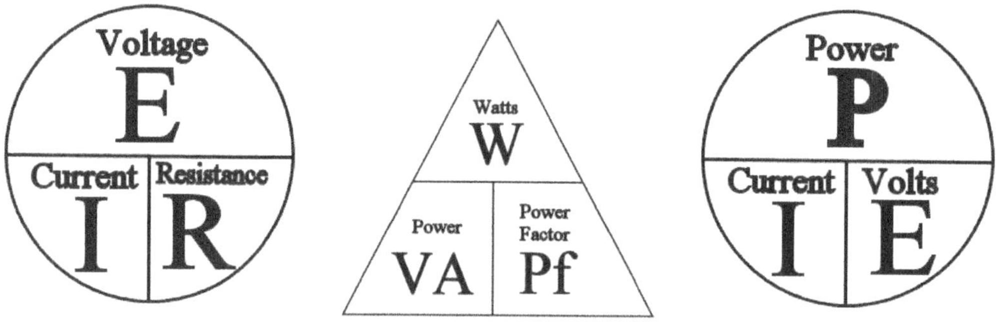

UNIT 1

BASIC ELECTRICAL FORMULAS

PIE CIRCLE FORMULAS

RELATED INFORMATION:

- The **PIE** formula circle illustrates the relationship between **power, current and voltage**.

- Power may be expressed as true power such as, **watts**, **kilowatts**, **kW** or **horsepower**; power may also be expressed in terms as apparent power such as, **volt-amps**, **VA**, **kilo volt-amps** or **kVA**.

- The letter "**P**" represents power.

- The letter "**I**" represents the intensity of current.

- The letter "**E**" represents voltage.

- The letter "**k**" is the abbreviation of kilo or one thousand (1,000).

- One **kW** equals 1,000 watts.

- One **kVA** equals 1,000 volt-amps.

- One **horsepower** equals 746 watts.

- Formulas used to determine the available power for a single-phase circuit, load or an electrical system are:

  P = I x E

  P = current x volts

  P = volts x amps

  P = VA

  P = kVA

  $kW = \frac{\text{current x volts}}{1{,}000}$

  $kVA = \frac{\text{current x volts}}{1{,}000}$

EXAMPLE – Determine the available power, in VA, for a 100 ampere, 240 volt, single-phase circuit.

A. 2,400 VA
B. 24,000 VA
C. 240,000 VA
D. 240 VA

ANSWER – (B) 24,000 VA

VA = I x E
VA = 100 amperes x 240 volts = 24,000 VA

EXAMPLE – Determine the apparent power, in kVA, for a 150 ampere, 120/240 Volt, single-phase electrical system.

A. 36 kVA
B. 3.60 kVA
C. 360 kVA
D. 3,600 kVA

ANSWER – (A) 36 kVA

$kVA = \frac{I \text{ x } E}{1{,}000}$

$kVA = \frac{\text{150 amps x 240 volts}}{1{,}000} = \frac{36{,}000}{1{,}000} = 36 \text{ kVA}$

- Formulas used to determine the available power for three-phase circuits, loads or electrical systems are:

  $P = I \times E \times 1.732$

  P = current x volts x 1.732

  P = volts x 1.732 x amps

  P = VA x 1.732

  $$kW = \frac{\text{current x volts x 1.732}}{1{,}000}$$

  $$kVA = \frac{\text{current x volts x 1.732}}{1{,}000}$$

EXAMPLE – Determine the available power, in VA, for a 100 ampere 208Y/120 volt, three-phase circuit.

A. 3,603 VA
B. 36,026 VA
C. 360,260 VA
D. 20,800 VA

ANSWER – (B) 36,026 VA

VA = I x E x 1.732
VA = 100 amps x 208 volts x 1.732 = 36,026 VA

*Note – In this situation we are to use 208 volts and multiply by 1.732 (the square root of 3), because we are to balance the load in the three current-carrying conductors.

EXAMPLE – A load that draws 50 amperes when connected to a 208Y/120 volt, three-phase source has a kW rating of ______.

A. 18 kW
B. 1.8 kW
C. 180 kW
D. 1,800 kW

ANSWER – (A) 18 kW

$$kW = \frac{\text{current x volts x 1.732}}{1{,}000}$$

$$kW = \frac{50 \times 208 \times 1.732}{1{,}000} = \frac{18{,}013}{1{,}000} = 18 \text{ kW}$$

- Current may be expressed in terms such as **amps**, **amperes**, **full-load current**, **FLC**, **full-load amps**, **FLA**, **load in amps** or **amperes**, **amperage**, **amperage draw** or **line load**.

- The letter "I" represents the intensity of the current.

- Formulas used to determine the current in a single-phase circuit, load or an electrical system are:

  $I = \frac{P}{E}$

  $I = \frac{\text{power}}{\text{voltage}}$

  $I = \frac{\text{watts}}{\text{volts}}$

  $I = \frac{\text{kW x 1,000}}{\text{volts}}$

  $I = \frac{\text{VA}}{\text{volts}}$

  $I = \frac{\text{kVA x 1,000}}{\text{volts}}$

EXAMPLE – Determine the current, in amperes, for a 120 volt, single-phase branch circuit that has only six (6) 100 watt incandescent luminaries (lighting fixtures) connected.

A. 5 amperes
B. 15 amperes
C. 20 amperes
D. 2 amperes

ANSWER – (A) 5 amperes

$I = \frac{\text{watts}}{\text{volts}} \quad I = \frac{600}{120} = 5$ amperes

EXAMPLE – Determine the current, in amperes, of a 2.4 kW load connected to a 240 volt, single-phase source.

A. .01 ampere
B. 1 ampere
C. 100 amperes
D. 10 amperes

ANSWER – (D) 10 amperes

$$I = \frac{2.4 \text{ kW} \times 1{,}000}{240} = \frac{2{,}400}{240} = 10 \text{ amperes}$$

- Formulas used to determine the current in a three (3)-phase circuit, load, or an electrical system are:

$$I = \frac{P}{E \times 1.732}$$

$$I = \frac{\text{power}}{\text{volts} \times 1.732}$$

$$I = \frac{\text{watts}}{\text{volts} \times 1.732}$$

$$I = \frac{\text{kW} \times 1{,}000}{\text{volts} \times 1.732}$$

$$I = \frac{\text{VA}}{\text{volts} \times 1.732}$$

$$I = \frac{\text{kVA} \times 1{,}000}{\text{volts} \times 1.732}$$

EXAMPLE – A 36,026 VA load connected to a 208Y/120-volt, three-phase circuit will draw ______ of current per phase.

A. 10 amperes
B. 173 amperes
C. 250 amperes
D. 100 amperes

ANSWER – (D) 100 amperes

$$I = \frac{\text{VA}}{E \times 1.732}$$

$$I = \frac{36{,}026 \text{ VA}}{208 \text{ volts} \times 1.732} = \frac{36{,}026}{360.25} = 100 \text{ amperes}$$

EXAMPLE – A balanced 60 kVA load connected to a 480Y/277-volt three-phase electrical system will have a full-load current draw of _____ per phase.

A. 72 amperes
B. 125 amperes
C. 720 amperes
D. 80 amperes

ANSWER – (A) 72 amperes

$$I = \frac{\text{kVA x 1,000}}{\text{volts x 1.732}}$$

$$I = \frac{\text{60 kVA x 1,000}}{\text{480 volts x 1.732}} = \frac{60{,}000}{831.36} = \text{72 amperes}$$

POWER FACTOR

RELATED INFORMATION:

- **Power factor (PF)** is the ratio between true power expressed as **watts**, **kilo watts** or **kW** and the apparent power expressed as **volt-amps**, **VA** or **kVA**.

- Power factor is expressed as a percent that does not exceed 100 percent or a decimal.

- True power, is expressed as **watts**, a unit of work, **kW** or **kilowatts**; this condition occurs in AC circuits or loads that contain only resistance. This is why electric ranges, ovens, cooktops, dryers and water heaters are all rated in **watts** or **kW**. The current and the voltage will be "in-phase", meaning that the voltage and the current will reach their peak and zero values at the same time. This is what we call unity or a power factor of 100 percent.

- True power (**watts**) equals apparent power (**VA**) in an electrical circuit or load containing only resistance.

- True power (**watts**) is less than apparent power (**VA**) in a circuit or load containing inductance or capacitance, such as motors, transformers, HID and fluorescent lighting.

- The true power (**watts**) of a single-phase circuit or load that contains inductance or capacitance can be calculated by the use of the following formula:

  Watts = volts x amperes x power factor

EXAMPLE – What is the true power, in watts, of a 10 ampere load supplied with 120 volts, having a power factor of 80 percent?

A. 1,000 watts
B. 1,200 watts
C. 2,400 watts
D. 960 watts

ANSWER – (D) 960 watts

Watts = volts x amperes x power factor
Watts = 120 volts x 10 amps x .8 = 960 watts

- The true power (watts) of a three-phase circuit or load that contains inductance or capacitance can be calculated by the use of the following formula:

Watts = volts x 1.732 x amperes x power factor

EXAMPLE – Determine the true power (watts) of a 7.5 ampere load with a power factor of 87 percent supplied from a three-phase, 208-volt source.

A. 1,375 watts
B. 2,350 watts
C. 2,700 watts
D. 3,132 watts

ANSWER – (B) 2,350 watts

Watts = volts x 1.732 x amperes x power factor
Watts = 208 volts x 1.732 x 7.5 amps x .87 = 2,350 watts

- In most **ac circuits** containing inductance or capacitance a phase shift exists, the current is **"out-of-phase"** with the voltage; the current and the voltage do not reach their peak and zero values at the same time. Apparent power (VA) is usually more than the power in watts when this condition occurs. Apparent power is calculated without considering the phase shift that may be present between total voltage and current in the circuit.

- Formulas used to determine the power factor are:

$$\text{Power factor} = \frac{\text{watts}}{\text{VA}}$$

$$\text{Power factor} = \frac{\text{watts}}{\text{volt amps}}$$

$$\text{Power factor} = \frac{\text{kW x 1,000}}{\text{volt amps}}$$

EXAMPLE - The power factor of a 5 kW load drawing 30 amperes of current when connected to a 208-volt, single-phase source is ______.

A. 92 percent
B. 46 percent
C. 80 percent
D. 83 percent

ANSWER – (C) 80 percent

$$PF = \frac{kW \times 1{,}000}{volt \times amperes}$$

$$PF = \frac{5\ kW \times 1{,}000}{208\ volts \times 30\ amps} = \frac{5{,}000}{6{,}240} = .80 \text{ or } 80\%$$

- Formulas used to determine the current of a single-phase electrical load or system when the voltage and power factor are known are:

$$I = \frac{watts}{volts \times PF}$$

$$I = \frac{kw \times 1{,}000}{volts \times PF}$$

EXAMPLE – A 300 watt industrial type HID luminaire (lighting fixture) has a power factor of 85 percent and is connected to a 120 volt branch circuit. The luminaire will draw ______ of current.

A. 2.94 amperes
B. 2.50 amperes
C. 3.25 amperes
D. 2.13 amperes

ANSWER – (A) 2.94 amperes

$$I = \frac{watts}{volts \times PF}$$

$$I = \frac{300\ watts}{120\ volts \times .85} = \frac{300}{102} = 2.94 \text{ amperes}$$

- Formulas used to determine the current of a three-phase load or system when the voltage and the power factor are known are:

$$I = \frac{watts}{volts \times 1.732 \times PF}$$

$$I = \frac{kw \times 1{,}000}{volts \times 1.732 \times PF}$$

EXAMPLE - A 5 kW load having a power factor of 90 percent will draw ______ when connected to a 208Y/120 volt, three-phase electrical system.

A. 37.47 amperes
B. 13.88 amperes
C. 17.87 amperes
D. 15.42 amperes

ANSWER – (D) 15.42 amperes

$$I = \frac{kW \times 1{,}000}{volts \times 1.732 \times PF}$$

$$I = \frac{5\ kW \times 1{,}000}{208\ volts \times 1.732 \times .9} = \frac{5{,}000}{324.2} = 15.42\ amperes$$

OHM'S LAW CIRCLE FORMULAS

RELATED INFORMATION:

- The Ohm's Law circle formula illustrates the relationship between **voltage**, **current** and **resistance**.

- The letter "**E**" represents electromotive force, or voltage.

- The letter "**I**" represents the intensity of the current.

- The letter "**R**" represents the friction opposite the flow of electrons in a conductor and is known as resistance; the unit of measurement is the ohm.

- In an alternating current circuit, factors that oppose current flow are conductor resistance, capacitive reactance, and inductive reactance. This total opposition to current flow is known as impedance and is also measured in ohms; the letter "**Z**" represents the impedance and may be substituted for the letter "**R**".

- The formula used to determine the current flow in an electrical circuit or load when the resistance and voltage are known is:

$$I = \frac{E}{R}$$

$$I = \frac{volts}{resistance}$$

EXAMPLE – A 120 volt circuit supplies an incandescent luminaire (lighting fixture) with a resistance of 200 ohms. Determine the current flow, in amperes, of the circuit.

A. 6.00 amperes
B. 0.60 amperes
C. 3.00 amperes
D. 1.60 amperes

ANSWER – (B) 0.60 amperes

$$I = \frac{\text{volts}}{\text{resistance}} = \frac{120 \text{ volts}}{200 \text{ ohms}} = 0.60 \text{ amperes}$$

- The formula used to determine the voltage or voltage drop in an electrical circuit when the current and resistance are known is:

$E = I \times R$

E = current x resistance

EXAMPLE – Determine the voltage drop of two size 10 AWG copper conductors that supply a 16 ampere load located 100 feet from the voltage source.

Given: The total resistance of the two conductors is 0.25 ohms.

A. 2.00 volts
B. 0.40 volts
C. 4.00 volts
D. 40.00 volts

ANSWER – (C) 4.00 volts

$E = I \times R$
E = 16 amperes x .25 ohms = 4 volts

- The formula used to determine the resistance in an electrical circuit or load when the voltage and current are known is:

$$R = \frac{E}{I}$$

$$R = \frac{\text{voltage}}{\text{current}}$$

EXAMPLE – Determine the resistance of the heating elements of an electric baseboard heater that draws 8 amperes when supplied from a 120 volt source.

A. 0.07 ohms
B. 960 ohms
C. 15 ohms
D. 150 ohms

ANSWER – (C) 15 ohms

$$R = \frac{\text{volts}}{\text{current}} = \frac{120 \text{ volts}}{8 \text{ amperes}} = 15 \text{ ohms}$$

UNIT 2

BRANCH CIRCUITS

Upon successfully completing this unit of study, the student will be familiar with the concept of sizing, rating and overcurrent protection of branch circuits as well as calculating the number required.

$$\text{\# of CIRCUITS} = \frac{\text{LOAD VA}}{\text{CIRCUIT VA}}$$

UNIT 2

BRANCH CIRCUITS

RELATED INFORMATION:

- The definition of a **branch circuit** is the circuit conductors between the final overcurrent device (circuit breaker or fuse) protecting the circuit and the outlet(s). **[Article 100]** In other words, that portion of a wiring system that is beyond the final overcurrent device protecting the circuit and the outlet(s).

- The rating of a **branch circuit** is determined by the maximum ampere rating of the overcurrent protective device (circuit breaker or fuse) and **NOT** by the size of the conductors used for the branch-circuit.

- In general, branch-circuit conductors shall have an allowable ampacity (current-carrying capacity) of **NOT** less than **125%** of the **continuous** load, plus **100%** of the **non-continuous** load to be served.

EXAMPLE – When a single branch-circuit serves a continuous load of 20 amperes and a non-continuous load of 10 amperes, the branch-circuit conductors are required to have an allowable current-carrying capacity of at least _____.

A. 30.00 amperes
B. 37.50 amperes
C. 35.00 amperes
D. 32.50 amperes

ANSWER – (C) 35.00 amperes

20 amperes x 1.25 = 25 amperes
10 amperes x 1.00 = 10 amperes
TOTAL = 35 amperes

- The definition of a **continuous** load is a load where the maximum current is expected to continue for **3 hours** or more.

- Examples of **continuous** loads are lighting loads for commercial and industrial occupancies that are expected to be operated for at least three (3) hours.

- Examples of **non-continuous** loads are general-purpose receptacle outlets provided for commercial, industrial, and residential occupancies and general-purpose lighting loads for residential occupancies.

- In general, overcurrent devices protecting branch-circuits shall have a rating of not less than **125%** of the **continuous** load to be served plus **100%** of the **non-continuous** load to be served. In other words, overcurrent devices protecting branch circuits are not to be loaded more than **80%** of their rated value when protecting **continuous** loads.

EXAMPLE - When a 100 ampere rated circuit breaker is used to protect a branch circuit serving a continuous load, the load shall not exceed _____.

A. 80 amperes
B. 100 amperes
C. 125 amperes
D. 115 amperes

ANSWER – (A) 80 amperes

100 amperes x .80 = 80 amperes

- Note the exception to **210.20(A)**. If the overcurrent device protecting the circuit is **listed** for **continuous operation**, it shall be permitted to have a rating of **100%** of the continuous load(s) to be served. **Be advised**, circuit breakers are **NOT** listed for continuous operation, unless they have a rating of at least 4**00 amperes** or more.

- In general, branch-circuit loads shall be calculated as shown in **220.12**, **220.14**, and **220.16** **[220.10]**

- In general, lighting loads are to be supplied by 15-and 20-ampere rated branch-circuits.

- Lighting loads for specific occupancies shall be based on the unit load per square foot depending on the type of occupancy as given on **Table 220.12**

General Lighting Loads by Occupancy (Non-Dwelling)

	UNIT LOAD	
Type of Occupancy	**Volt-Amperes/ m^2**	**Volt-Amperes/ft^2**
Automotive facility	16	1.5
Convention center	15	1.4
Courthouse	15	1.4
Dormitory	16	1.5
Exercise center	15	1.4
Fire station	14	1.3
Gymnasium[a]	18	1.7
Health care clinic	17	1.6
Hospital	17	1.6
Hotels and motels, including apartment houses without provision for cooking by tenants[b]	18	1.7
Library	16	1.5
Manufacturing facility[c]	24	2.2
Motion picture theater	17	1.6
Museum	17	1.6
Office[d]	14	1.3
Parking garage[e]	3	0.3
Penitentiary	13	1.2
Performing arts theater	16	1.5
Police station	14	1.3
Post office	17	1.6
Religious facility	24	2.2
Restaurant[f]	16	1.5
Retail[g,h]	20	1.9
School/university	33	3
Sports area	33	3
Town hall	15	1.4
Transportation	13	1.2
Warehouse	13	1.2
Workshop	18	1.7

- General lighting loads are to be calculated from the outside dimensions of the building.

- To determine the area, in square feet, of a building, simply multiply the length of the building times the width of the building.

EXAMPLE - A building has outside dimensions of 100 feet in length and 75 feet in width. The building has a total area of _____.

A. 750 square feet
B. 175 square feet
C. 7,500 square feet
D. 1,750 square feet

ANSWER - (C) 7,500 sq. ft.

100 ft. x 75 ft. = 7,500 sq. ft.

- When calculating the area, in square feet, of a multi-story building, multiply the length of the building by the width of the building by the number of stories.

EXAMPLE - A three (3) story building having outside dimensions of 100 feet by 75 feet has a total area of _____.

A. 2,225 square feet
B. 7,500 square feet
C. 15,000 square feet
D. 22,500 square feet

ANSWER - (D) 22,500 sq. ft.

100 ft. x 75 ft. x 3 (stories) = 22,500 sq. ft.

- When calculating lighting loads for **dwelling units** do **NOT** include open porches, garages or unfinished spaces not adaptable for future use.

- Remember, in general, lighting loads for habitable spaces of dwelling units and guest rooms of hotels and motels are **not considered** as continuous use. But lighting loads of commercial and industrial occupancies **are considered** as continuous use.

- The formula used to determine the minimum number of general lighting branch-circuits required for a dwelling unit is:

$$\text{Number of Circuits} = \frac{\text{load VA}}{\text{circuit VA}}$$

EXAMPLE – A dwelling unit having 2,000 sq. ft. of habitable space is required to have at least _____ 15-ampere, 120-volt general-purpose lighting branch-circuits.

A. two
B. three
C. four
D. five

ANSWER - (C) four

$$\frac{2{,}000 \text{ sq. ft.} \times 3 \text{ VA}}{120 \text{ volts} \times 15 \text{ amperes}} = \frac{6{,}000 \text{ VA}}{1{,}800 \text{ VA}} = 3.3 = 4 \text{ circuits}$$

- When calculating branch-circuits, when your calculation is more than a whole number, ex. 3.3, you must go to the next whole number. In other words, you cannot install part of a circuit or circuit breaker.

- Multifamily apartment dwellings without provisions for cooking by tenants are to be calculated at the same value, **1.7 VA** per square foot, as hotels and motels when determining the minimum of general lighting branch-circuits required for the living units.

EXAMPLE - A multifamily condo, without cooking facilities provided for the tenants, having 12,000 sq. ft. of living area, is required to have at least _____ 20 ampere, 120-volt general lighting branch-circuits, or at least _____ 15 ampere, 120-volt general lighting branch-circuits.

A. ten – ten
B. fourteen – fourteen
C. ten – thirteen
D. nine – twelve

ANSWER – (D)nine – twelve

$$\frac{12{,}000 \text{ sq. ft.} \times 1.7 \text{ VA}}{120 \text{ volts} \times \mathbf{20} \text{ amperes}} = \frac{20{,}400 \text{ VA}}{2{,}400 \text{ VA}} = 8.5 = 9 \text{ circuits}$$

$$\frac{12{,}000 \text{ sq. ft.} \times 2 \text{ VA}}{120 \text{ volts} \times \mathbf{15} \text{ amperes}} = \frac{20{,}400 \text{ VA}}{1{,}800 \text{ VA}} = 11.3 = 12 \text{ circuits}$$

- A formula used to determine the minimum number of required general lighting branch-circuits for an office building, store, bank, restaurant, etc. is :

$$\text{Number of Circuits} = \frac{\text{load VA} \times \mathbf{125\%}}{\text{circuit VA}}$$

EXAMPLE - A 10,000 sq. ft. restaurant is required to be provided with at least _____ 20-ampere, 120-volt general lighting branch-circuits.

A. eight
B. nine
C. ten
D. eight

ANSWER - (D) eight

$$\frac{10{,}000 \text{ x } 1.5\text{VA x } \mathbf{125\%}}{120 \text{ volts x } 20 \text{ amps}} = \frac{18{,}750 \text{ VA}}{2{,}400 \text{ VA}} = 7.8 = 8 \text{ circuits}$$

➢ Because the circuit breakers protecting the branch-circuits are not permitted to be loaded to more than **80 percent** of their rated value, we can also use this formula:

$$\text{number of circuits} = \frac{\text{load VA}}{\text{circuit VA x } \mathbf{80\%}}$$

$$\text{number of circuits} = \frac{10{,}000 \text{ x } 1.5 \text{ VA}}{120 \text{ x } 20 \text{ x } \mathbf{80\%}} = \frac{15{,}000 \text{ VA}}{1{,}920 \text{ VA}} = 7.8 = 8 \text{ circuits}$$

➢ Notice that **Table 220.12** reflects minimum requirements for general lighting loads. Many commercial, particularly mercantile, occupancies have luminaries (lighting fixtures) installed for display, specialty, enhancement or accent lighting in addition to the general lighting. These loads are required to be included when calculating lighting loads.

EXAMPLE - A 15,000 sq. ft. retail store has 10,000 VA of accent lighting in addition to the general lighting. How many 120-volt, 20-ampere branch-circuits are required for the accent and general lighting loads?

A. 21
B. 24
C. 36
D. 32

ANSWER - (A) 21 circuits

$$\text{General ltg. circuits} = \frac{15{,}000 \text{ x } 1.9 \text{ VA}}{120 \text{ x } 20 \text{ x } 80\%} = \frac{28{,}500}{1{,}920} = 14.8 = 15$$

$$\text{Accent ltg. circuits} = \frac{10{,}000 \text{ VA}}{120 \text{ x } 20 \text{ x } 80\%} = \frac{10{,}000}{1{,}920} = 5.2 = 6$$

15 + 6 = 21 circuits total

➢ When reviewing **Table 220.12** notice the subscript **(b)** opposite of banks and office buildings which refers you to **220.14(K)**. This article indicates when the number of general-purpose receptacle outlets to be installed in the building has not yet been determined, **one VA** per square foot is to be added to the calculation for the outlets. The NEC® initiated this requirement because it is common practice for banks and office buildings to have future tenant spaces and the actual number of general-purpose receptacle outlets to be installed have not been determined prior to complete construction of the building.

- For non-dwelling units, receptacle outlets are to be calculated at a value of not less than **180 volt-amperes** for each single or duplex receptacle. **[220.14(I)]** In banks and office buildings, the receptacle loads are to be calculated to be the larger of (1) the calculated load from **220.14(I)** or (2) one VA per square ft.

- The formula used to determine the maximum number of receptacle outlets permitted on a branch-circuit is:

$$\text{Number of Receptacles} = \frac{\text{circuit VA}}{\text{180 VA}}$$

EXAMPLE - No more than ______ duplex receptacle outlets installed in a commercial establishment may be supplied from a single 20-ampere rated, 120-volt branch-circuit.

A. ten
B. twelve
C. thirteen
D. fourteen

ANSWER - (C) thirteen

$$\frac{\text{120 volts x 20 amperes}}{\text{180 VA}} = \frac{2{,}400}{180} = 13.3 = 13 \text{ receptacles}$$

- When determining the minimum number of required branch-circuits for general-purpose receptacle outlets when the specific number of receptacle outlets to be installed in a commercial building is known, this formula may be used:

$$\text{number of circuits} = \frac{\text{180 VA x number of receptacles}}{\text{circuit VA}}$$

EXAMPLE - You are to install one hundred (100) duplex receptacle outlets in an existing office building. How many 20-ampere, 120-volt, branch-circuits will need to be added to supply the additional receptacles?

A. twelve
B. ten
C. seven
D. eight

ANSWER - (D) eight

$$\frac{180\ VA \times 100}{120\ volts \times 20\ amps} = \frac{18{,}000}{2{,}400} = 7.5 = 8\ circuits$$

➢ Section **220.14(G)** indicates two methods are permitted when calculating branch-circuits for show window lighting.
(1) 180 VA per receptacle outlet in compliance with **210.62**, which requires one receptacle per twelve linear feet of the show window.
(2) 200 volt-amps per linear foot of the show window.

The linear foot calculation method is the most commonly used method. The following formula may be used:

$$\text{number of circuits} = \frac{200\ VA \times \text{linear ft.} \times \mathbf{125\%}}{\text{circuit } VA}$$

EXAMPLE - A retail department store is to have seventy five (75) continuous linear feet of show window space. Using the linear foot method of calculation, how many 20-ampere, 120-volt, branch-circuits must be provided for the show window lighting?

A. eight
B. seven
C. six
D. five

ANSWER - (A) eight

$$\frac{200\ VA \times 75\ ft. \times \mathbf{125\%}}{20\ amps \times 120\ volts} = \frac{18{,}750}{2{,}400} = 7.8 = 8\ circuits$$

➢ When calculating the number of required branch-circuits for multioutlet assemblies installed in commercial, industrial and educational locations, the calculation is to be based on the use of the supplied cord-connected equipment that is expected to be used at the same time.

➢ When calculating the required branch-circuits for fixed multioutlet assemblies where the cord-connected appliances are **unlikely** to be used simultaneously, you can use the following formula:

$$\text{number of circuits} = \frac{(\text{linear ft.}/5) \times 180\ VA}{\text{circuit } VA}$$

EXAMPLE - A small cabinet makers shop is to install fifty (50) feet of multioutlet assembly where the appliances to be used are unlikely to be operated simultaneously. Where 20-ampere, 120-volt branch-circuits are used to supply the assembly, what is the minimum required?

A. one
B. two
C. three
D. four

ANSWER - (A) one

$$\frac{(50/5) \times 180}{120 \text{ volts} \times 20 \text{ amps}} = \frac{(10) \times 180}{2{,}400} = \frac{1{,}800}{2{,}400} = .75 \text{ or } 1 \text{ circuit}$$

➢ When calculating the branch-circuits required for fixed multioutlet assemblies where the cord-connected appliances are **likely** to be used simultaneously, the following formula may be used:

$$\text{number of circuits} = \frac{\text{linear ft.} \times 180 \text{ VA}}{\text{circuit VA}}$$

EXAMPLE - Seventy five (75) feet of fixed multioutlet assembly is to be wall-mounted in a retail outlet displaying television sets where most of the TV sets are operating simultaneously. How many 20-ampere, 120-volt branch-circuits are needed to supply this installation?

A. two
B. five
C. six
D. seven

ANSWER - (C) six

$$\frac{75 \text{ ft.} \times 180 \text{ VA}}{120 \text{ volts} \times 20 \text{ amps}} = \frac{13{,}500}{2{,}400} = 5.6 = 6 \text{ circuits}$$

➢ The definition of an individual branch-circuit is a branch-circuit that supplies only one utilization equipment. Examples of individual branch circuits would be branch-circuits supplying electric water heaters, dryers, ranges, cooktops, air conditioners, etc. **[Article 100]**

➢ For **other than** individual branch-circuits the rating of the circuits shall be 15, 20, 30, 40 and 50 amperes. **Individual** branch circuits may also have ratings of the same size, in addition they may have ratings of 25, 35, 45 and 60 amperes or more. See **Table 240.6(A)** for the standard size ampere ratings of fuses and circuit breakers.

➢ When selecting ampere ratings of overcurrent protective devices, if the conductors being protected are **NOT** part of a multi-outlet branch circuit supplying receptacles for cord-and-plug-connected portable loads and the ampacity of the conductors do not correspond with the standard ampere rating of a fuse or circuit breaker and the next higher standard rating selected does **not exceed 800 amperes**, the next higher standard overcurrent device shall be permitted to be used.

➢ When selecting overcurrent protective devices where the overcurrent device is rated **over 800 amperes**, if the ampacity of the conductors do not correspond with the standard rating of a fuse or a circuit breaker you must go **down** to the next standard size fuse or circuit breaker.

➢ The overcurrent protection for small conductors, sizes 14 AWG through 10 AWG, shall be as listed in **240.4(D)**. Do not get overcurrent confused with ampacity.

- When sizing branch-circuits and overcurrent protection for appliances such as water heaters and cooktops, they are to be sized per **Article 422**. Branch-circuits for household cooking appliances shall be permitted to be in accordance with **Table 220.55**, which will be discussed later.

- Fixed storage-type water heaters with a capacity of 120 gallons or less shall be considered a continuous load when sizing branch-circuits.

EXAMPLE - The branch-circuit conductors supplying a 5 kW, 240-volt, single-phase water heater, are required to have an ampacity of at least _____.

A. 15.0 amperes
B. 20.8 amperes
C. 26.0 amperes
D. 31.2 amperes

ANSWER - (C) 26.0 amperes

$$I = \frac{5 \text{ kW} \times 1{,}000}{240 \text{ volts}} = \frac{5{,}000}{240} = 20.8 \times \mathbf{125\%} = 26.04 \text{ amperes}$$

*NOTE - To solve this problem you should refer to **422.13** and **422.10(A)**.

EXAMPLE - The MAXIMUM size circuit breaker that may be used to protect a 5 kW, 240-volt, single-phase electric water heater has a rating of _____.

A. 20 amperes
B. 25 amperes
C. 30 amperes
D. 35 amperes

ANSWER - (D) 35 amperes

$$I = \frac{5{,}000}{240} = 20.8 \text{ amps} \times 150\% = 31.2 \text{ amperes}$$

*NOTE - The next standard size circuit breaker has a rating of 35 amperes. To solve this problem you should refer to **422.11(E)(3)** and **240.6(A)**.

- When sizing branch-circuits and overcurrent protection for fixed electric space-heating equipment, they are to be sized in compliance with **Article 424**.

- Fixed electric space-heating equipment shall be considered as **continuous loads**.

EXAMPLE - The branch-circuit conductors supplying a 15 kW, 240 volt, single-phase fixed electric space-heater, are required to have an ampacity of at least _____.

A. 42 amperes
B. 52 amperes
C. 63 amperes
D. 78 amperes

ANSWER - (D) 78 amperes

$$I = \frac{15 \times 1{,}000}{240} = \frac{15{,}000}{240} = 62.5 \times \mathbf{125\%} = 78 \text{ amperes}$$

➢ The following formula may be used to determine the minimum number of a required branch-circuits to supply fixed electric space-heating equipment:

$$\text{number of circuits} = \frac{\text{load VA} \times \mathbf{125\%}}{\text{circuit VA}}$$

EXAMPLE - What is the minimum number of 20-ampere, 240-volt branch-circuits required for twelve (12) baseboard heaters, each rated 1,250 watts at 240-volts, single-phase?

A. three
B. four
C. six
D. eight

ANSWER – (B) four

$$\frac{1{,}250 \times 12 \times \mathbf{125\%}}{240 \text{ volts} \times 20 \text{ amps}} = \frac{18{,}750}{4{,}800} = 3.9 = 4 \text{ circuits}$$

UNIT 3

COOKING EQUIPMENT & APPLIANCE DEMAND LOADS

Upon successfully completing this study unit, the student will be familiar with the concept of calculating demand loads for household cooking equipment and appliances.

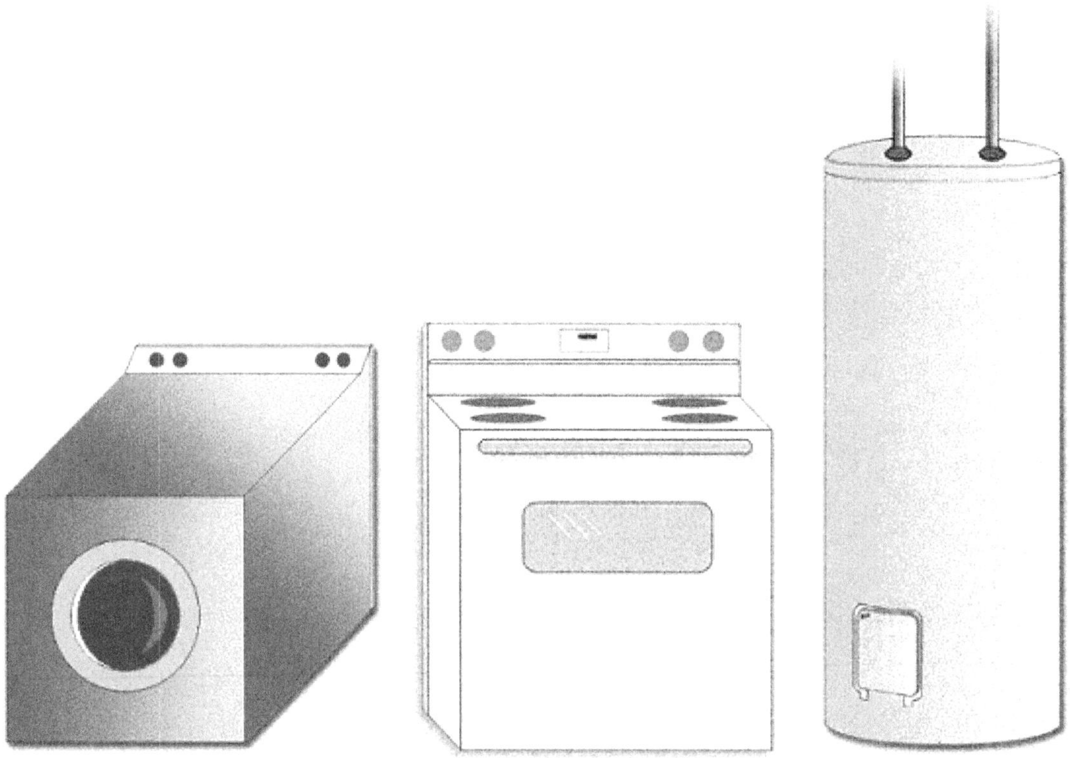

Unit 3

COOKING EQUIPMENT & APPLIANCE DEMAND LOADS

RELATED INFORMATION:

- The definition of **demand factor** is the ratio of the maximum demand of a system, or part of a system, to the total connected load of a system or the part of the system under consideration.

- The **demand load** of an electrical system or an electrical appliance is the MAXIMUM load of the system or appliance that may be required at a given time. In other words, **demand factors** are applied because all of the electrical loads are not used at the same time; all of the luminaires (lighting fixtures) will not be on at the same time, neither will all the receptacle outlets and appliances be fully loaded at the same time.

- A good example of this concept would be an electric range having a **connected load** rating of **12 kW**. The range-top has four heating elements, the oven has one heating element, another heating element is required for the broiler, and accessories such as timers and lights are included in the total connected load. Therefore, we can apply **demand factors** as shown in **Table 220.55** which reflects a **demand load** of **8 kW**, because we would not be using all of the heating elements and the accessories at their **MAXIMUM** value at any given time.

- **Table 220.55** and its related notes are to be used to apply **demand factors** for household electric ranges, wall-mounted ovens, counter-mounted cooking units, and other household cooking appliances over **1¾ kW** rating. This table is to be used when applying **demand factors** when sizing services, feeders and branch circuits for dwelling units and instructional programs for educational institutions.

Table 220.55 Demand Factors and Loads for Household Electric Ranges, Wall-Mounted Ovens, Counter-Mounted Cooking Units, and Other Household Cooking Appliances over 1¾ kW Rating (Column C to be used in all cases except as otherwise permitted in Note 3).

Demand Factor (Percent) (See Notes)

Number of Appliances	Column A (Less than 3½ kW Rating)	Column B (3½ kW to 8¾ kW Rating)	Column C Maximum Demand (kW) (See Notes) (Not over 12 kW Rating)
1	80	80	8
2	75	65	11
3	70	55	14
4	66	50	17
5	62	45	20
6	59	43	21
7	56	40	22
8	53	36	23
9	51	35	24
10	49	34	25
11	47	32	26
12	45	32	27
13	43	32	28
14	41	32	29
15	40	32	30
16	39	28	31
17	38	28	32
18	37	28	33
19	36	28	34
20	35	28	35
21	34	26	36
22	33	26	37
23	32	26	38
24	31	26	39
25	30	26	40
26-30	30	24	15 kW + 1 kW for each range
31-40	30	22	
41-50	30	20	25 kW + ¾ kW for each range
51-60	30	18	
61 and over	30	16	

1. Over 12 kW through 27 kW ranges all of same rating. For ranges individually rated more than 12 kW but not more than 27 kW, the maximum demand in Column C shall be increased 5 percent for each additional kilowatt of rating or major fraction thereof by which the rating of individual ranges exceeds 12 kW.
2. Over 8¾ kW through 27 kW ranges of unequal ratings. For ranges individually rated more than 8¾ kW and of different ratings, but none exceeding 27 kW, an average value of rating shall be calculated by adding together the ratings of all ranges to obtain the total connected load (using 12 kW for any range rated less than 12 kW) and dividing by the total number of ranges. Then the maximum demand in Column C shall be increased 5 percent for each kilowatt or major fraction thereof by which this average value exceeds 12 kW.
3. Over 1¾ kW through 8¾ kW. In lieu of the method provided in Column C, it shall be permissible to add the nameplate ratings of all household cooking appliances rated more than 1¾ kW but not more than 8¾ kW and multiply the sum by the demand factors specified in Column A and Column B for the given number of appliances. Where the rating of cooking appliances falls under both Column A and Column B, the demand factors for each column shall be applied to the appliances for that column, and the results added together.
4. Branch-Circuit Load. It shall be permissible to calculate the branch-circuit load for one range in accordance with Table 220.55. The branch-circuit load for one wall-mounted oven or one counter-mounted cooking unit shall be the nameplate rating of the appliance. The branch-circuit load for a counter-mounted cooking unit and not more than two wall-mounted ovens, all supplied from a single branch circuit and located in the same room, shall be calculated by adding the nameplate rating of the individual appliances and treating this total as equivalent to one range.
5. This table also applies to household cooking appliances rated over 1¾ kW and used in instructional programs.

- Take notice that household electric ranges having a rating of **8.75 kW** or **more** are required to be supplied by at least a **40 ampere** rated branch circuit. **[210.19(A)(3)]** Also, **note 4** to **Table 220.55** states the branch circuit load for **one** wall-mounted oven or **one** counter-mounted cooking unit shall be the **nameplate rating** of the appliance. Therefore, demand factors are **not** to be applied when sizing branch circuits for these single cooking units.

- **Table 220.55** is separated into four columns. The first column shows the number of appliances. **Column A** is to be used when determining demand factors of cooking equipment of **less than 3½ kW rating** and is expressed in **percent**. **Column B** is used for equipment rated **3½ to 8¾ kW** and is also expressed in **percent**. **Column C** lists applicable demand factors for equipment rated **not over 12 kW** and is expressed in **kW**. When applying demand factors be sure you are in the correct column and on the right line, because the maximum demand changes in relationship with the number of appliances.

- As per **note 3**, When the rating of cooking appliances fall under **both** Column A and B, the demand factors for each column shall be applied for that column and the results added together.

EXAMPLE – A small residential duplex has a 3 kW counter-mounted cooktop and a 4 kW wall-mounted oven installed in each unit. Determine the demand load, in kW, to be added to the ungrounded service-entrance conductors for the cooking equipment.

A. 9.7 kW
B. 14.0 kW
C. 11.2 kW
D. 10.5 kW

ANSWER - (A) 9.7 kW

Col. A – 3 kW + 3 kW = 6 kW x **75%** = 4.5 kW
Col. B – 4 kW + 4 kW = 8 kW x **65%** = 5.2 kW
TOTAL = 9.7 kW demand

- When a single range having a rating of **3½ kW to 8¾ kW** is used as cooking equipment for households, we may use the demand factors shown in **Column B** when sizing branch-circuits, (**note 4**) feeders and service-entrance conductors.

EXAMPLE – What is the demand load, in kW, for the branch-circuit conductors supplying an 8 kW residential electric range?

A. 8.0 kW
B. 6.4 kW
C. 6.0 kW
D. 7.2 kW

ANSWER – (B) 6.4 kW

8 kW x 80% = 6.4 kW demand load

➢ Column C is to be used when applying demand factors for electric ranges of **not over 12 kW** rating.

EXAMPLE - Determine the demand load, in kW, to be added to the ungrounded service-entrance conductors for a 9.6 kW residential electric range.

A. 9.6 kW
B. 8.0 kW
C. 10.0 kW
D. 12.0 kW

ANSWER - (B) 8.0 kW

Column C of Table 220.55 shows a demand of **8 kW** for one range not over 12 kW rating.

➢ When we have multiple ranges of **equal ratings** up to **12 kW** we are to also use **Column C**.

EXAMPLE - A ten (10) unit apartment complex is to have a 10 kW electric range installed in each unit. When sizing the ungrounded service-entrance conductors, the total demand load for the multiple ranges is ______.

A. 30 kW
B. 80 kW
C. 25 kW
D. 100 kW

ANSWER - (C) 25 kW

Column C of Table 220.55 shows a demand of 25 kW for ten ranges of not over 12 kW rating.

➢ When applying maximum demand factors for ranges all of the **same rating over 12 kW through 27 kW**, we are to apply **note 1 and Column C** of **Table 220.55**, which states we are to increase the Column C demand value by **5%** for each kW that exceeds 12 kW.

EXAMPLE - What is the branch-circuit demand load, in amperes, for one 16 kW, 240 volt, single-phase residential electric range?

A. 33 amperes
B. 50 amperes
C. 40 amperes
D. 67 amperes

ANSWER – (C) 40 amperes

16 kW – 12 kW = 4 kW x 5% = 20% increase in Column C
Col. C demand (1 range) = 8 kW x 120% = 9.6 kW demand

I = <u>9.6 kW x 1,000</u> = <u>9,600</u> = 40 amperes

240 volts 240

➢ When applying demand factors for **multiple ranges**, all having the **same** nameplate rating of **more than 12 kW**, but **not more than 27 kW**, we are to also apply **note 1 and Column C** of **Table 220.55**.

EXAMPLE - A four (4) unit residential town house has a 14 kW electric range installed in each unit. What is the demand load for the ranges, in kW, to be added to the ungrounded service-entrance conductors when sizing the service?

A. 56.0 kW
B. 44.8 kW
C. 28.0 kW
D. 18.7 kW

ANSWER - (D) 18.7 kW

14 kW – 12 kW = 2 kW x 5% = 10% increase in Column C
Col. C demand (4 ranges) = 17 kW x 110% = 18.7 kW

➢ When applying maximum demand factors of ranges having **unequal ratings** of **8¾ kW through 27 kW** we are to apply **note 2 and Column C** of **Table 220.55.**

EXAMPLE - The vocational education department of a high school is to have three (3) electric ranges installed in a classroom; one 10 kW, one 11 kW and one 12 kW. The ranges are to be supplied by a 208 volt, single-phase feeder from a sub-panel. What is the demand load, in amperes, on the ungrounded feeder conductors?

A. 58 amperes
B. 67 amperes
C. 136 amperes
D. 142 amperes

ANSWER - (B) 67 amperes

In this situation you simply refer to Column C, which shows demand of 14 kW for three ranges, because not any of the ranges have a nameplate rating above 12 kW.

$$I = \frac{14\text{ kW} \times 1{,}000}{208\text{ volts}} = \frac{14{,}000}{208} = 67.3\text{ amperes}$$

➢ When calculating demand factors for ranges of **unequal ratings** of **8¾ through 27 kW**, when the nameplate rating of any **range less than 12 kW** you are to use **12 kW** as a **minimum** and add the ratings together and divide by the number of ranges to obtain the average, then apply the same steps as per **note 1**. **[Note 2, Table 220.55]**

EXAMPLE - Refer to the previous example. Another classroom in the high school is to install two electric ranges, one 16 kW and one 11 kW. Determine the demand load, in amperes, on the 208 volt, single-phase ungrounded feeder conductors.

A. 67 amperes
B. 76 amperes
C. 58 amperes
D. 63 amperes

ANSWER – (C) 58 amperes

$$12 \text{ kW (minimum)} + 16 \text{ kW} = \frac{28 \text{ kW}}{2 \text{ (ranges)}} = 14 \text{ kW average}$$

14 kW – 12 kW = 2 kW x **5%** = **10%** increase in Column C
Col. C demand (2 ranges) = 11 kW x **110%** = 12.1 kW demand

$$I = \frac{12.1 \text{ kW} \times 1{,}000}{208 \text{ volts}} = \frac{12{,}100}{208} = 58 \text{ amperes}$$

➢ **Note 4** of **Table 220.55** addresses **branch-circuits**; it states it is permissible to calculate the branch-circuit load for one range in accordance with **Table 220.55**, as we have shown. As mentioned before, the branch-circuit load for **one wall-mounted oven** or **one counter-mounted cooking unit** shall be the **nameplate rating** of the appliance. When sizing branch-circuit loads for a **single branch-circuit** supplying a counter-mounted cooking unit and not more than two (2) wall-mounted ovens, it is permissible to add the nameplate ratings of the appliances together and treat the result as one range.

EXAMPLE - A 240-volt, single-phase branch-circuit (home run) is to supply one (1) 6 kW rated counter-mounted cooking unit and two (2) wall-mounted 4 kW rated ovens in a residential kitchen. What is the demand load, in amperes, on the branch-circuit for the appliances?

A. 22 amperes
B. 27 amperes
C. 33 amperes
D. 37 amperes

ANSWER - (D) 37 amperes

6 kW + 4 kW + 4 kW = 14 kW connected load
14 kW – 12 kW = 2 kW x 5% = **10%** increase in Column C
Col. C demand (1 range) = 8 kW x 110% = 8.8 kW demand load

$$I = \frac{8.8 \text{ kW} \times 1{,}000}{240 \text{ volts}} = \frac{8{,}800}{240} = 36.6 \text{ amperes}$$

➢ **Section 220.61(B)(1)** permits an additional demand factor of **70 percent** for the **neutral** (grounded) conductor, for a feeder or service supplying household electric ranges, wall-mounted ovens, counter mounted cooking units, and electric dryers after apply the applicable demand factors of **Table 220.55** for ranges and **Table 220.54** for dryers.

EXAMPLE - A four (4) unit apartment house is to have a 10.5 kW electric range installed in each unit. Determine the demand load, in kW, on the grounded (neutral) service-entrance conductor for the ranges.

A. 11.9 kW
B. 13.6 kW
C. 17.0 kW
D. 10.4 kW

ANSWER - (A) 11.9 kW

Column C shows a demand of 17 kW for the demand on the ungrounded conductors for the four (4) electric ranges.

17 kW x **70%** = 11.9 kW neutral demand

- In a residential occupancy, a **75%** demand factor is permitted to be applied when **four(4) or more** fastened in place appliances such as water heaters, trash compactors, garage door openers, dishwashers, garbage disposers, sump pumps, attic fans, etc., are supplied from the same feeder or service. **[220.53]** **Note** this section does not apply to ranges, clothes dryers, space-heating and air-conditioning equipment.

EXAMPLE - A one-family dwelling unit is to have the following fastened in place appliances installed:

one – 1,200 VA dishwasher
one – 4,000 VA water heater
one – 1,150 VA garbage disposer
one - 700 VA attic fan
one – 1,920 VA garage door opener

The demand load, in VA, on the ungrounded service-entrance conductors for the listed appliances is _____.

A. 7,728 VA
B. 6,728 VA
C. 6,276 VA
D. 8,970 VA

ANSWER - (B) 6,728 VA

1,200 VA dishwasher
4,000 VA water heater
1,150 VA garbage disposer
700 VA attic fan
1,920 VA garage door opener
8,970 VA connected load x **75%** = 6,728 VA demand

- In residential occupancies, demand factors may also be applied to electric clothes dryers; the use of demand factors in **Table 220.54** shall be permitted when sizing feeders and service entrance conductors. Each dryer shall be calculated at a **minimum of 5,000 watts (volt-amperes)** or the nameplate rating, whichever is larger. **[220.54]**

EXAMPLE - An eight (8) unit multifamily dwelling is to have the following electric clothes dryers installed in the laundry rooms of the tenants:

two – 4.5 kW rated
two – 5.5 kW rated
two – 6.0 kW rated
two – 6.5 kW rated

The demand load, in kW, to be added to the ungrounded feeder conductors for the listed electric dryers is _____.

A. 27.0 kW
B. 27.6 kW
C. 34.5 kW
D. 33.8 kW

ANSWER - (B) 27.6 kW

two dryers @ 5.0 kW (minimum)	= 10 kW
two dryers @ 5.5 kW	= 11 kW
two dryers @ 6.0 kW	= 12 kW
two dryers @ 6.5 kW	= 13 kW
connected load	= 46 kW x **60%** = 27.6 kW

- An additional demand factor of **70 percent** is permitted for the **neutral** (grounded conductor) for a feeder or service supplying electric clothes dryers for dwelling units. **[220.61(B)(1)]**

EXAMPLE - Refer to the previous example. The demand, in kW, on the grounded (neutral) conductor of the feeder conductors is _____.

A. 32.20 kW
B. 27.60 kW
C. 19.32 kW
D. 18.90 kW

ANSWER - (C) 19.32 kW

27.6 kW (demand) load x **70%** (neutral demand) = 19.32 kW

- For commercial cooking related equipment, branch-circuits and overcurrent protection are sized according to the nameplate rating on the appliance. When sizing feeder and service conductors we may apply demand factors in accordance with **Table 220.56**. These demand factors shall not apply to space heating, ventilating or air-conditioning equipment. However, the feeder or service demand load is **not** permitted to be less than the sum of the **largest two** kitchen equipment loads. **[220.56]**

EXAMPLE - A feeder is to supply the following cooking related equipment in the kitchen of a restaurant:

oven	- 10 kW
booster heater	- 15 kW
dishwasher	- 2 kW
garbage disposal	- 1 kW
water heater	- 6 kW
steamer	- 4 kW

What is the demand load on the ungrounded feeder conductors for the appliances?

A. 38.0 kW
B. 24.7 kW
C. 26.6 kW
D. 25.0 kW

ANSWER - (D) 25.0 kW

oven	- 10 kW
booster heater	- 15 kW
dishwasher	- 2 kW
garbage disposal	- 1 kW
water heater	- 6 kW
steamer	- 4 kW

Total = 38 kW (connected load)
X **65%** (demand)
= 24.7 kW **demand load**

But, the **two largest** loads are rated 10 kW and 15 kW which totals **25 kW**.

UNIT 4

CONDUCTOR AMPACITY AND SIZING

Upon successfully completing this unit of study, the student will be familiar with the concept of determining the ampacity of conductors, application of ampacity correction factors, proper sizing, and insulation ratings of conductors.

$$\text{Required Ampacity} = \frac{\text{Load}}{\text{Correction Factors}}$$

UNIT 4

CONDUCTOR AMPACITY AND SIZING

RELATED INFORMATION:

- The definition of **ampacity** is the maximum current, in amperes, that a conductor can carry continuously under the conditions of use **without exceeding** its temperature rating. **[Article 100]** To get a better understanding of **ampacity**, perhaps we might consider it as **current-carrying capacity**, or the maximum amperage a conductor can carry without damaging the conductor and/or its insulation.

- When determining the ampacity of a conductor, or sizing a conductor, there are several factors needed to be taken into consideration; the ambient temperature, the type and temperature rating of the conductor insulation, the number of current-carrying conductors contained in the raceway or cable, the temperature rating of the terminations, characteristics of the load to be served, the environment the conductor will be subject to and voltage drop, which will be discussed later.

- **Table 310.4(A)** lists the various types of insulated conductors, rated 600 volts, that includes maximum operating temperatures, application provisions and insulation characteristics. Some conductors are dual rated in regard to the location in which they are installed. For example, type **THHW** is rated **75 deg. C** for wet locations and **90 deg. C** for dry locations.

- **Table 310.16** lists the ampacity values for copper, aluminum or copper clad aluminum conductors, up to 2000 volts, with temperature ratings of 60 deg. C through 90 deg. C. This table is based on **not more than three** current-carrying conductors in a raceway, cable or directly buried in the earth at an ambient temperature (temperature surrounding the wire) of **30 deg. C or 86 deg. F**.

Table 310.16 Ampacities of Insulated Conductors with Not More Than Three Current-Carrying Conductors in Raceway, Cable or Earth (Directly Buried)

	Temperature Rating of Conductor (See Table 310.4(A)						
	60°C (140°F)	75°C(167°F)	90°C(194°F)	60°C(140°F)	75°C (167°F)	90° (194°F)	
	Types TW, UF	Types RHW, THHW,THW, THWN,XHHW, USE, ZW	Types TBS, SA, SIS, FEP, FEPB, MI, RHH, RHW-2, THHN, THHW, THW-2, THWN-2, USE-2, XHH, XHHW, XHHW-2, ZW-2	Types TW, UF	Types RHW, THHW,THWT HWN, XHHW, USE	Types TBS, SA, SIS, THHN, THHW, THW-2, THWN-2, RHH, RHW-2, USE-2, XHH, XHHW, XHHW-2, ZW-2	
Size AWG or kcmil	COPPER			ALUMINUM OR COPPER-CLAD ALUMINUM			Size AWG or kcmil
18*	-	-	14	-	-	-	-
16*	-	-	18	-	-	-	-
14*	15	20	25	-	-	-	-
12*	20	25	30	15	20	25	12*
10*	30	35	40	25	30	35	10*
8	40	50	55	35	40	45	8
6	55	65	75	40	50	55	6
4	70	85	95	55	65	75	4
3	85	100	115	65	75	85	3
2	95	115	130	75	90	100	2
1	110	130	145	85	100	115	1
1/0	125	150	170	100	120	135	1/0
2/0	145	175	195	115	135	150	2/0
3/0	165	200	225	130	155	175	3/0
4/0	195	230	260	150	180	205	4/0
250	215	255	290	170	205	230	250
300	240	285	320	195	230	260	300
350	260	310	350	210	250	280	350
400	280	335	380	225	270	305	400
500	320	380	430	260	310	350	500
600	350	420	475	285	340	385	600
700	385	460	520	315	375	425	700
750	400	475	535	320	385	435	750
800	410	490	555	330	395	445	800
900	435	520	585	355	425	480	900
1000	455	545	615	375	445	500	1000
1250	495	590	665	405	485	545	1250
1500	525	625	705	435	520	585	1500
1750	545	650	735	455	545	615	1750
2000	555	665	750	470	560	630	2000

1. Section 310.15(B) shall be referenced for ampacity correction factors where the ambient temperature is other than 30°C (86°F).
2. Section 310.15(C)(1) shall be referenced for more than three current-carrying conductors.
3. Section 310.16 shall be referenced for conditions of use.
*Section to 240.4(D) shall be referenced for conductor overcurrent protection limitations, except as modified elsewhere in the Code.

- The body of **Table 310.16** lists ampacities of conductors used in areas where the ambient temperature is 30 deg. C or 86 deg. F, this is called **normal operating temperature**. The left half of the table is for **copper** conductors and the right half of the table is for **aluminum or copper clad aluminum** conductors.

- The temperature rating of a conductor is the maximum temperature, at any location along its length, that the conductor can withstand over a prolonged period of time without serious damage occurring. **[310.15(A)(3), INF. Note #1]**

- When conductors are subject to ambient temperatures above 86 deg. F, the resistance of the conductors are also increased proportionately. The greater the elevated ambient temperature, the greater the resistance. When the **resistance** of a conductor **increases** the **ampacity** of the conductor **decreases**. When this condition occurs, you must apply the appropriate temperature correction factors given in **Table 310.15(B)(1).**

Table 310.15(B)(1) Ambient Temperature Correction Factors Based on 30°C (86°F)				
For ambient temperatures other than 30°C (86°F), multiply the allowable ampacities specified in the ampacity table by the appropriate correction factor shown below.				
Ambient Temp. (°C)	**Temperature Rating of Conductor**			**Ambient Temp. (°F)**
	60° C	**75°C**	**90° C**	
10 or less	1.29	1.20	1.15	50 or less
11-15	1.22	1.15	1.12	51-59
16-20	1.15	1.11	1.08	60-68
21-25	1.08	1.05	1.04	69-77
26-30	1.00	1.00	1.00	78-86
31-35	0.91	0.94	0.96	87-95
36-40	0.82	0.88	0.91	96-104
41-45	0.71	0.82	0.87	105-113
46-50	0.58	0.75	0.82	114-122
51-55	0.41	0.67	0.76	123-131
56-60	-	0.58	0.71	132-140
61-65	-	0.47	0.65	141-149
66-70	-	0.33	0.58	150-158
71-75	-	-	0.50	159-167
76-80	-	-	0.41	168-176
81-85	-	-	0.29	177-185

EXAMPLE - When a size 3 AWG copper conductor, with THW insulation, is installed in an area where the ambient temperature is 114 deg. F, the wire has an allowable ampacity of _____.

A. 100 amperes
B. 75 amperes
C. 82 amperes
D. 58 amperes

ANSWER - (B) 75 amperes

100 amperes x .75 = 75 amperes

To solve this problem, first we locate the wire size on the left side of **Table 310.16** and look to the right under the copper THW column, with a temperature rating of 75°C, and note the ampacity of the wire is 100 amperes at normal operating temperature. Then, we apply the values as shown in **Table 310.15(B)(1).** Look to the right side of the table where the ambient temperature is shown as **°F** and find the ambient temperature. Next, we follow that line to the left where the line intersects with the **75° C column** (temperature rating of conductor) to find our correction factor of **.75**, or 75%. Finally, to find the allowable ampacity of the conductor, multiply the two values together.

EXAMPLE - When a size 1/0 AWG THWN aluminum conductor is installed in an ambient temperature of 45 deg. C, the conductor has an allowable ampacity of _____.

A. 100 amperes
B. 90 amperes
C. 98 amperes
D. 104 amperes

ANSWER - (C) 98 amperes

1/0 THWN aluminum ampacity before derating = 120 amperes
120 amps x .82 (correction factor) = 98.4 amperes

We use the same steps as before. First, we find the wire size which has an ampacity of 120 amperes. **[Tbl. 310.15(B)(16)]** Then, we find the ambient temperature, this time on the left portion of **Table 310.15(B)(2)(a)**, and go to the right under the THWN aluminum column (temperature rating of conductor) to find the correction factor of **.82**. Next, multiply the two values together.

- The temperature correction factors on **Table 310.15(B)(2)(a)** are to be applied when sizing conductors for a given load located in an area with an elevated ambient temperature. The following formula should be used:

$$\text{Required ampacity} = \frac{\text{load}}{\text{correction factor}}$$

EXAMPLE - Where a 100 ampere load is to be supplied with THWN copper conductors in an area where the ambient temperature will reach 110 deg. F, size _____ THWN conductors are required to serve the load.

A. 1 AWG
B. 2 AWG
C. 3 AWG
D. 1/0 AWG

ANSWER - (A) 1 AWG

$$\text{required ampacity} = \frac{100 \text{ amps}}{.82} = 122 \text{ amperes}$$

Table 310.16 indicates size 1 AWG copper conductors with an ampacity of 130 amperes, should be selected. To cross reference:

130 amperes x .82 (correction factor) = 107 amperes

- Conductors are to be sized in accordance with the lowest temperature rating of the terminal, device or conductor of the circuit. **[110.14(C)]** In other words, conductors must be sized to the **lowest temperature rating** of the wire, circuit breaker, terminal or device.

- Conductors with temperature ratings higher than that of the terminations are permitted to be used for ampacity adjustment and/or correction. **[110.14(C)]** Today, most terminations are rated at **60 deg. C or 75 deg. C**. This permits us to use THHN conductors for derating purposes, but the conductor size is based on the lower terminal rating of the circuit breaker, equipment or device, not the 90 deg. C rating of the conductor insulation.

EXAMPLE - The load on a size 6 AWG THHN copper conductor is limited to _____ where connected to a circuit breaker with a termination rated at 60° C.

A. 75 amperes
B. 65 amperes
C. 60 amperes
D. 55 amperes

ANSWER - (D) 55 amperes

Table 310.15(B)(16) lists the ampacity of size 6 AWG, copper, 60° C rated conductors to be 55 amperes.

EXAMPLE - The load, in amperes, on a size 6 AWG THHN copper conductor is permitted to be no more than _____ where connected to a fusible disconnect switch with terminals rated at 75 deg. C.

A. 75 amperes
B. 65 amperes
C. 60 amperes
D. 55 amperes

ANSWER - (B) 65 amperes

Table 310.16 lists the ampacity of size 6 AWG copper 75 deg. C rated conductors to be 65 amperes.

- Many circuit breakers and disconnect switches now have dual ratings marked **60/75 deg. C**. Under this condition, for 60 deg. C conductors, derating and ampacity values are to be based on the 60 deg. C terminal ratings; 75 deg. C and 90 deg. C conductors derating and ampacity values may be based on either the 60 deg. C or 75 deg. C terminal ratings.

- Many conductors now are dual rated such as **THWN/THHN**. The ampacity rating is based on the THWN, 75 deg. C values, but the derating factor(s) may be based on the THHN 90 deg. C values.

- The allowable **ampacity** of **Types NM**, **NMC** and **NMS** cable shall be in accordance with the **60 deg. C** conductor temperature rating. The **90 deg. C** rating shall be permitted to be used for **ampacity derating** purposes, provided the final ampacity does not exceed that for a 60 deg. C rated conductor. **[334.80]**

EXAMPLE - A size 12/2 AWG w/ground copper NM cable is to be installed in an attic of a dwelling where the ambient temperature is 125 deg. F. Determine the ampacity of the cable.

A. 22.8 amperes
B. 14.5 amperes
C. 24.6 amperes
D. 17.4 amperes

ANSWER - (A) 22.8 amperes

Ampacity of 12 AWG at 90 deg. C before derating = 30 amperes
30 amperes x .76 (temperature correction) = 22.8 amperes

Under this condition, the ampacity of 22.8 amperes is NOT permitted, because this value is more than the 20 ampere rating of the 12 AWG conductors at the 60 deg. C temperature rating.

EXAMPLE - A size 10/3 AWG w/ground copper NM cable is to be installed in the crawl space of a dwelling where the ambient temperature is 100 deg. F. Determine the ampacity of the cable.

A. 24.6 amperes
B. 36.4 amperes
C. 32.3 amperes
D. 30.0 amperes

ANSWER - (D) 30.0 amperes

Ampacity of 10 AWG at 90 deg. C before derating = 40 amperes
40 amperes x .91 (temp. correction) = 36.4 amperes

Under this condition the ampacity of 36.4 amperes is also NOT permitted, because this value is more than the 30 ampere rating of 10 AWG conductors at the 60 deg. C rating.

➢ When there are more than three (3) current-carrying conductors in a raceway or cable, the ability of the conductors to dissipate heat is reduced. Therefore, when this condition exists in a raceway or cable longer than 24 inches the allowable ampacity of each conductor shall be reduced as shown in **Table 310.15(B)(3)(a)**.

EXAMPLE - What is the allowable ampacity of a size 1/0 AWG THW copper conductor installed in a conduit longer than 24 inches, when there are three (3) other current-carrying conductors contained in the same pipe?

A. 150 amperes
B. 120 amperes
C. 105 amperes
D. 140 amperes

ANSWER - (B) 120 amperes

150 amperes x .8 (adjustment factor) = 120 amperes

First, find the ampacity of the conductor, before derating, as shown in **Table 310.116.** Then, apply the appropriate adjustment factor as shown in **Table 310.15(C)(1).**

➢ When there are four (4) or more current-carrying conductors in a raceway or cable, longer than 24 inches, installed in an area with an elevated temperature, **both** the temperature correction and the adjustment factor for the number of current-carrying conductors must be applied.

EXAMPLE - Determine the allowable ampacity of a size 2 AWG THWN aluminum conductor installed in a 20 foot long conduit with seven (7) other current-carrying conductors of the same size and insulation, where the ambient temperature is 99 deg. F.

A. 59 amperes
B. 71 amperes
C. 55 amperes
D. 63 amperes

ANSWER - (C) 55 amperes

Size 2 AWG THWN AL ampacity before derating = 90 amperes
90 amperes x .88 (temp. correction) x .7 (adj. factor) = 55 amps

First, find the ampacity of the conductor as shown in **Table 310.16** before derating. Then, apply the temperature correction factor. **[Table 310.15(B)(1)]** Next, apply the adjustment factor for the multiple current-carrying conductors as shown in **Table 310.15(C)(1),** and multiply the three values together.

- When sizing conductors for a given load in an area with an elevated ambient temperature, installed in a raceway or cable more than 24 inches in length, the following formula may be used when there are more than three current-carrying conductors in the raceway or cable.

$$\text{Required ampacity} = \frac{\text{Load}}{\text{temp. correction x adj. factor}}$$

EXAMPLE - A 100 ampere load is located in an environment where the temperature reaches 115 deg. F, and is to be supplied with four (4) 75 deg. C rated copper current-carrying conductors. Determine the proper size wire to serve the load. All terminations are rated at 75 deg. C.

A. 1/0 AWG
B. 2/0 AWG
C. 1 AWG
D. 3 AWG

ANSWER - (B) 2/0 AWG

$$\text{ampacity} = \frac{\text{100 amperes (load)}}{\text{.76 (temp.) x .8 (adj.)}} = \frac{100}{0.6} = 167 \text{ amperes}$$

*NOTE – Size 2/0 AWG copper conductors rated at 75 deg. C with an ampacity of 175 amperes are required.

When considering current-carrying conductors, the neutral conductor is **not counted** when the neutral carries only the **unbalanced current** of the circuit; for example, 120/240-volt single-phase systems. **[310.15(E)(1)]** The neutral does carry current, but is not required to be counted.

- The neutral **is considered** a current-carrying conductor on a 4-wire, 3-phase wye circuit where the major portion of the load consists of **nonlinear loads**. **[310.15(E)(3)]** Examples of nonlinear loads are high intensity discharge (HID) lighting and fluorescent lighting, information technology equipment, computers, and data processing equipment.

- As per Section **310.12(A)&(B)** for sizing **120/240-volt, 3-wire, single-phase** service and feeder conductors rated 100 through 400 amperes, for one-family dwelling units and individual units of a multi-family dwelling, they are permitted to have an ampacity not less than 83 percent of the service or feeder rating.

EXAMPLE - A one-family dwelling is supplied with a 120/240-volt, single-phase electrical system from the local utility company and has a demand load of 200 amperes. What is the MINIMUM size THWN/THHN aluminum service-entrance conductors required?

A. 250 kcmil
B. 4/0 AWG
C. 3/0 AWG
D. 2/0 AWG

ANSWER - (B) 4/0 AWG

200 amperes x .83 = 166 amperes

Size 4/0 AWG THWN/THHN aluminum service-entrance conductors with an ampacity of 180 amperes should be selected from **Table 310.16.**

- When single-insulated conductors are installed in free air, they can dissipate the heat caused by the current flowing in the conductors more readily than when installed in raceways. The conductors have a greater allowable ampacity therefore, **Table 310.17** may be applied in the same manner as previously referenced in this unit.

EXAMPLE - When ambient temperature is not a consideration, when installed in free air, a size 6 AWG THWN copper conductor has a MAXIMUM allowable ampacity of _____.

A. 65 amperes
B. 75 amperes
C. 105 amperes
D. 95 amperes

ANSWER - (D) 95 amperes

Table 310.17 shows size 6 AWG THWN copper conductors to have an allowable ampacity of 95 amperes.

UNIT 5

BOX AND RACEWAY SIZING

Upon successfully completing this unit of study the student will be familiar with the concept of properly sizing electrical boxes and raceways.

$$\text{Number of Wires Permitted} = \frac{\text{Allowable Fill}}{\text{Wire Size}}$$

UNIT 5

BOX AND RACEWAY SIZING

Outlet and Device Box Sizing

RELATED INFORMATION:

- Device and junction boxes are required to be of a sufficient size to house conductors and/or devices, clamps and support fittings without damaging the conductor's insulation. Therefore, when sizing boxes, conductors, clamps and support fittings are required to be counted in order to select the proper size box. **[314.16]**

- To properly size outlet boxes you must count the conductors within the box correctly. **Section 314.16(B)(1)** is to be used as a guideline to count the conductors as follows:

    1) Conductors that originate outside the box or that are spliced within the box are counted **one** for each conductor.

    2) Conductors unbroken within the box, less than 12 inches in length, that pass through the box without splicing or terminating are counted **one** for each conductor.

    3) Conductors 12 inches or longer that are looped and unbroken are counted as **two** for a single conductor.

    4) Conductors that originate within the box and do not leave the box such as, bonding jumpers and pigtails are **not counted**.

    5) Conductors from a domed luminaire (fixture) that terminate within the box are **not counted**.

- When sizing device and junction boxes, the insulation of the conductors are not required to be taken into consideration. The volume required for the individual conductors is expressed in **cubic inches** and/or **cubic centimeters**, no matter what the insulation characteristics of the conductor(s) is/are.

- To determine the volume, in cubic inches, of a box simply multiply the length times the width times the depth of the box.

EXAMPLE - A box that measures 6 inches x 6 inches and is 4 inches deep has a volume of _____.

A. 96 cubic inches
B. 144 cubic inches
C. 24 cubic inches
D. 36 cubic inches

ANSWER - (B) 144 cubic inches

6 in. x 6 in. x 4 in. = 144 cubic inches

- **Table 314.16(A)** may be used to determine the **MINIMUM** size outlet box required for a given number of conductors, or when determining the **MAXIMUM** number of conductors permitted in an outlet box when all of the conductors in the box are of the **same size**.

EXAMPLE - Determine the MAXIMUM number of size 12 AWG THWN conductors permitted in a 4 x 1½ in. square box.

A. seven
B. eight
C. nine
D. ten

ANSWER - (C) nine

The right hand side of **Table 314.16(B)** under the **12** column shows nine conductors permitted in the box.

EXAMPLE - Of the following listed, which one of the boxes is the MINIMUM required to house three (3) size 12 AWG THWN/THHN conductors and three (3) size 12 AWG THW conductors?

A. 4 x 1½ in. octagon
B. 4 x 2¼ in. octagon
C. 4 x 1½ in. square
D. 4 x 2¼ in. square

ANSWER - (A) 4 x 1½ in. octagon

Table 314.16(B) permits six (6) size 12 AWG conductors in 4 x 1½ in. octagon box.

- **Table 314.16(A)** shall apply where no fittings or devices, such as cable clamps, luminaire studs, hickeys, receptacles, switches or dimmers, are enclosed in the box. **Table 314.16(A)** does not take into consideration the fill requirements for these fittings or devices; where one or more of these items are contained in the box, the number of conductors permitted as shown in the table shall be reduced as follows:

1) **cable clamps** – One or more internal cable clamps present in the box are counted as **one** conductor, based on the **largest** conductor in the box. **[314.16(B)(2)]**

2) **support fittings** – One or more luminaire (fixture) studs and/or hickeys in the box are counted as **one** conductor for each type of fitting, based on the **largest** conductor in the box. **[314.16(B)(3)]**

3) **devices** – For each yoke or strap containing one or more device present in the box, they are to be counted as **two wires**, based on the **largest** conductor connected to the device. **[314.16(B)(4)]**

4) **equipment grounding conductors** – One or more equipment grounding conductors or bonding jumpers contained in a box are to be counted as **one** conductor, based on the **largest** equipment grounding conductor or bonding jumper in the box. **[314.16(B)(5)]** Where an **additional set** of

isolated equipment grounding conductors are in the box, they are to be counted as **one** conductor, based on the **largest** equipment grounding conductor in the additional set.

➢ When doing box fill calculations we must take into consideration the volume taken up by all conductors, fittings and devices contained in the box to properly size the box.

EXAMPLE - A device box contains two (2) internal clamps, two (2) equipment grounding conductors, one (1) bonding jumper and one (1) duplex receptacle. The number of conductors permitted in the box is to be reduced by _____ conductors.

A. three
B. four
C. five
D. six

ANSWER - (B) four

clamps	= 1 wire
receptacle	= 2 wires
equip. grounding & bonding wires	= 1 wire
TOTAL	= 4 wires

➢ When calculating the proper size outlet box to be used when the conductors are of different sizes, you are to determine the volume of the conductors, in cubic inches, by applying **Table 314.16(B)**, and then size the box by using **Table 314.16(A)**.

EXAMPLE - Determine which one of the following listed outlet boxes is the MINIMUM size required to enclose the following conductors:

- six (6) size 12 AWG conductors
- two (2) size 14 AWG conductors
- one (1) size 14 AWG equipment grounding conductors

A. 4 x 1½ in. octagon
B. 4 x 1½ in. square
C. 4 x 2¼ in. square
D. 4¼ x 1½ in. square

ANSWER - (B) 4 x 1½ in. square

Size 12 AWG = 2.25 cu. in. x 6	= 13.5 cubic inches
Size 14 AWG = 2.00 cu. in. x 2	= 4.0 cubic inches
Size 14 AWG Equip. grounding x 1	= 2.0 cubic inches
	19.5 cubic inches

Table 314.16(A) requires a 4 x 1½ inch square box having a volume of 21 cubic inches.

Junction and Pull Box Sizing

RELATED INFORMATION:

- **Section 314.16** states when boxes enclosing conductors of size **4 AWG or larger** are used as pull or junction boxes, they are to comply with the provisions of **314.28**. Under this condition, pull and junction boxes are to be sized by the raceways entering the box(es) and not by the size of the conductors contained in the box.

- In straight pulls, the length of the box shall not be less than **eight times** the trade diameter of the largest raceway entering the box. **[314.28(A)(1)]**

EXAMPLE - Determine the MINIMUM length of a pull box that has a trade size 3½ inch conduit entering at each end, and containing conductors of size 250 kcmil, when a straight pull of the conductors is to be made.

A. 21 inches
B. 24 inches
C. 28 inches
D. 32 inches

ANSWER - (C) 28 inches

3.5 in. (conduit) x 8 = 28 inches

- Where splices, angle or U-pulls are made, the distance between each raceway entry inside the box and opposite wall of the box shall not be less than **six (6) times** the trade size of the raceway in a row. **[314.28(A)(2)]** Then, you are to add the sum of the trade size diameter of any additional raceways entering the box. In other words, for angle or U-pulls, the proper size junction box can be determined by multiplying the largest raceway by six (6) and add any additional conduits.

EXAMPLE - A junction box is to be installed where the conductors are larger than size 4 AWG and an angle (90 deg.) pull of the conductors is to be made. Two (2) trade size 3 inch conduits are to enter the box from the top and two (2) trade size 3 inch conduits are to enter the box from the side. Determine the MINIMUM size pull box required.

A. 36 in. x 36 in.
B. 27 in. x 27 in.
C. 24 in. x 24 in.
D. 21 in. x 21 in.

ANSWER - (D) 21 in. x 21 in.

Top to bottom – 3 in. (largest conduit) x 6 = 18 in. + 3 in. = 21 in.
Side to side – 3 in. (largest conduit) x 6 = 18 in. + 3 in. = 21 in.

EXAMPLE - A pull box has one (1) trade size 2 inch conduit and one (1) trade size 1½ inch conduit entering the top and two (2) trade size 2 inch conduits on the left side. Where conductors are larger than 4 AWG and an angle (90 deg.) pull of the conductors is to be made, determine the MINIMUM distance required from the top wall to the bottom wall.

A. 13½ inches
B. 11 inches
C. 12 inches
D. 16 inches

ANSWER - (A) 13½ inches

2 in. (largest conduit) x 6 = 12 + 1½ in. = 13½ inches

Conduit and Tubing Sizing

RELATED INFORMATION:

- When electrical conduit or tubing enclose conductors of the same size, with the same type of insulation, when the conduit or tubing is more than 24 inches in length, application of **Annex C, Tables C.1 through C.13(A)** is permitted to be used when determining the MAXIMUM number of conductors permitted. **[Chapter 9, Table 1]** This is the fastest and easiest method of determining the MAXIMUM number of conductors allowed in a standard trade size conduit or tubing.

- Located at the first part of **Annex C** there is a listing of the various types of standard electrical conduits. Use this table to find the particular type of conduit you are going to use when determining conduit fill.

EXAMPLE - Determine the MINIMUM trade size electrical metallic tubing (EMT), more than 24 inches in length, permitted to enclose twelve (12) size 10 AWG THWN conductors.

A. 3/4 in.
B. 1 in.
C. 1¼ in.
D. 1½ in.

ANSWER - (B) 1 inch

First locate **Table C.1** of **Annex C**. Next, refer to the type of insulation **(THWN)** of the conductors. Then, locate the wire size **(10 AWG)**, and you will find for twelve (12) size 10 AWG THWN conductors a trade size 1 inch EMT is required.

EXAMPLE - A trade size 1½ inch Schedule 40 PVC conduit, 25 feet in length, is permitted to enclose no more than _____ size 2 AWG XHHW compact aluminum conductors.

A. six
B. seven
C. eight
D. ten

ANSWER - (C) eight

First, locate **Table C.11(A)** of **Annex C**. Next, find the insulation type **(XHHW)** of the conductors. Then, locate the conduit size **(1½ in.)** and conductor size **(2 AWG)**, and you will find a trade size 1½ inch Schedule 40 PVC is permitted to enclose eight (8) size 2 AWG XHHW compact aluminum conductors.

- When conduit or tubing enclose conductors of different sizes and/or insulations, **Chapter 9**, **Tables 4, 5 and 5A**, with their related notes, are to be applied to determine the proper fill.

- **Table 1** of **Chapter 9** shows the permitted fill, in percent of conduit and tubing, when one, two or over two conductors are installed; for example, when more than two (2) conductors are installed in a conduit or tubing they shall be permitted to be filled to **40 percent** of their cross-sectional area.

- Where conduit or tubing nipples have a MAXIMUM length not to exceed 24 inches between boxes and enclosures, the nipples shall be permitted to be filled to **60 percent** of their total cross-sectional area.
  [Chapter 9, Note 4]

- **Table 4, Chapter 9** list the various types of conduit and tubing. Each type of conduit or tubing is shown as a separate table. At the top of each table is shown the internal diameter and the percent of fill. Under the percent of fill heading you will find the allowable fill of each size conduit or tubing expressed in square inches and millimeters. On the left side of the table the trade size and metric designator of the conduit or tubing are listed. To find the allowable fill of a specific conduit or tubing simply locate the conduit or tubing size and extend to the right under the proper **percent** of fill heading.

EXAMPLE - When more than two (2) conductors are installed in a trade size 2 inch electrical metallic tubing (EMT) longer than 24 inches, the EMT has an allowable fill of _____.

A. 2.013 square inches
B. 1.778 square inches
C. 1.040 square inches
D. 1.342 square inches

ANSWER - (D) 1.342 square inches

Under this condition the 2 in. EMT is permitted to have an allowable fill of 40 percent. **[Table 4, Chapter 9]**

EXAMPLE - When four (4) current-carrying conductors are installed in a trade size 2 inch electrical metallic tubing (EMT) nipple 18 inches long, the EMT has a MAXIMUM allowable fill of _____.

A. 2.013 square inches
B. 1.778 square inches
C. 1.040 square inches
D. 1.342 square inches

ANSWER - (A) 2.013 square inches

Under this condition the 2 in. EMT is permitted to have an allowable fill of 60 percent. **[Table 4, Chapter 9]**

➢ **Table 5, Chapter 9** shows the various sizes and insulations of conductors expressed in millimeters and square inches in accordance with appropriate diameter and area. In most cases we relate to the **approximate area** in **square inches** on the right side of the table.

EXAMPLE - A size 8 AWG THWN copper conductor has an approximate area of ______.

A. 0.0437 square inches
B. 0.0366 square inches
C. 0.0835 square inches
D. 0.2160 square inches

ANSWER - (B) 0.0366 square inches

First, we locate the insulation **(THWN)** of the conductor. Then, the size **(8 AWG)**, and look to the extreme right side of the table to find the approximate area in square inches. **[Table 5, Chapter 9]**

➢ **Table 5A, Chapter 9** shows the various sizes and insulations of **compact aluminum conductors** expressed in millimeters and square inches with approximate diameter and area, much like **Table 5 of Chapter 9**. This table is structured different than **Table 5** but, is easier to use because there is only four (4) types of conductor insulations listed. Again, refer to the approximate area in square inches of the conductor when calculating raceway fill.

EXAMPLE - What is the area, in square inches, of a size 3/0 AWG XHHW compact aluminum conductor.

A. 0.590 square inches
B. 0.2733 square inches
C. 0.2290 square inches
D. 0.1885 square inches

ANSWER - (C) 0.2290 square inches

First, from **Table 5A of Chapter 9**, locate the insulation **(XHHW)** of the conductor. Then, locate the wire size, **(3/0 AWG)**, and look under the **in.^{2}** heading to find the area.

➢ Where equipment grounding or bonding conductors are installed in conduit or tubing, they shall be included when calculating the permitted fill. **[Chapter 9, Note 3]** If insulated, use the **Table 5** to find the approximate area; if bare find the area in square inches from **Table 8 of Chapter 9**, look under the heading of **in²**.

EXAMPLE - A size 8 AWG solid bare equipment grounding conductor has an area of _____.

A. 0.128 square inches
B. 0.146 square inches
C. 0.017 square inches
D. 0.013 square inches

ANSWER - (D) 0.013 square inches

First, locate the wire size and stranding properties from **Table 8 of Chapter 9**.
Next, extend to the right under the **in.²** heading to find the area.

- Conduits or tubing enclosing different size conductors and/or conductors having different insulations are sized by locating the area, in square inches, of each conductor per **Table 5**, **Table 5A** or **Table 8** and multiplying by the number of conductors. This total is used to select the proper size raceway using **Table 4** in **Chapter 9**.

EXAMPLE - Determine the MINIMUM trade size intermediate metal conduit (IMC) permitted to enclose three (3) size 8 AWG XHHW copper branch-circuit conductors and six (6) size 12 AWG THWN copper control-circuit conductors. The IMC is to be fifty (50) feet in length.

A. 1/2 in.
B. 3/4 in.
C. 1 in.
D. 1¼ in.

ANSWER - (B) 3/4 in.

8 XHHW = .0437 sq. in. x 3 conductors = .1311 square inches
12 THWN = .0133 sq. in. x 6 conductors = .0798 square inches
TOTAL = .2109 square inches

A trade size 3/4 in. IMC having an allowable fill @ 40% of 0.235 square inches is the MINIMUM required.

EXAMPLE - Determine the MINIMUM trade size, one (1) foot long, rigid metal conduit (RMC) to enclose the following listed copper conductors.

- four (4) – 3/0 AWG THWN
- four (4) – 4/0 AWG THHN

A. 3 in.
B. 2 in.
C. 3½ in.
D. 2½ in.

ANSWER - (D) 2½ inches

3/0 THWN	= .2679 x 4 conductors	= 1.0716 square inches
4/0 THHN	= .3237 x 4 conductors	= 1.2948 square inches
	TOTAL	= 2.3664 square inches

A trade size 2½ in. RMC nipple having an allowable fill @ 60% of 2.919 square inches is the MINIMUM required.

➢ When determining the number of conductors, all of the same size, permitted in a conduit or tubing 24 inches or less in length, simply divide the allowable fill area of the conduit or tubing by the area of one (1) conductor.

EXAMPLE - Determine the MAXIMUM number of size 2/0 AWG THHN copper conductors permitted to be installed in a trade size 2 in. electrical metallic tubing (EMT) 18 inches long.

A. seven
B. eight
C. nine
D. ten

ANSWER - (C) nine

$$\frac{2.013 \text{ sq. in. (allowable fill)}}{.2223 \text{ sq. in. (area of wire)}} = 9.05 \text{ or } 9 \text{ wires}$$

➢ When calculating the MAXIMUM number of conductors, all of the same size, permitted in a conduit or tubing, when the calculation results in a decimal of **0.8** or larger, an additional wire of the same size may be installed. **[Chapter 9, Note 7]**

EXAMPLE - Determine the MAXIMUM number of size 1/0 AWG THWN copper conductors permitted to be installed in a trade size 1¼ in. rigid metal conduit (RMC) nipple.

A. four
B. five
C. six
D. seven

ANSWER - (B) five

$\frac{0.916 \text{ sq. in. (allowable fill)}}{.1855 \text{ sq. in. (area of wire)}} = 4.9$ or 5 wires

Wireway and Gutter Sizing

RELATED INFORMATION:

- When calculating the number of conductors, all of the same size, permitted in a metal or nonmetallic wireway, or an auxiliary gutter, the fill shall not exceed **20 percent** of the interior cross-sectional area of the wireway or gutter where splices or taps are not made. **[366.22(A)&(B)]**, **[376.22(A)]** and **[378.22]** Use the same steps as before; first, find the allowable fill and divide by the area of one (1) conductor. Disregard the length of the wireway or gutter.

EXAMPLE - Determine the MAXIMUM number of size 4/0 AWG XHHW copper conductors permitted to be installed in a 4 in. x 4 in. metal wireway.

A. ten
B. eleven
C. twenty
D. sixteen

ANSWER - (A) ten

4 in. x 4 in. = 16 sq. in. x 20% = 3.2 sq. in. permitted fill

$\frac{3.2 \text{ sq. in. (permitted fill)}}{.3197 \text{ sq. in. (area of wire)}} = 10$ wires

- When conductors are of different sizes and/or insulations, **wireways** and **gutters** can be properly sized by dividing the total area, in square inches, of the conductors by the **20 percent** permitted fill area, where splices or taps are not made. Or find the area, in square inches, of a specific wireway or gutter and multiply by **20 percent** to find the allowable fill. Using this method you may have to try more than one size gutter or wireway to find the proper size.

EXAMPLE - A wireway is to contain the following listed conductors.

- three – size 250 kcmil THHN compact aluminum
- three – size 4/0 AWG THHN compact aluminum
- three – size 1/0 AWG THHN compact aluminum

Which one of the following listed wireways is the MINIMUM size required to house the conductors?

A. 4 in. x 4 in.
B. 6 in. x 6 in.
C. 8 in. x 8 in.
D. 12 in. x 12 in.

ANSWER - (A) 4 in. x 4 in.

First, go to **Table 5A of Chapter 9** to determine the area of the conductors.

250 kcmil THHN compact AL = .3525 sq. in. x 3 = 1.0575 sq. in.
4/0 AWG THHN compact AL = .2780 sq. in. x 3 = 0.8340 sq. in.
1/0 AWG THHN compact AL = .1590 sq. in. x 3 = 0.4770 sq. in.
TOTAL = 2.3685 sq. in.

$$\frac{2.3685 \text{ (area of wires)}}{20\% \text{ (permitted fill)}} = 11.8425 \text{ sq. in. required area}$$

A 4 in. x 4 in. wireway with an area of 16 square inches is required.

To cross-check:
4 in. x 4 in. = 16 sq. in. x 20% = 3.2 square inches allowable fill
This wireway having an allowable fill of 3.2 square inches may contain the conductors having an area of 2.3685 square inches.

UNIT 6

VOLTAGE DROP CALCULATIONS

Upon successfully completing this unit of study the student will be familiar with the concept of calculating voltage drop in conductors, causes of voltage drop, as well as the means to prevent excessive voltage drop in three-phase and single-phase circuits.

$$VD = \frac{2 \times K \times I \times D}{CM}$$

UNIT 6

VOLTAGE DROP CALCULATIONS

RELATED INFORMATION:

- The conductors of an electrical system should be of sufficient size so that the voltage drop is not excessive. Typical results of excessive voltage drop are as follows:

    1) luminaires (lighting fixtures) dimming when appliances or motors are turned on,
    2) overheating of motors and appliances,
    3) shortened life span of appliances such as computers, TVs, refrigerators and freezers,
    4) nuisance tripping of circuit breakers,
    5) delayed starting of high-intensity discharge lighting.

- The loss of voltage, known as voltage drop, is apparent in all electrical circuits due to the resistance of the circuit conductors. This loss of voltage varies with conductor material, conductor size, conductor length, ambient temperature and intensity of the current.

- The NEC® recommends the MAXIMUM voltage drop to be limited to 3 percent at the farthest outlet for branch circuits and 5 percent on both feeder and branch circuits to the farthest outlet. **[210.19(A)(1) IN#4]** and **[215.2(A)(3) IN#2]** In practical work, many engineers try to limit the voltage drop for lighting and power branch circuits to 2 percent and 4 percent for feeders.

- **The smaller the wire size, the greater the resistance** because, the small cross-sectional area of the conductor restricts the flow of electrons; thus, the greater the voltage drop. **The larger the wire size, the less the resistance** because, the larger cross-sectional area of the conductor permits the electrons to flow more freely; thus, the less voltage drop. So, the most practical way to limit voltage drop is increase the wire size. Although not always practical, voltage drop may be decreased by:

    1) increasing the voltage, which reduces the intensity of the current,
    2) change the conductor material say, from aluminum to copper which reduces the resistance,
    3) move the load closer to its source voltage, which reduces the conductor resistance.

- A useful and common formula that may be used to determine the voltage drop in a single-phase circuit is:

$$VD = \frac{2 \times K \times I \times D}{CM}$$

Formula Definitions:

VD – Volts dropped from a circuit.

2 – Multiplying factor for single-phase circuits. The **2** represents the conductor length in a single-phase circuit.

K – Approximate resistivity of the conductor per mil foot at an operating temperature of 75°C/167°F. A mil foot is a wire one (1) foot long and one (1) mil in diameter. The approximate **K** value (constant) for copper wire is **12.9 ohms** and for aluminum wire is **21.2 ohms**.

I – Current or amperage draw of the load at 100 percent.

D – The distance, in feet, from the source voltage to the load.

CM – The area of the conductor expressed in **circular mils**, which can be found in **Chapter 9, Table 8**, which lists wire sizes from 18 AWG through 2,000 kcmil. For example, a size 10 AWG conductor has a cross-sectional area of 10,380 circular mils. For conductors of size 250 kcmil through size 2,000 kcmil, the cross-sectional area in circular mils can be determined by adding three (3) zeros to the kcmil size. For example, a size 300 kcmil conductor has a cross-sectional area of 300,000 circular mils.

EXAMPLE - A 120-volt, single-phase branch circuit, using size 12 AWG copper conductors, is supplying a 15 ampere load located sixty (60) feet from the panelboard. Determine the approximate voltage drop. (K = 12.9)

A. 2 volts
B. 4 volts
C. 6 volts
D. 8 volts

ANSWER - (B) 4 volts

CM = 6,530 (12 AWG)
K = 12.9 ohms (copper)
I = 15 amperes
D = 60 feet

$$VD = \frac{2 \times 12.9 \times 15 \times 60}{6{,}530} = \frac{23{,}220}{6{,}530} = 3.55 \text{ volts}$$

➢ A useful and common formula that may be used to determine the voltage drop in a **three-phase** circuit is:

$$VD = \frac{1.732 \times K \times I \times D}{CM}$$

- The multiplying factor for **three-phase** circuits is **1.732**. The square root of 3 represents the conductor length in a three-phase circuit. The only difference between the single-phase and the three-phase formulas is that "**1.732**" has replaced "2".

EXAMPLE - A 208Y/120-volt, three-phase feeder, using size 4 AWG aluminum conductors is to supply an 80 ampere load located one hundred (100) feet from the switchboard. Determine the approximate voltage drop.
(K = 21.2)

A. 9.3 volts
B. 5.0 volts
C. 7.0 volts
D. 9.0 volts

ANSWER - (C) 7.0 volts

CM = 41,740 (4 AWG)
K = 21.2 ohms (aluminum)
I = 80 amperes
D = 100 feet

$$VD = \frac{1.732 \times 21.2 \times 80 \times 100}{41,740} = \frac{293,747}{41,740} = 7.0 \text{ volts}$$

- As stated before, the size of the conductor affects voltage drop because of the resistance variables. Conductors are to be sized to prevent excessive voltage drop. A useful formula that may be used to size the conductors and prevent excessive voltage drop in a single-phase circuit is:

$$CM = \frac{2 \times K \times I \times D}{VD}$$

- When determining wire size, VD is the actual volts allowed to be dropped from the circuit. For example, the recommended voltage drop in a 240 volt, single-phase branch circuit is 3 percent; 3 percent of 240 volts is 7.2 volts. DO NOT enter 3 percent in the VD position in the formula, enter the value of the actual voltage permitted to be lost or dropped.

EXAMPLE - A 240-volt, single-phase, 52 ampere load is located two-hundred (200) feet from the panelboard. What MINIMUM size copper branch circuit conductors should be used to supply this load when voltage drop is to be limited to 3 percent? (K = 12.9)

A. 8 AWG
B. 6 AWG
C. 4 AWG
D. 2 AWG

ANSWER - (C) 4 AWG

VD = 240 x 0.03 = 7.2 volts
K = 12.9 ohms (copper)
I = 52 amperes
D = 200 feet

$$CM = \frac{2 \times 12.9 \times 52 \times 200}{7.2} = \frac{268{,}320}{7.2} = 37{,}267 \text{ CM}$$

In this situation, a size 4 AWG conductor with a circular mil area (CMA) of 41,740 CM is required because, a size 6 AWG conductor with a CMA of 26,240 CM would not limit the voltage drop to 3 percent.

- A useful formula that may be used to size conductors in a three-phase circuit to prevent excessive voltage drop is:

$$CM = \frac{1.732 \times K \times I \times D}{VD}$$

EXAMPLE - A 208Y/120-volt, 3-phase, 150 ampere load is located two hundred and fifty (250) feet from the main distribution switchboard. What MINIMUM size copper feeder conductors are required to supply the load when voltage drop is to be limited to 3 percent? (K = 12.9)

A. 4/0 AWG
B. 1/0 AWG
C. 2/0 AWG
D. 3/0 AWG

ANSWER - (D) 3/0 AWG

VD = 208 x 0.03 = 6.24 volts
K = 12.9 ohms (copper)
I = 150 amperes
D = 250 feet

$$CM = \frac{1.732 \times 12.9 \times 150 \times 250}{6.24} = \frac{83{,}786}{6.24} = 134{,}272 \text{ CM}$$

A size 3/0 AWG conductor with a CMA of 167,800 CM is required to limit the voltage drop to 6.24 volts.

- Voltage drop can be limited in a circuit by limiting the length of the circuit conductors. The following formula can be used to determine the approximate distance circuit conductors may be installed to prevent excessive voltage drop in a single-phase circuit.

$$D = \frac{CM \times VD}{2 \times K \times I}$$

EXAMPLE - What is the approximate MAXIMUM distance a 120-volt, single-phase, 1,800 VA load, supplied with size 12 AWG copper branch circuit conductors can be located from the panelboard, when the permitted voltage drop is to be not more than three percent?

A. 60 feet
B. 75 feet
C. 90 feet
D. 120 feet

ANSWER - (A) 60 feet

CM = 6,530 (12 AWG)
VD = 120 volts x .03 = 3.6 volts
K = 12.9 ohms

$$I = \frac{VA}{volts} = \frac{1{,}800\ VA}{120\ volts} = 15\ amperes$$

$$D = \frac{6{,}530 \times 3.6}{2 \times 12.9 \times 15} = \frac{23{,}508}{387} = 60.7\ feet$$

➢ When determining the approximate distance circuit conductors may be installed in three-phase circuits to prevent excessive voltage drop, the following formula can be used:

$$D = \frac{CM \times VD}{1.732 \times K \times I}$$

EXAMPLE - A transformer having a 208Y/120-volt, 3-phase secondary is to supply a panelboard with a 130 ampere demand load. The feeder conductors are size 1/0 AWG THWN copper. What is the MAXIMUM approximate distance the panelboard can be located from the transformer so that the voltage drop does not exceed three percent?

A. 125 feet
B. 65 feet
C. 225 feet
D. 200 feet

ANSWER - (C) 225 feet

CM = 105,600 (1/0 AWG)
VD = 208 volts x .03 = 6.24 volts
K = 12.9 ohms
I = 130 amperes

$$D = \frac{105{,}600 \times 6.24}{1.732 \times 12.9 \times 130} = \frac{658{,}944}{2{,}905} = 227\ feet$$

➢ Another way of limiting voltage drop is to limit the intensity of the current on the conductors. Perhaps, you may have an existing installation and if additional loads are added, this may cause excessive voltage drop on the feeder conductors. The following formula can be used to determine the MAXIMUM load permitted when limiting voltage drop on single-phase circuits:

$$I = \frac{CM \times VD}{2 \times K \times D}$$

EXAMPLE - A 240-volt, single-phase feeder with size 2/0 AWG THWN aluminum conductors is supplying an existing panelboard located 260 feet from the main switchboard. What is the MAXIMUM load that can be placed on the panelboard so that the voltage drop is limited to three percent?

A. 143 amperes
B. 175 amperes
C. 122 amperes
D. 87 amperes

ANSWER - (D) 87 amperes

CM = 133,100 CM (2/0 AWG)
VD = 240 volts x .03 = 7.2 volts
K = 21.2 ohms (aluminum)
D = 260 feet

$$I = \frac{133{,}100 \times 7.2}{2 \times 21.2 \times 260} = \frac{958{,}320}{11{,}024} = 86.9 \text{ amperes}$$

➢ The following formula can be used to determine the MAXIMUM load permitted when limiting the voltage drop on three-phase circuits:

$$I = \frac{CM \times VD}{1.732 \times K \times D}$$

EXAMPLE - An existing 208Y/120-volt, three-phase, 4-wire, panelboard is supplied with size 2 AWG THW copper feeder conductors from the main switchboard. The panelboard is located three-hundred (300) feet from the main switchboard. What is the MAXIMUM load, in amperes, the conductors can carry without exceeding a three percent voltage drop?

A. 62 amperes
B. 54 amperes
C. 38 amperes
D. 79 amperes

ANSWER - (A) 62 amperes

CM = 66,360 (2 AWG)
VD = 208 x .03 = 6.24 volts
K = 12.9 ohms (copper)
D = 300 feet

$$I = \frac{66{,}360 \times 6.24}{1.732 \times 12.9 \times 300} = \frac{414{,}086}{6{,}703} = 61.77 \text{ amperes}$$

➢ Another method of determining the voltage drop of the conductors for **single-phase circuits only** is to apply the Ohm's Law Method, using the following formula:

VD = I x R

FORMULA DEFINITIONS:

VD = Volts dropped from a circuit

I = Intensity of the current, or the load, in amperes, at 100 percent.

R = Total conductor resistance, which can be found in **Chapter 9**, **Table 8** of the NEC®, under the ohm/KFT column. Using this method, you must take into consideration the **total length** of both the conductors to find total resistance.

EXAMPLE - Two (2) size 12 AWG THWN/THHN 120-volt, single-phase, copper branch circuit conductors are to supply a 15 ampere load located one-hundred (100) feet from the panelboard. Determine the approximate voltage drop.

A. 3 volts
B. 6 volts
C. 9 volts
D. 12 volts

ANSWER - (B) 6 volts

R = 1.98 ohms per 1,000 feet **(Chapter 9, Table 8)**

$$R = \frac{1.98}{1{,}000} = 0.00198 \text{ ohms per ft.} \times 200 \text{ ft} = .396 \text{ ohms total}$$

I = 15 amperes

VD = 15 amps x .396 ohms = 5.94 volts

EXAMPLE - A 240-volt, single-phase branch circuit is to supply a 32 ampere load with size 8 AWG THWN copper conductors. The load is one-hundred and fifty (150) feet from the panelboard; determine the voltage drop.

A. 4 volts
B. 15 volts
C. 7.5 volts
D. 6 volts

ANSWER - (C) 7.5 volts

R = .778 ohms per 1,000 feet **(Chapter 9, Table 8)**

$R = \frac{.788}{1,000} = 0.000788$ ohms per ft. x 300 ft. = .2334 ohms total

VD = 32 amps x .2334 ohms = 7.46 volts

UNIT 7

AC MOTOR CALCULATIONS

Upon successfully completing this unit of study the student will be familiar with the concept of properly sizing conductors, overcurrent protection, overload protection, and disconnects for single-phase and three-phase ac electric motors.

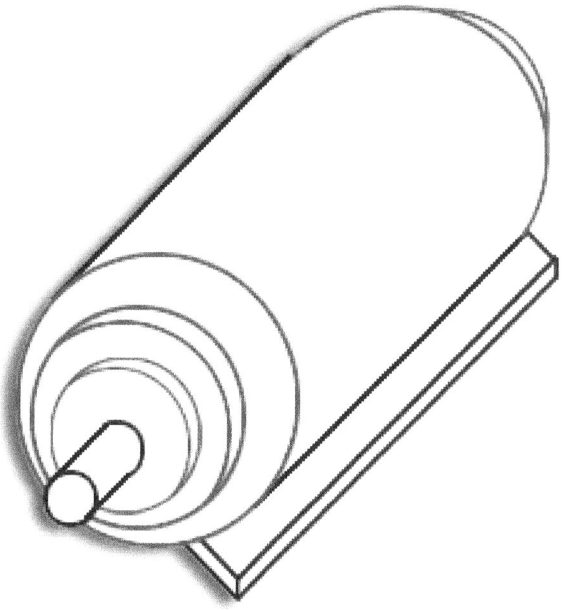

UNIT 7

AC MOTOR CALCULATIONS

RELATED INFORMATION:

- In general, when sizing the conductors, disconnecting means and overcurrent protection for **continuous-duty** ac motors, the full-load current values of the motor(s) given in **Tables 430.247** through **430.250** shall be used, instead of the actual current rating marked on the motor nameplate. **[430.6(A)(1)]** Note this rule does not apply for motors built for low speeds (less than 1,200 RPM) or high torque which may have higher full-load currents and multispeed motors which will have full-load current varying with the speed. For these motors the current values given on the motor(s) nameplate shall be used instead of the NEC® tables.

- **All** motors shall be considered to be for **continuous-duty** unless the nature of the apparatus it drives is such that the motor cannot operate continuously with load under any condition of use. **[430.33]** Examples of motors **not** considered as continuous duty are motors operating elevators, cranes and assembly line machines.

- In general, in order to properly size branch circuit conductors supplying a single continuous duty motor you are to comply with **430.22** which requires the conductors to have an ampacity of at least **125 percent** of the motor's full-load current (FLC) rating as determined in the related tables in the NEC®. The actual conductor sizes are to be selected from **Tables 310.15(B)(16)** or from **Table 400.5(A)**. The conductors are to be sized according to the temperature ratings (60°C or 75°C) of the equipment terminations.

EXAMPLE - Determine the MINIMUM size THHN copper conductors required to supply a 3 hp, 240-volt, single-phase continuous-duty motor when all terminations have a rating of 75°C.

A. 14 AWG
B. 12 AWG
C. 10 AWG
D. 8 AWG

ANSWER - (B) 12 AWG

motor FLC = 17 amperes **[Table 430.248]**
17 amperes x 125% **[430.22]** = 21.25 amperes
Size 12 AWG THHN is rated at 25 amperes at 75°C
[Table 310.15(B)(16)]

- Conductors that supply a motor used in a short-time, intermittent, or varying duty application are permitted to have an ampacity of not less than the percentage values shown on **Table 430.22(E)**, based the full-load current rating indicated on the **motor's nameplate**.

EXAMPLE - Conductors supplying a 40 hp, 480-volt, three-phase, 5 minute rated elevator motor with an ampere rating of 50 amperes marked on the nameplate, shall have an ampacity of at least _____.

A. 42.5 amperes
B. 45.9 amperes
C. 62.5 amperes
D. 67.5 amperes

ANSWER - (A) 42.5 amperes

motor FLA = 50 amperes x 85% **[Table 430.22(E)]** = 42.5 amps

- In general, conductors that supply more than one continuous-duty motor on a single circuit and/or motor(s) and other load(s), are required to have an ampacity of not less than **125 percent** of the full-load current rating of the **highest** rated motor in the group plus **100 percent** of the full-load current ratings of all the **remaining motors** in the group, also the ampacity required for the other load(s).**[430.24]**

EXAMPLE - Determine the MINIMUM size THWN/THHN copper feeder conductors required to supply two (2) induction type, 208-volt, three-phase, continuous-duty motors; one (1) 10 hp and one (1) 15 hp. Consider all terminations are rated 75°C.

A. 6 AWG
B. 4 AWG
C. 3 AWG
D. 2 AWG

ANSWER - (C) 3 AWG

10 hp FLC = 30.8 amps **[Tbl. 430.250]** x 100% = 30.80 amperes
15 HP FLC = 46.2 amps **[Tbl. 430.250]** x 125% = <u>57.75 amperes</u>
88.55 amperes

Size 3 AWG THWN is rated at 100 amperes. **[Table 310.15(B)(16)]**

- Each motor and its accessories is required to have branch circuit, short-circuit and ground fault protection by the use of overcurrent protective devices such as fuses or circuit breakers. The overcurrent protective devices are to be sized no larger than the percentage values given in **Table 430.52. [430.52(C)(1)]** Where the values for overcurrent protection determined from **Table 430.52** does not correspond with the standard sizes or ratings as listed per **240.6(A)** the next higher standard overcurrent protection device is permitted to be used. **[430.52(C)(1), Ex 1]** This is known as **initial sizing**.

EXAMPLE - Determine the MAXIMUM initial rating of nontime delay fuses to be used for branch-circuit, short-circuit and ground-fault protection for a 5 hp, 230-volt, three-phase, squirrel cage, continuous-duty motor.

A. 40 amperes
B. 45 amperes
C. 50 amperes
D. 60 amperes

ANSWER - (C) 50 amperes

5 hp FLC = 15.2 amperes **[Table 430.250]**
15.2 amperes x 300% = 45.6 amperes **[Table 430.52]**

Since 45.6 amperes is not a standard rating for nontime delay fuses, as per **430.52(C)(1) Ex. 1**, you are permitted to go up to the next standard size fuse which is rated at 50 amperes.

➢ When sizing overcurrent protection for motors, the selected rating or setting, if adjustable, should be as low as possible for MAXIMUM protection. However, if the motor is under severe starting conditions, the rating or setting designated in **Table 450.52** or as permitted by **430.52(C)(1) Ex. 1** is not large enough for the starting current of the motor, you are permitted to go up to a higher value as allowed by **430.52(C)(1) Ex. 2**. This is known as **MAXIMUM** or **absolute MAXIMUM** sizing.

EXAMPLE - Determine the absolute MAXIMUM standard size time-delay fuses permitted for short-circuit, branch-circuit and ground-fault protection for a 40 hp, 480-volt, three-phase, induction type, continuous-duty motor.

A. 100 amperes
B. 110 amperes
C. 115 amperes
D. 125 amperes

ANSWER - (B) 110 amperes

40 hp FLC = 52 amperes **[Table 430.250]**
52 amperes x 225% = 117 amperes **[430.52(C)(1)Ex.2(b)]**

Since you are NOT permitted to exceed 225% of the FLC of the motor, you must go down to the next smaller standard size fuse as listed in **240.6(A).**

➢ In general, to properly size the overcurrent protection device for **feeder** conductors supplying two or more motors, the rules as specified in **430.62(A)** are to be applied which states, the protective device is to be sized by:

(1) not greater than the largest overcurrent protection device provided for any motor in the group,

(2) plus the sum of the full-load currents of the other motors of the group.

When sizing **feeder** overcurrent protection for motors, when the value you select does not correspond with a standard rating as listed per **240.6(A)** you are NOT permitted to go up to the next standard size, you must go **down**.

EXAMPLE - What standard size time-delay fuses are required for the feeder overcurrent protection of a feeder supplying four (4), 15 hp, 480-volt, three-phase, continuous-duty induction-type motors, each protected with 40 ampere rated time-delay fuses?

A. 100 amperes
B. 110 amperes
C. 125 amperes
D. 150 amperes

ANSWER - (A) 100 amperes

15 hp FLC = 21 amperes **[Table 430.250]**

40 A (largest OCP in group) + 21 A + 21 A + 21 A = 103 amps

You are required to go down to 100 ampere rated fuses. **[240.6(A)]**

- In addition to overcurrent protection, most continuous-duty electric motors rated more than 1 hp and motors automatically started having a rating of 1 hp or less, are required to be protected from harmful **overloads**. **[430.32(A)]** To properly size the overload protective devices, they shall be selected to trip at no more than the percentage values of the motors nameplate rating given in **430.32(A)(1), (MINIMUM)** or **430.32(C), (MAXIMUM)** instead of the full-load current values from Tables 430.248, 430.249 and 430.250. Today, many manufacturers have adjustable overloads installed in motor controllers or starters for protecting the motor against overloads, which are harmful to it.

- The ampere trip setting value of the separate overloads is based upon **service factor** and **temperature rise** of the motor, as indicated on the motor **nameplate**. The running overload protection may range from **115%** to **125% (MINIMUM) [430.32(A)(1)]** to no more than **140% (MAXIMUM) [430.32(C)]** of the motor's ampere **nameplate** rating. The service factor indicated on the nameplate usually ranges from **1.00** to **1.30**. For example, if a motor has a service factor rating of 1.15 this means that the motor can operate up to **115%** of its rating without undue harm where the ambient temperature is not more than 104°F or 40°C. The temperature rise indicated on the motors nameplate relates to the heating effect of the motor when it is running properly in relation to the ambient temperature. The higher the temperature rise indicated on the nameplate the hotter the motor runs. For example, a motor with a 40°C temperature rise means, under normal operating conditions the motor should not get warmer than 40°C or 104°F. If too great a load is put on the motor or the ambient temperature is elevated, the motor will become excessively hot, causing probable injury to the insulation of the windings.

EXAMPLE - What is the MINIMUM (initial) size running overload protection, in amperes, required for a 2 hp, 208-volt, single-phase, squirrel cage motor with a temperature rise of 42°C and a FLA of 12 amperes indicated on the nameplate?

A. 13.20 amperes
B. 15.18 amperes
C. 15.00 amperes
D. 13.80 amperes

ANSWER - (D) 13.80 amperes

2 hp FLA (nameplate) = 12 amperes

12 amps x 115% (all other motors) = 13.8 amps **[430.32(A)(1)]**

EXAMPLE - Refer to the previous example. Assume the ampere rating you have selected is not sufficient to start the motor and trips. Determine the MAXIMUM size overload protection permitted.

A. 15.00 amperes
B. 15.60 amperes
C. 16.80 amperes
D. 17.16 amperes

ANSWER - (B) 15.60 amperes

2 hp FLA (nameplate) = 12 amperes

12 amps x 130% (all other motors) = 15.60 amps **[430.32(C)]**

➢ Some motors are provided with a **thermal protector integral** with the motor, located inside the motor housing, for overload protection. **[430.32(A)(2)]** Under this condition, the ultimate trip setting, in amperes, shall not exceed the percentage values as expressed in **430.32(A)(2)**, multiplied by the motor's full-load current as given in **Table 430.248**, **Table 430.249** or **Table 430.250**.

EXAMPLE - Determine the MAXIMUM current setting permitted for overload protection for a motor that has a thermal protector integral with the motor, given the following:

- 1 hp – squirrel cage
- single-phase, 120-volts

A. 24.96 amperes
B. 20.80 amperes
C. 22.40 amperes
D. 27.20 amperes

ANSWER - (A) 24.96 amperes

1 hp FLC = 16 amperes **[Table 430.248]**

16 amperes x 156% **[430.32(A)(2)]** = 24.96 amperes

➢ In general, each motor must be provided with some form of approved manual **disconnecting means**. The disconnecting means is required to have an ampere rating of not less than **115 percent** of the full-load current rating of the motor as determined in **Table 430.248** through **430.250**.**[430.110(A)]** For motors rated 2 hp through 100 hp the disconnecting means may be a general-use switch, rated in horsepower, a circuit breaker, or a manual motor controller when marked **"Suitable as Motor Disconnect"**. **[430.109(A)(6)]**

EXAMPLE - When an inverse time circuit breaker is used as a disconnecting means only for a 7½ hp, single-phase, 240-volt, ac motor, the circuit breaker must have a standard ampacity rating of at LEAST _____.

A. 40 amperes
B. 50 amperes
C. 100 amperes
D. 46 amperes

ANSWER - (B) 50 amperes

7½ hp FLA = 40 amperes **[Table 430.248]**

40 amperes x 115% = 46 amperes **[430.110A]**

As per **240.6(A),** the next standard size circuit breaker has a rating of 50 amperes.

➢ For stationary ac motors of 2 hp or less and 300 volts or less the disconnecting means is permitted to be an ac general-use snap switch where the motor full-load current rating is not more than **80 percent** of the ampere rating of the switch. **[430.109(C)(2)]**

EXAMPLE - A 20 ampere rated ac general-use snap switch is permitted for use as a disconnecting means for a 120-volt, single-phase, ac motor when the motor has a rating of 2 hp or less and a full-load current rating of _____ or less.

A. 20 amperes
B. 16 amperes
C. 12 amperes
D. 25 amperes

ANSWER - (B) 16 amperes

20 amperes (switch rating) x 80% = 16 amperes
[430.109(C)(2)]

UNIT 8

SINGLE-FAMILY DWELLING SERVICE CALCULATIONS

After completing this unit of study, the successful student will be familiar with the concept of properly sizing services for one-family dwellings.

UNIT 8

SINGLE-FAMILY DWELLING SERVICE CALCULATIONS

RELATED INFORMATION:

- A single-family dwelling is considered a building consisting solely of one dwelling unit with living and sleeping quarters and having permanent provisions for cooking, cleaning, and laundering.

- In order to properly size services for dwelling units you are to comply with the requirements as set forth in **Article 220** of the NEC® and additional Articles such as **210**, **230** and **240** that may also apply. As indicated in **Section 310.12(A)**, for sizing residential **120/240-volt, 3-wire, single phase** ungrounded (line) service conductors rated **100 through 400 amperes,** they are permitted to have an ampacity not less than **83 percent** of the service rating. For example, if the dwelling unit has a service rating of 150 amperes, the service-entrance conductors are permitted to have a rating of 125 amperes. 150 amperes x .83 = 124.5 amperes

- The NEC® recognizes two (2) methods when calculating dwelling services, the **general method**, also known as the **standard method** and the **optional method**. The standard method starts at **220.11** and the optional method starts at **220.80.** Generally, the optional method is easier to use because you simply add the nameplate values of the utilization equipment together and apply only one demand factor. With the general method, there are several demand factors applied. With either method the most common service provided for a one-family dwelling unit is 120/240-volts, single-phase.

- When using either calculation method, the **MINIMUM** size service for a one-family dwelling is required to be rated **100 amperes** because the ampacity for the ungrounded conductors shall not be less than the rating of the service disconnecting means **[230.42(B)]** and the service disconnecting means shall have a rating of not less than **100 amperes**. **[230.79(C)]**

- **Annex D** of the NEC® shows examples of both calculation methods and the steps and procedures to be used. We will follow these examples and steps to learn how to properly size services for one-family dwellings. First, we will look at the general (standard) method of calculation.

General Calculation Method

<u>**Step 1**</u> - Determine the total connected load, in VA, of the general lighting and general-purpose receptacles by applying **Table 220.14 (J)**. Use the outside dimension of the house but, do not include garages, open porches and enclosed areas not adaptable for future use. **[220.11]**

EXAMPLE - What is the total connected load, in VA, for the general lighting and general-use receptacles of a one-family dwelling having 30 feet by 60 feet of livable space?

A. 2,100 VA
B. 3,600 VA
C. 5,400 VA
D. 6,300 VA

ANSWER - (C) 5,400 VA

First, find the area, in square feet, of the livable space, then multiply by the value given in **Table 220.14(J).**

30 ft. x 60 ft. = 1,800 sq. ft. x 3 VA **[Table 220.14(J)]** = 5,400 VA

Step 2 - Find the total connected load of the small appliance and laundry branch circuits. A MINIMUM of **two (2)** small appliance branch circuits are required **[210.11(C)(1)]** and they shall be calculated at **1,500 VA** per circuit. **[220.52(A)]** A MINIMUM of **one (1)** branch circuit is required to supply the laundry **[210.11(C)(2)]** and shall be calculated at **1,500 VA** per circuit. **[220.52(B)]**

EXAMPLE - What is the MINIMUM total connected load, in VA, for the small appliance and laundry loads in a single-family dwelling?

A. 4,500 VA
B. 3,000 VA
C. 6,000 VA
D. 1,500 VA

ANSWER - (A) 4,500 VA

2 small appl. circuits @ 1,500 VA each	= 3,000 VA
1 laundry circuit @ 1,500 VA	= 1,500 VA
TOTAL	= 4,500 VA

Step 3 - Apply the demand factors specified in **Table 220.42** for the general-purpose lighting and receptacle loads, plus the loads required for the small appliance and laundry branch circuits. **[220.42]**

EXAMPLE - What is the demand load, in VA, for a dwelling unit having a 5,400 VA total connected lighting load and a 4,500 VA connected load for small appliance and laundry branch-circuits?

A. 9,900 VA
B. 5,415 VA
C. 6,780 VA
D. 3,465 VA

ANSWER - (B) 5,415 VA

5,400 VA (ltg.) + 4,500 VA (laundry & sm. appl.) = 9,900 VA total

1st 3,000 VA @ 100% **[Table 220.42]**	= 3,000 VA
9,900 VA – 3,000 VA = 6,900 VA (remainder) x 35%	= 2,415 VA
DEMAND LOAD	= 5,415 VA

Step 4 - Apply a demand factor of **75 percent** of the nameplate rating of **four (4)** or more fastened in place appliances.

*NOTE – This rule does **not apply** for electric ranges, clothes dryers, space heating or air-conditioning equipment. **[220.53]**

EXAMPLE - A one-family dwelling is to have the following fastened in place appliances:

garbage disposal – 864 VA
dishwasher – 1,100 VA
trash compactor – 1,188 VA
water heater – 4,500 VA
attic fan – 750 VA
swimming pool pump – 1,250 VA
Where using the standard method of calculation for dwelling units, determine the demand load.

A. 7,652 VA
B. 9,652 VA
C. 6,757 VA
D. 7,239 VA

ANSWER - (D) 7,239 VA

garbage disposal	- 864 VA
dishwasher	- 1,100 VA
trash compactor	- 1,188 VA
water heater	- 4,500 VA
attic fan	- 750 VA
pump	- 1,250 VA
TOTAL =	9,652 VA (connected load)
	x 75%
	7,239 VA (demand load)

Step 5 - Determine the electric clothes dryer demand load, using **5,000 watts (volt – amperes)** as a MINIMUM or the nameplate rating, **whichever is larger**, for each dryer served. **[220.54]** You are permitted to use the demand factors shown in **Table 220.54**. A demand of **70 percent** of this value may be applied to the **neutral** (grounded) conductor. **[220.61(B)(1)]**

EXAMPLE - When a one-family dwelling is to have only one (1) 4,500 VA electric clothes dryer installed, the demand load will be _____ on the ungrounded service-entrance conductors and _____ on the grounded (neutral) conductor.

A. 4,500 VA – 3,500 VA
B. 3,500 VA – 4,500 VA
C. 4,500 VA – 5,000 VA
D. 5,000 VA – 3,500 VA

ANSWER - (D) 5,000 VA – 3,500 VA

5,000 VA MINIMUM ungrounded conductors **[220.54]**
5,000 VA x 70% = 3,500 VA neutral conductor **[220.61(B)(1)]**

<u>Step 6</u> - Determine the demand load for the cooking appliances in accordance with **Table 220.55**. **[220.55]** This is explained in **Unit 3** of this book. A further demand of **70 percent** of the demand load on the ungrounded conductors may be applied to the **neutral** (grounded) conductor. **[220.61(B)(1)]**

EXAMPLE - A 12 kW electric range installed in a one-family dwelling will have a demand load of _____ on the ungrounded service-entrance conductors and a demand load of _____ on the grounded neutral conductor.

A. 8,000 VA – 5,600 VA
B. 12,000 VA – 8,400 VA
C. 12,000 VA – 8,000 VA
D. 8,000 VA – 3,920 VA

ANSWER - (A) 8,000 VA – 5,600 VA

ungrounded conductors demand – 8 kW = 8,000 VA
[Table 220.55, Col. C]
grounded conductor – 8,000 VA x 70% = 5,600 VA
[220.61(B)(1)]

<u>Step 7</u> - Determine the demand load for the fixed electric space heating or air-conditioning load; you are permitted to **omit the smaller** of the two because these loads are considered noncoincident loads, meaning, they are unlikely to be in use simultaneously. **[220.60]**

EXAMPLE - A one-family dwelling unit to be constructed will have a 10 kW (kVA), 240-volt, single-phase, fixed electric space heating unit and a 32 ampere, 240-volt, single-phase air-conditioning unit. When calculating the total load on the dwelling unit, what is the demand that should be applied to the service-entrance conductors?

A. 10,000 VA
B. 10,800 VA
C. 9,600 VA
D. 19,600 VA

ANSWER - (A) 10,000 VA

First, compare the two loads.

A/C unit - P = I x E P = 32 amperes x 240 volts = 7,680 VA
Heating unit - 10 kW = 10 kW x 1,000 = 10,000 VA

*NOTE – The heating unit is the larger of the loads, this value should be applied.

Step 8 - Add an additional **25 percent** of the full-load current of the **largest motor** in the dwelling. **[220.50]** Generally, the largest motor in the house is the air-conditioning unit.

EXAMPLE - A one-family dwelling will have the following motor loads installed:

garbage disposal – 864 VA
trash compactor – 1,188 VA
attic fan – 750 VA
pump motor – 1,250 VA

When applying the largest motor rule for residential service calculations, how many VA should be added?

A. 1,013 VA
B. 1,563 VA
C. 1,266 VA
D. 313 VA

ANSWER - (D) 313 VA

Largest motor (pump) 1,250 VA x 25% = 313 VA

Step 9 - Add together the values determined from steps 3-8 to find the required volt-amperes. Next, apply the current formula **(I=P/E)** to determine the demand load. Then, multiply the current value by **83%** and size the service-entrance conductors using **Table 310.16**. Use **Table 250.66** for sizing the grounding electrode conductor.

EXAMPLE - After all demand factors have been taken into consideration for a one-family dwelling unit, a demand load of 35,967 VA is determined. What MINIMUM size THWN aluminum ungrounded service-entrance conductors are required when the house is to have a 120/240-volt, single-phase, electrical system?

A. 1 AWG
B. 1/0 AWG
C. 2/0 AWG
D. 3/0 AWG

ANSWER - (C) 2/0 AWG

First, find the load in amperes and multiply by 83%.

$$I = \frac{P}{E} = \frac{35{,}967}{240 \text{ volts}} = 150 \text{ amperes} \times 83\% = 124.5 \text{ amperes}$$

Table 310.16 indicates size 2/0 AWG aluminum conductors having an ampacity of 135 amperes should be selected.

STANDARD CALCULATION: ONE-FAMILY DWELLING

1. GENERAL LIGHTING & RECEPTACLES: *Table* ***220.14(J)***

_____ sq. ft. x 3 VA = _____ VA

2. SMALL APPLIANCES ***220.52(A)*** **& LAUNDRY** ***220.52(B)***

1,500 VA x _____ circuits = _____ VA

3. APPLY DEMAND FACTORS: *Table* ***220.42***

Total of gen. ltg. & small appl. _____ VA

First 3000 VA x 100% = 3,000 VA

Next _____ VA x 35% = _____ VA **LINE** **NEUTRAL**

Remaining _____ VA x 25% = _____ VA

Total _____ VA _____ VA _____VA

4. FIXED APPLIANCES: ***220.53***

Water Heater = _____ VA

Disposal = _____ VA

Compactor = _____ VA

Dishwasher = _____ VA

_______ = _____ VA

_______ = _____ VA

_______ = _____ VA

Total _____ VA (x 75% if 4 or more)= _____ VA _____ VA

5. DRYER: ***220.54***; *Table* ***220.54***

_____ VA = _____ VA x 70%= _____ VA

6. COOKING EQUIPMENT: *Table* ***220.55*** *& Notes*

Col A _____ VA x _____% = _____ VA

Col B _____ VA x _____% = _____ VA

Col C _____ VA = _____ VA

Total _____ VA _____ VA x 70%=_____ VA

7. HEATING or A/C (largest): ***220.60***

Heating unit = _____ VA x 100% = _____ VA

A/C unit = _____ VA x 100% = _____ VA

Heat pump = _____ VA x 100% = _____ VA

Largest Load _____ VA

8. LARGEST MOTOR: ***220.14(C)***

_____ VA x 25% = _____ VA _____ VA

9. TOTAL _____ VA _____ VA

Line I = _______ VA = _____ amperes
240 volts

Neutral I = _______ VA = _____ amperes
240 volts

Conductors are permitted to be sized @ 83% of the demand load if 120/240-volts, single-phase and not greater than 400 amperes.

STANDARD CALCULATION: ONE-FAMILY DWELLING

1. GENERAL LIGHTING & RECEPTACLES: *Table 220.14(J)*
1,800 sq. ft. x 3 VA = 5,400 VA

2. SMALL APPLIANCES ***220.52(A)*** **& LAUNDRY** ***220.52(B)***
1,500 VA x 3 circuits = 4,500 VA

3. APPLY DEMAND FACTORS: *Table 220.42*

			LINE	NEUTRAL
Total of gen. ltg. & small appl.	9,900 VA			
First 3000 VA x 100%	=	3,000 VA		
Next 6,900 VA x 35%	=	2,415 VA		
Remaining -0- VA x 25%	=	-0- VA		
Total		5,415 VA	5,415 VA	5,415 VA

4. FIXED APPLIANCES: ***220.53***

			LINE	NEUTRAL
Water Heater =	4,500 VA			
Disposal =	864 VA			
Compactor =	1,188 VA			
Dishwasher =	1,110 VA			
Attic fan =	750 VA			
Pump =	1,250 VA			
-0- =	-0- VA			
Total	9,652 VA	(x 75% if 4 or more)=	7,239 VA	7,239 VA

5. DRYER: ***220.54***; *Table 220.54*
5,000 VA = 5,000 VA x 70%= 3,500 VA

6. COOKING EQUIPMENT: *Table 220.55 & Notes*

			LINE	NEUTRAL
Col A -0- VA x -0- % =	-0- VA			
Col B -0- VA x -0- % =	-0- VA			
Col C 8,000 VA =	8,000 VA			
Total	8,000 VA		8,000 VA x 70%=	5,600 VA

7. HEATING or A/C (largest): ***220.60***

Heating unit	= 10,000 VA x 100%	=	10,000 VA
A/C unit	= 7,680 VA x 100%	=	7,680 VA
Heat pump	= -0- VA x 100%	=	-0- VA
Largest Load			10,000 VA

8. LARGEST MOTOR: ***220.14(C)***
1,250 VA x 25% = 313 VA 313 VA

9. TOTAL 35,967 VA 22,067 VA

Line $I = \frac{35,967 \text{ VA}}{240 \text{ volts}} = 150$ amperes

Neutral $I = \frac{22,067 \text{ VA}}{240 \text{ volts}} = 92$ amperes

Conductors are permitted to be sized @ 83% of the demand load if 120/240-volts, single-phase and not greater 400 amperes.

Optional Calculation Method

- In general, the **optional calculation method** for dwelling units provides an easier and less complex method than the standard (general) method for computing the total demand load for service-entrance conductors. The optional calculation method is reserved for dwelling units served by a single service with a connected load of **100 amperes or greater. [220.82(A)]** Therefore, since most one-family homes currently being constructed have a connected load of 100 amperes or more, this calculation method is frequently used.

- When using the **optional calculation method**, the calculated load shall not be less than **100 percent** of the **first 10 kW**, plus **40 percent** of the remainder of the **"general loads"**, including, general lighting and receptacles, laundry and small appliance branch circuits and nameplate VA rating of all fastened in place motors and appliances, plus the larger of the air-conditioner or heating load. **[220.82(A)]** The following steps may be applied when using the optional calculation method for dwellings.

Step 1 - Compare the heating and air-conditioning loads. As per **220.82(C)**, include the **largest** of the following:

1. 100 percent of the nameplate rating(s) of the air-conditioning equipment.
2. 100 percent of the nameplate rating(s) of the heat pump(s) only.
3. 100 percent of the nameplate ratings of electric thermal storage and other heating systems where the usual load is expected to be continuous.

4. 100 percent of the nameplate rating(s) of the heat pump compressor and 65 percent of the supplemental electric heating for central electric space heating systems. If the heat pumps compressor is interlocked with the supplementary heat in a manner that both cannot be operated at the same time, the heat pump does not need to be added.

5. 65 percent of the nameplate rating(s) of electric space heating, if there are less than four (4) units having separate controls.

6. 40 percent of the nameplate rating(s) of electric space heating, if there are four (4) or more units with separate controls.

EXAMPLE - A one-family dwelling is to have the following heating and air-conditioning equipment:

two (2) 10 kW (kVA) electric space heating systems
two (2) 240-volt, single-phase, 50 ampere rated air-conditioners

When using the optional method of calculation for one-family dwellings, what demand, in VA, should be applied to the ungrounded service-entrance conductors for the heating or air-conditioning loads?

A. 20,000 VA
B. 24,000 VA
C. 15,600 VA
D. 13,000 VA

ANSWER - (B) 24,000 VA

Space heaters **[220.82(C)(5)]**
10 kVA + 10 kVA = 20 kVA x 1,000 = 20,000 VA
20,000 VA x 65% = 13,000 VA

A/C Equipment **[220.82(C)(1)]**
50 amps + 50 amps = 100 amperes x 240 volts = 24,000 VA

The A/C equipment with a computed load of 24,000 VA is to be used for this calculation.

<u>Step 2</u> - Determine the connected load, in VA, of the general lighting and general-use receptacles; calculated from the outside dimensions of the dwelling using 3 VA per square foot. Do not include open porches, garages or unused or unfinished spaces not adapted for future use. **[220.82(B)(1)]**

EXAMPLE - Before demand factors are taken into consideration, determine the connected load, in VA, for the general lighting and general-use receptacles for a one-family dwelling having 5,000 square feet of livable space, a 600 square foot garage and a 350 square foot open porch.

A. 15,000 VA
B. 17,500 VA
C. 17,850 VA
D. 5,000 VA

ANSWER - (A) 15,000 VA

5,000 sq. ft. x 3 VA **[220.82(B)(1)]** = 15,000 VA

Step 3 - Find the total connected load of the small appliance and laundry branch circuits; each circuit is to be calculated at **1,500 VA each**. **[220.82(B)(2)]** A MINIMUM of two (2) small-appliance branch circuits are required **[210.11(C)(1)]** and a MINIMUM of one (1) laundry branch circuit is required. **[210.11(C)(2)]**

EXAMPLE - A one-family dwelling is to have three (3) small-appliance branch circuits and one (1) laundry branch circuit installed. Before demand factors are taken into consideration, what is the total connected load of these circuits?

A. 1,500 VA
B. 3,000 VA
C. 4,500 VA
D. 6,000 VA

ANSWER - (D) 6,000 VA

Small appliance circuits 3 x 1,500 VA = 4,500 VA **[220.52(A)]**
Laundry circuit 1 x 1,500 VA = 1,500 VA **[220.52(B)]**
TOTAL Connected Load = 6,000 VA

Step 4 - Find the total connected load of all fastened in place appliances, such as electric ranges, cooktops, ovens, clothes dryers and water heaters. This total is to be based on the nameplate rating of the appliances. **[220.82(B)(3)]** Also include the nameplate ratings of all motors, such as attic fans, sump pumps and water well and swimming pool pumps. **[220.82(B)(4)]**

EXAMPLE - A single family dwelling is to have the following fastened in place appliances and motors:

one – 12 kVA electric range
one – 6 kVA electric clothes dryer
one – 1,250 VA dishwasher
one – 1,176 VA trash compactor
one – 1,656 VA garbage disposer
one – 6,000 VA water heater
one – 1,176 VA attic fan
one – 1,250 VA microwave oven

What is the total connected load of this utilization equipment?

A. 26,508 VA
B. 30,508 VA
C. 25,508 VA
D. 26,805 VA

ANSWER - (B) 30,508 VA

range - 12 kVA x 1,000	= 12,000 VA
clothes dryer - 6 kVA x 1,000	= 6,000 VA
dishwasher	= 1,250 VA
trash compactor	= 1,176 VA
garbage disposer	= 1,656 VA
water heater	= 6,000 VA
attic fan	= 1,176 VA
microwave oven	= 1,250 VA
TOTAL Connected Load	= 30,508 VA

Step 5 - Total the **"general load"** as determined in steps 2, 3 and 4, then apply the demand factors as per **220.82(B)**, **100 percent** of the **first 10 kVA (10,000 VA)**, plus **40 percent** of the remainder.

EXAMPLE - Using the optional calculation method for one-family dwellings, determine the demand load on the ungrounded service-entrance conductors for a dwelling that has the following total connected general loads:

General lighting and receptacles	- 15,000 VA
Small appliance and laundry circuits	- 6,000 VA
Fastened in place appliances and motors	- 30,500 VA

A. 51,500 VA
B. 25,000 VA
C. 26,600 VA
D. 25,600 VA

ANSWER - (C) 26,600 VA

General lighting and receptacles	- 15,000 VA
Small appliance and laundry circuits	- 6,000 VA
Fastened in place appliances and motors	- 30,500 VA
TOTAL General Load	= 51,500 VA
1st 10,000 VA @ 100%	- 10,000 VA
Remainder (total – 10,000) = 41,500 VA @ 40%	- 16,600 VA
DEMAND LOAD	= 26,600 VA

Step 6 - Add together the values determined from steps 1 and 5 to find the required volt-amperes. Next, apply the current formula **(I=P/E)** to determine the demand load. Then, multiply the current value by **83%** and size the service-entrance conductors using **Table 310.16**. Use **Table 250.66** for sizing the grounding electrode conductor.

EXAMPLE - When applying the optional method of calculation for a one-family dwelling, after all demand factors have been considered, a demand load of 50,600 VA is determined. Using standard overcurrent protective devices, determine the MAXIMUM ampere rating of the service overcurrent protective device and the MINIMUM size of 75ºC aluminum ungrounded service-entrance conductors required. The electrical system is 120/240-volts, single-phase.

A. 200 amperes OCP – 4/0 AWG aluminum conductors
B. 250 amperes OCP – 4/0 AWG aluminum conductors
C. 250 amperes OCP – 250 kcmil aluminum conductors
D. 225 amperes OCP – 4/0 AWG aluminum conductors

ANSWER - (D) 225 amperes – 4/0 AWG aluminum conductors

First, find the load in amperes.

$$I = \frac{P}{E} = \frac{50{,}600\ VA}{240\ volts} = 210.8\ \text{amperes (demand load)}$$

This value does not correspond with the standard ampere rating of an overcurrent protective device. Therefore, as per **240.4(B)**, the next higher standard overcurrent device is permitted to be used. **Table 240.6(A)** indicates a **225 ampere** rating is the next higher standard OCP rating.

To find the required ampacity of the conductors:

210.8 amperes **x 83% = 175 amperes**

Size 4/0 AWG 75ºC aluminum conductors with an ampacity of 180 amperes should be selected from **[Table 310.16].**

OPTIONAL CALCULATION: ONE-FAMILY DWELLING

1. HEATING or A/C: ***220.82(C)(1-6)***

Heating units (3 or less) = ____ VA x 65%	= _____ VA		
Heating units (4 or more) = ____ VA x 40%	= _____ VA		
A/C unit = _____ VA x 100%	= _____ VA		
Heat pump = _____ VA x 100%	= _____ VA	**LINE**	
Largest Load	= _____ VA		
Total	= _____ VA	_____ VA	

2. GENERAL LIGHTING: ***220.82(B)(1)***

			NEUTRAL
_____ sq. ft. x 3 VA per sq. ft.	= _____ VA		_____ VA

3. SMALL APPLIANCE & LAUNDRY LOADS: ***220.82(B)(2)***

1,500 VA x _____ circuits	_____ VA		_____VA

4. FIXED APPLIANCES & MOTORS: ***220.82(B)(3)&(4)***

Dishwasher =	_____ VA		_____ VA
Disposal =	_____ VA		_____ VA
Compactor =	_____ VA		_____ VA
Water heater =	_____ VA		_____ VA
Range =	_____ VA	@ 70%	_____ VA
Cooktop =	_____ VA	@ 70%	_____ VA
Oven =	_____ VA	@ 70%	_____ VA
Dryer =	_____ VA	@ 70%	_____ VA
__________ =	_____ VA		_____ VA
__________ =	_____ VA		_____ VA
__________ =	_____ VA		_____ VA
Total =	_____ VA		_____ VA

5. APPLY DEMAND FACTORS: ***220.82(B)***

First 10,000 VA x 100% =	10,000 VA		
Remaining _____ VA x 40% =	_____ VA		
Total	_____ VA	_____ VA	_____ VA

6. TOTAL _____ VA _____ VA

LINE $I = \frac{VA}{240\text{ volts}}$ = ____amperes

NEUTRAL $I = \frac{VA}{240\text{ volts}}$ = ____amperes

Conductors are permitted to be sized @ 83% of the demand load if 120/240-volts, single-phase, or 100% if 208Y/120-volts, three-phase, or the load is greater than 400 amperes.

OPTIONAL CALCULATION: ONE-FAMILY DWELLING

1. HEATING or A/C: *220.82(C)(1-6)*

Heating units (3 or less) = 20,000 VA x 65% =13,000 VA
Heating units (4 or more) = ____ VA x 40% =_____ VA
A/C unit = 24,000 VA x 100% = 24,000 VA
Heat pump = _____ VA x 100% = _____ VA **LINE**
Largest Load = 24,000 VA
Total = 24,000 VA 24,000 VA

2. GENERAL LIGHTING: *220.82(B)(1)* **NEUTRAL**

5,000 sq. ft. x 3 VA per sq. ft. = 15,000 VA 15,000 VA

3. SMALL APPLIANCE & LAUNDRY LOADS: *220.82(B)(2)*

1,500 VA x 4 circuits = 6,000 VA 6,000 VA

4. FIXED APPLIANCES & MOTORS: *220.82(B)(3)&(4)*

Dishwasher	=	1,250 VA		1,250 VA
Disposal	=	1,656 VA		1,656 VA
Compactor	=	1,176 VA		1,176 VA
Water heater	=	6,000 VA		6,000 VA
Range	=	12,000 VA	@ 70%	8,400 VA
Cooktop	=	-0- VA	@ 70%	-0- VA
Oven	=	-0- VA	@ 70%	-0- VA
Dryer	=	6,000 VA	@ 70%	4,200 VA
Attic fan	=	1,176 VA		1,176 VA
Microwave	=	1,250 VA		1,250 VA
__________	=	_____ VA		____ VA
	Total =	51,508 VA		____ VA

5. APPLY DEMAND FACTORS: *220.82(B)*

First 10,000 VA x 100% = 10,000 VA
Remaining 41,508 VA x 40% = 16,603 VA
Total = 26,603 VA 26,603 VA 46,108 VA

6. TOTAL 50,603 VA 46,108 VA

LINE I = 50,603 VA / 240 volts = 211 amperes

NEUTRAL I = 46,108 VA / 240 volts = 192 amperes

Conductors are permitted to be sized @ 83% of the demand load if 120/240-volts, single-phase and not greater 400 amperes.

UNIT 9

MULTI-FAMILY DWELLING SERVICE CALCULATIONS

After successfully completing this unit of study, the student will have the ability to properly size services for multiple-family dwelling units.

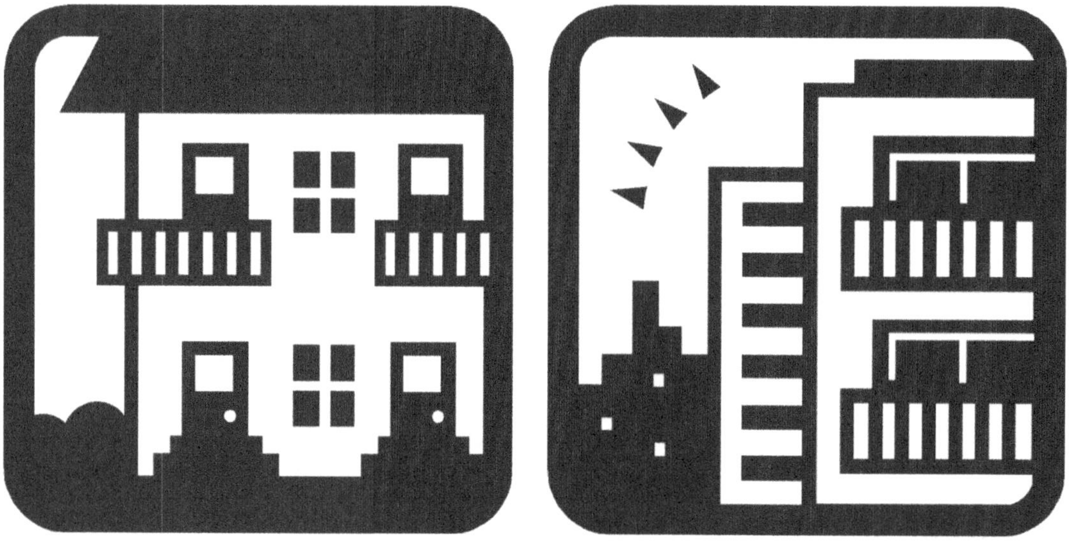

UNIT 9

MULTI-FAMILY DWELLING SERVICE CALCULATIONS

RELATED INFORMATION:

- A multi-family dwelling unit is considered a building containing three or more dwelling units; examples are apartments, condominiums, and town houses.

- Many similarities exist between multi-family dwelling service calculations and one-family dwelling service calculations. Both can be calculated using the **standard (general) method** as well as the **optional method**. I suggest you become familiar with one-family dwelling calculations before attempting multi-family dwelling calculations.

- For multi-family dwellings the service-entrance conductor sizes are to be selected from **Table 310.16.** The neutral load is permitted to be determined per **Section 220.61**. The rule in **Section 310.12** that permits a reduction in the ampacity of service conductors, is reserved for one-family dwellings and individual units in a two-family or multifamily dwelling.

- **Annex D** of the NEC® shows examples of both calculation methods and the steps and procedures to be used. We will follow these examples and steps to learn to properly size services for multi-family dwellings. First, we will look at the general (standard) method of calculation.

General Calculation Method

Step 1 - Determine the total connected load, in VA, of the general lighting and general-use receptacles. Simply multiply the number of units by the square footage of one unit, when they are all the same size, and multiply by **3 VA** per Table **220.14(J)**. Do not include open porches, garages, and enclosed areas not adaptable for future use. **[220.11]**

EXAMPLE - What is the total connected load, in VA, for the general lighting and general-use receptacles for a six (6) unit multi-family dwelling, when each apartment is 750 square feet?

A. 2,250 VA
B. 4,500 VA
C. 13,500 VA
D. 15,300 VA

ANSWER – (C) 13,500 VA

First, find the area, in square feet, of the habitable spaces.

6 units X 750 sq.ft. = 4,500 sq.ft.

Next, multiply by 3 VA **[Table 220.14(J)]**

4,500 sq. ft. X 3 VA = 13,500 VA

Step 2 - Find the total connected load of the small appliance and laundry branch circuits. A minimum of **two (2)** small appliance branch circuits are required per unit **[210.11(C)(1)]** and they shall be calculated at **1,500 VA** per circuit. **[220.52(A)]**. A minimum of **one (1)** branch circuit calculated at **1,500 VA** is required to supply the laundry of each unit having a laundry. **[210.11(C)(2)] & [220.52(B)]**. When the multi-family dwelling unit has a common laundry facility provided on the premises and available to all building occupants, this is considered a "house load" and the laundry load can be omitted in this step.

EXAMPLE - What is the minimum total connected load, in VA, for the small appliance and laundry loads for a six (6) unit multi-family dwelling, having laundry facilities in each unit?

A. 27,000 VA
B. 18,000 VA
C. 12,000 VA
D. 9,000 VA

ANSWER - (A) 27,000 VA

2 small appl. circuits @ 1,500 VA X 6 units = 18,000 VA
1 laundry circuit @ 1,500 VA X 6 units = 9,000 VA
Total = 27,000 VA

Step 3 - Apply the demand factors specified in **Table 220.42** for the general purpose lighting and receptacle loads, plus the loads required for the small appliance and laundry branch circuits. **[220.42]**

EXAMPLE - What is the demand load, in VA, for a multi-family dwelling unit having a total connected general-purpose receptacle and lighting load of 13,500 VA and a total connected small appliance and laundry branch circuit load of 27,000 VA? (Use general method of calculation.)

A. 13,125 VA
B. 16,125 VA
C. 37,500 VA
D. 40,500 VA

ANSWER - (B) 16,125 VA

General purpose lighting & receptacles = 13,500 VA
Laundry & small appliances = 27,000 VA
Total Connected Load = 40,500 VA

1st 3,000 VA @ 100% **[Table 220.42]** = 3,000 VA
40,500 VA – 3,000 VA = 37,500 VA
37,500 VA (Remainder) X 35% = 13,125 VA
Demand Load = 16,125 VA

Step 4 - Apply a demand factor of **75%** of the nameplate rating of **four (4)** or more fastened in place appliances. Examples include, water heater, dishwasher, trash compactor, garbage disposal, etc. **[220.53]** Note that this rule **does not apply** for electric ranges, clothes dryers, space heating or air conditioning equipment.

EXAMPLE - Using the standard (general) method of calculation for dwellings, determine the demand load, in VA, of a six (6) unit multi-family dwelling unit having the following fixed appliances installed in each unit:

dishwasher - 1,100 VA
water heater - 3,500 VA
garbage disposal - 850 VA

A. 32,700 VA
B. 23,700 VA
C. 22,890 VA
D. 24,525 VA

ANSWER - (D) 24,525 VA

Dishwasher - 1,100 VA X 6 = 6,600 VA
Water Heater - 3,500 VA X 6 = 21,000 VA

Garbage Disposal - 850 VA X 6 = 5,100 VA
Total Connected Load = 32,700 VA
X 75% (demand)
Demand Load = 24,525 VA

Step 5 - Determine the electric clothes dryer demand load, using **5,000 watts** (volt amperes) as the minimum or the nameplate rating, **whichever is larger**, for each dryer served. **[220.54]** Apply the demand factors listed in **Table 220.54**. A further demand of **70 percent** of this value may be applied to the **neutral** (grounded) conductor. **[220.61(B)(1)]**

EXAMPLE - When the standard (general) method of calculation for dwellings is applied, where a six (6) unit multifamily apartment building having a 3.5 kW electric clothes dryer in each unit, the demand load, in VA, On the ungrounded (line) service-entrance conductors is ____________.

A. 15,750 VA
B. 21,000 VA
C. 22,500 VA
D. 30,000 VA

ANSWER - (C) 22,500 VA

5,000 VA (minimum) x 6 = 30,000 VA
Demand **[Table 220.54]** x 75 %
22,500 VA

STEP 6 - Determine the demand load for the cooking appliances in accordance with **Table 220.55 [220.55]**. This is explained in **Unit 3** of this book. A further demand of **70 percent** of the demand load on the ungrounded conductors may be applied to the **neutral** (grounded) conductor. **[220.61(B)(1)]**

EXAMPLE - An 8 kW electric range installed in each unit of a six (6) unit multifamily apartment building will have a demand load of _______ on the ungrounded (line) service-entrance conductors and demand load of ________ on the grounded (neutral) conductor, when the standard method of calculation for dwellings is applied.

A. 43,000 VA – 30,100 VA
B. 20,640 VA – 14,448 VA
C. 48,000 VA – 33,600 VA
D. 43,000 VA – 32,250 VA

ANSWER - (B) 20,640 VA – 14,448 VA

ungrounded conductor – **[Table 220.55, Column B.]**
8 kW x 6 units x 43% = 20.64 kW
20.64 kW x 1,000 = 20,640 VA

grounded conductor – **[220.61(B)(1)]**

20,640 VA x 70% = 14,448 VA

STEP 7 - Determine the demand load for the fixed electric space heating or air conditioning load; the smaller of the two is permitted to be omitted, because these loads are considered noncoincident loads, meaning they are unlikely to be used at the same time. **[220.60]**

EXAMPLE - A six (6) unit multifamily apartment building to be constructed will have a 3 kW (kVA), 240-volt, single-phase, fixed electric space heating unit and a 17 ampere, single-phase, 240-volt, air conditioning unit, installed in each dwelling unit. When using the standard (general) method of calculation for dwellings, what is the demand, in VA, that should be applied to the ungrounded (line) service-entrance conductors?

A. 24,480 VA
B. 18,000 VA
C. 7,080 VA
D. 42,840 VA

ANSWER - (A) 24,480 VA

First compare the two loads.
A/C unit – P = I x E P= 17 amps x 240 volts = 4,080 VA
Heating unit – 3 kW x 1,000 = 3,000 VA

4,080 VA (larger) x 6 units = 24,480 VA

STEP 8 - Add the values determined from steps 3 – 7 together to find the required volt ampere rating of the service. Next, apply the current formula **(I = P ÷ E)**, and size the ungrounded service-entrance conductors using **Table 310.16**.

EXAMPLE - After all demand factors have been taken into consideration for a multifamily dwelling unit, a demand load of 108,270 VA is determined for the ungrounded service-entrance conductors. What minimum size THWN copper ungrounded conductors are required for the dwelling service? (120/240-volt, 3-wire, single-phase electrical system.)

A. 400 kcmil
B. 500 kcmil
C. 600 kcmil
D. 700 kcmil

ANSWER - (D) 700 kcmil

First, find the load in amperes.

$I = P \div E$

$$I = \frac{108{,}270\ VA}{240\ volts} = 451.125$$

Table 310.16 is to be used for sizing the conductors. Size 700 kcmil conductors with an ampacity of 460 amperes should be selected.

STANDARD CALCULATION: MULTI-FAMILY DWELLING

1. GENERAL LIGHTING & RECEPTACLES: ***Table 220.14(J)***

_____ sq. ft. x 3 VA = _____ VA

2. SMALL APPLIANCES *220.52(A)* & LAUNDRY *220.52(B)*

1,500 VA x _____ circuits = _____ VA

3. APPLY DEMAND FACTORS: ***Table 220.42***

Total of gen. ltg. & small appl. _____ VA

First 3000 VA x 100% = 3,000 VA

Next _____ VA x 35% = _____ VA **LINE** **NEUTRAL**

Remaining _____ VA x 25% = _____ VA

Total = _____ VA _____ VA _____VA

4. FIXED APPLIANCES: ***220.53***

Water Heater _____ VA x _____ units = _____ VA

Disposal _____ VA x _____ units = _____ VA

Compactor _____ VA x _____ units = _____ VA

Dishwasher _____ VA x _____ units = _____ VA

_______ _____ VA x _____ units = _____ VA

_______ _____ VA x _____ units = _____ VA

_______ _____ VA x _____ units = _____ VA

Total = (x 75% if 4 or more) _____ VA = _____ VA _____ VA

5. CLOTHES DRYERS: ***220.54****;* ***Table 220.54***

_____ VA x _____ units = _____VA x _____%_____ VA x 70%= _____ VA

6. COOKING EQUIPMENT: ***Table 220.54 & Notes***

Col A _____ VA x _____units x _____ % =_____ VA

Col B _____ VA x _____units x _____ % =_____ VA

Col C _____ VA x _____units = _____ VA

Total = _____ VA _____ VA x 70%=_____ VA

7. HEATING or A/C at 100% (largest): ***220.60***

Heating unit =_____ VA x _____ units =_____ VA

A/C unit =_____ VA x _____ units =_____ VA

Heat pump =_____ VA x _____ units =_____ VA

Largest Load = _____ VA

8. TOTAL _____ VA _____ VA

Line I = _______ VA = _____ amperes
240 volts

Neutral I = _______ VA = _____ amperes
240 volts

Conductors are to be sized per Table 310.16.

STANDARD CALCULATION: MULTI-FAMILY DWELLING

1. GENERAL LIGHTING & RECEPTACLES: *Table 220.14(J)*

4,500 sq. ft. x 3 VA = 13,500 VA

2. SMALL APPLIANCES *220.52(A)* & LAUNDRY *220.52(B)*

1,500 VA x 18 circuits = 27,000 VA

3. APPLY DEMAND FACTORS: *Table 220.42*

Total of gen. ltg. & small appl. 40,500 VA

			LINE	NEUTRAL
First 3000 VA x 100%	=	3,000 VA		
Next 37,500 VA x 35%	=	13,125 VA		
Remaining _____ VA x 25%	=	_____ VA		
Total		16,125 VA	16,125 VA	16,125 VA

4. FIXED APPLIANCES: *220.53*

Water Heater 3,500 VA x 6 units = 21,000 VA
Disposal 850 VA x 6 units = 5,100 VA
Compactor _____ VA x _____ units = _____ VA
Dishwasher 1,100 VA x 6 units = 6,600 VA
_______ _____ VA x _____ units = _____ VA
_______ _____ VA x _____ units = _____ VA
_______ _____ VA x _____ units = _____ VA

Total (x 75% if 4 or more) 32,700 VA = 24,525 VA 24,525 VA

5. CLOTHES DRYERS: ***220.54****; Table* ***220.54***

5,000 VA x 6 units = 30,000 VA x 75 % 22,500 VA x 70% = 15,750 VA

6. COOKING EQUIPMENT: *Table* ***220.54*** *& Notes*

Col A _____ VA x _____ units x _____ % = _____ VA
Col B 8,000 VA x 6 units x 43 % = 20,640 VA
Col C _____ VA x _____ units = _____ VA
Total = 20,640 VA 20,640 VA x 70% = 14,448 VA

7. HEATING or A/C at 100% (largest): ***220.60***

Heating unit = 3,000 VA x _____ units = _____ VA
A/C unit = 4,080 VA x 6 units = 24,480 VA
Heat pump = _____ VA x _____ units = _____ VA
Largest Load = 24,480 VA

8. TOTAL 108,270 VA 70,848 VA

Line $I = \frac{108{,}270 \text{ VA}}{240 \text{ volts}} = 451$ amperes **220.61(B)(2)**

Neutral $I = \frac{70{,}848 \text{ VA}}{240 \text{ volts}} = 295$ amperes – First 200 amps @ 100% = 200 amperes
Next 95 amps @70% = 67 amperes
TOTAL NEUTRAL = 267 amperes

Conductors are to be sized per Table 310.16.

OPTIONAL CALCULATION METHOD

- When calculating the service size for multi-family dwellings, the **optional calculation method** is commonly applied, because it is an easier and less complex calculation method than the general (standard) method; less steps are used and it results in a smaller service size. The optional method is specifically designed for dwelling units having an electrical load of greater than 100 amperes. **[220.82(A)]**

- In general, the optional calculation method for multifamily dwellings may be applied when all of the following conditions are met: **[220.84(A)]**

  1. No dwelling unit is supplied by more than one feeder.
  2. Each dwelling unit is equipped with electric cooking equipment.
  3. Each dwelling unit is equipped with either electric space heating or air conditioning, or both.

- The following steps may be applied when using the optional calculation method for multifamily dwellings. Notice the first two steps are the same for both calculation methods.

<u>**STEP 1**</u> - Determine the total connected load, in VA, of the general lighting and general-use receptacle. Simply multiply the number of units by the square footage of all units of the same size and multiply by 3 VA per square foot. **[220.84(C)(1)]** Do not include open porches, balconies, and garages.

EXAMPLE - What is the connected load, in VA, for the general lighting and general-use receptacles for an eight (8) unit multifamily dwelling, when each apartment has 840 square feet of livable space?

A. 20,160 VA
B. 10,080 VA
C. 16,020 VA
D. 6,720 VA

ANSWER - (A) 20,160 VA

First, find the total area in square feet.

8 units x 840 sq. ft. = 6,720 sq. ft.

Next, multiply by 3 VA **[220.84(C)(1)]**

6,720 sq. ft. x 3 VA = 20,160 VA

<u>**STEP 2**</u> - Find the connected load of the small appliances and laundry branch circuits. **[220.84(C)(2)]** Each unit is required to have at least **two (2)** small appliance branch circuits, **[210.11(C)(1)]** and **one (1)** laundry branch circuit, **[210.11(C)(2)]** and they shall be calculated at **1,500** VA per circuit. **[220.52(A)&(B)]**

EXAMPLE - Determine the minimum connected load, in VA, for the small appliance and laundry loads for an eight (8) unit multifamily apartment building having a laundry facility in each unit.

A. 24,000 VA
B. 36,000 VA
C. 42,000 VA
D. 12,000 VA

ANSWER- (B) 36,000 VA

2 small appl. circuits @ 1,500 VA x 8 units	=	24,000 VA
1 laundry circuit @ 1,500 va x 8 units	=	12,000 VA
TOTAL		36,000 VA

STEP 3 - Calculate the connected load, at the nameplate rating, of all fastened in place appliances, such as electric ranges, cooktops, ovens, clothes, dryers, dishwashers, garbage disposers, and water heaters. **[220.84(C)(3)]**

EXAMPLE - An eight (8) unit multifamily apartment building is to have the following fastened in place appliances installed in each unit.

water heater	– 3.6 kW	– 240 volts
electric range	– 8 kW	– 240 volts
dishwasher	– 1.1 kW	– 120 volts
garbage disposal	– 850 VA	– 120 volts
clothes dryer	– 3.5 kW	– 240 volts

Determine the total connected load, in VA, for the appliances.

A. 17,050 VA
B. 102,300 VA
C. 136,400 VA
D. 51,150 VA

ANSWER - (C) 136,400 VA

water heater	- 3,600 VA x 8 units =	28,800 VA
electric range	- 8,000 VA x 8 units =	64,000 VA
dishwasher	- 1,100 VA x 8 units =	8,800 VA
garbage disposal	- 850 VA x 8 units =	6,800 VA
clothes dryer	- 3,500 VA x 8 units =	28,000 VA
	TOTAL	136,400 VA

STEP 4 - Calculate the connected load of the larger of the air-conditioning or space heating equipment. Omit the smaller. **[220.84(C)(5)]**

EXAMPLE - An eight (8) unit multifamily apartment building to be constructed will have a 3.5 kW (kVA), 240 volt, single-phase, fixed electric space heating unit and a 17 ampere, single-phase, 240-volt air-conditioning unit installed in each dwelling unit. When applying the optional method of calculations for multifamily dwellings for services and feeders, what MINIMUM value, in VA, is permitted to be used?

A. 60,640 VA
B. 28,000 VA
C. 24,480 VA
D. 32,640 VA

ANSWER - (D) 32,640 VA

First, compare the two loads.
A/C unit – P = I x E P= 17 amps x 240 volts = 4,080 VA
Heating unit – 3.5 kW x 1,000 = 3,500 VA

4,080 (larger) x 8 units = 32,640 VA

STEP 5 - Add steps 1 through 4 to determine the total connected VA load of the dwelling units and apply the demand factors as per **Table 220.84**.

EXAMPLE - An eight (8) unit multifamily apartment building has the following total connected loads:

general lighting & receptacles – 20,160 VA
small appliances & laundry circuits – 36,000 VA
Fixed appliances - 136,400 VA
A/C- heating equipment – 32,640 VA

Use the optional method of calculation for multifamily dwellings, and determine the demand load, in VA, on the ungrounded service-entrance conductors.

A. 96,836 VA
B. 222,500 VA
C. 225,500 VA
D. 99,088 VA

ANSWER - (A) 93,836 VA

20,160 VA	
36,000 VA	
136,400 VA	
32,640 VA	
225,200 VA	(connected load)
x 43%	**Table 220.84**
96,836 VA	(demand load)

STEP 6 - Add the "house loads" at the nameplate rating of the equipment. When the multifamily dwelling has a common laundry facility provided on the premises and available to all building occupants, this is considered a commercial occupancy and dwelling demand factors are **not** to be applied. If there are no "house loads," this step is omitted.

STEP 7 - Add the values determined from steps 5 and 6 (if any) together to find the required volt ampere rating of the service. Next, apply the current formula **(I = P ÷ E)** and size the service-entrance conductors using **Table 310.16**. The neutral load is determined per **220.61**.

EXAMPLE - After all demand factors have been taken into consideration for a multifamily dwelling, a demand load of 96,836 VA is determined for the ungrounded service-entrance conductors. What minimum size THWN/THHN copper ungrounded conductors are required for the service? (120/240-volts, single-phase electrical system)

A. 500 kcmil
B. 600 kcmil
C. 700 kcmil
D. 750 kcmil

ANSWER - (B) 600 kcmil

First, find the load in amperes.

$I = P \div E$

$I = \frac{96{,}836 \text{ VA}}{240 \text{ volts}} = 403 \text{ amperes}$

Select 75°C rated conductors from **Table 310.16.** Size 600 kcmil conductors with an ampacity of 420 amperes should be selected.

OPTIONAL CALCULATION: MULTI-FAMILY DWELLING

1. GENERAL LIGHTING & RECEPTACLES: ***220.84(C)(1)*** **Line** **Neutral**

_____ sq. ft. x 3 VA = (____) VA (_____) VA

2. SMALL APPLIANCES & LAUNDRY ***220.84(C)(2)***

		Line	Neutral
Small Appl.	1,500 VA x _____ circuits x _____ units=	_____ VA	_____ VA
Laundry	1,500 VA x _____ circuits x _____ units=	_____ VA	_____ VA
Total =		(_____) VA	(_____) VA

3. FIXED APPLIANCES: ***220.84(C)(3)***

		Line	Neutral
Water Heater	_____ VA x _____ units =	_____ VA	_____ VA
Disposal	_____ VA x _____ units =	_____ VA	_____ VA
Compactor	_____ VA x _____ units =	_____ VA	_____ VA
Dishwasher	_____ VA x _____ units =	_____ VA	_____ VA
Range	_____ VA x _____ units =	_____ VA x 70%	_____ VA
Cooktop	_____ VA x _____ units =	_____ VA x 70%	_____ VA
Oven	_____ VA x _____ units =	_____ VA x 70%	_____ VA
Dryer	_____ VA x _____ units =	_____ VA x 70%	_____ VA
_______	_____ VA x _____ units =	_____ VA	_____ VA
_______	_____ VA x _____ units =	_____ VA	_____ VA
Total =		(_____) VA	(_____) VA

4. HEATING or A/C at 100% (largest): ***220.84(C)(5)***

			Line	Neutral
Heating unit	= _____ VA x _____ units	= _____ VA		
A/C unit	= _____ VA x _____ units	= _____ VA		
Heat pump	= _____ VA x _____ units	= _____ VA		
Largest Load	= _____ VA x _____ units	= _____ VA	(_____) VA	(_____) VA

5. APPLY DEMAND FACTORS: ***Table 220.84 Total of steps 1 -4***

LINE	_____ VA x _____ % =	[_____] VA
NEUTRAL	_____ VA x _____ % =	[_____] VA

6. HOUSE LOADS: ***220.84(B)***

		Line	Neutral
Lighting	_____ VA	_____ VA	_____ VA
Receptacles	_____ VA	_____ VA	_____ VA
Motors	_____ VA	_____ VA	_____ VA
_____	_____ VA	_____ VA	_____ VA
_____	_____ VA	_____ VA	_____ VA
Total =		[____] VA	[____] VA

7. TOTAL of STEPS 5 & 6 _____ VA _____ VA

Line I = _______ VA = _____ amperes
240 volts

Neutral I = _______ VA = _____ amperes
240 volts

Conductors are to be sized per Table 310.16.

OPTIONAL CALCULATION: MULTI-FAMILY DWELLING

	Line	Neutral
1. GENERAL LIGHTING & RECEPTACLES: ***220.84(C)(1)***		
6,720 sq. ft. x 3 VA =	(20,160) VA	(20,160) VA
2. SMALL APPLIANCES & LAUNDRY ***220.84(C)(2)***		
Small Appl. 1,500 VA x 2 circuits x 8 units=	24,000 VA	24,000 VA
Laundry 1,500 VA x 1 circuits x 8 units=	12,000 VA	12,000 VA
Total =	(36,000) VA	(36,000) VA
3. FIXED APPLIANCES: ***220.84(C)(3)***		
Water Heater 3,600 VA x 8 units =	28,800 VA	28,800 VA
Disposal 850 VA x 8 units =	6,800 VA	6,800 VA
Compactor _____ VA x ____ units =	_____ VA	_____ VA
Dishwasher 1,100 VA x 8 units =	8,800 VA	8,800 VA
Range 8,000 VA x 8 units =	64,000 VA x 70%	44,800 VA
Cooktop _____ VA x _____ units =	_____ VA x 70%	_____ VA
Oven _____ VA x _____ units =	_____ VA x 70%	_____ VA
Dryer 3,500 VA x 8 units =	28,000 VA x 70%	19,600 VA
_______ _____ VA x _____ units =	_____ VA	_____ VA
_______ _____ VA x _____ units =	_____ VA	_____ VA
Total =	(136,400) VA	108,800) VA
4. HEATING or A/C at 100% (largest): ***220.84(C)(5)***		
Heating unit = 3,500 VA x _____ units = _____ VA		
A/C unit = 4,080 VA x 8 units = 32,640 VA		
Heat pump = ____ VA x _____ units = _____ VA		
Largest Load = 4,080 VA x 8 units = 32,640 VA	(32,640) VA	(0) VA
5. APPLY DEMAND FACTORS: ***Table 220.84 Total of steps 1 -4***		
LINE 225,200 VA x 43 % =	[96,836] VA	
NEUTRAL 164,960 VA x 43 % =		[70,933] VA
6. HOUSE LOADS: ***220.84(B)***		
Lighting _____ VA	_____ VA	_____ VA
Receptacles _____ VA	_____ VA	_____ VA
Motors _____ VA	_____ VA	_____ VA
_____ _____ VA	_____ VA	_____ VA
_____ _____ VA	_____ VA	_____ VA
Total =	[_____] VA	[_____] VA
7. TOTAL of STEPS 5 & 6	96,836 VA	70,933 VA

Line I = 96,836 VA = 403 amperes
240 volts **220.61(B)(2)**

Neutral I = 70,933 VA = 296 amperes – First 200 amps @100% = 200 amperes
240 volts Next 96 amps @ 70% = 67 amperes
TOTAL NEUTRAL = 267 amperes

Conductors are to be sized per Table 310.16.

UNIT 10

COMMERCIAL LOAD CALCULATIONS

Upon successfully completing this unit of study, the student will be familiar with the concept of properly sizing overcurrent protection, branch circuit, feeder, and service conductors for commercial occupancies.

UNIT 10

COMMERCIAL LOAD CALCULATIONS

RELATED INFORMATION:

- Examples of commercial occupancies are office buildings, banks, retail stores, restaurants, warehouses, laundries, mobile home and recreational vehicle (RV) parks, automobile dealerships, sporting facilities, motels, etc.

- The loads in commercial locations are diversified and are to be calculated based upon the type of occupancy, how the loads are to be used in the electrical system, and the requirements of the equipment to be supplied. A good example of a commercial occupancy with diverse loads would be a motel or hotel. The sleeping rooms are calculated much like residential occupancies but the lobby, hallways, meeting rooms, restaurant, and area lighting are considered commercial locations. Let's look at some of the requirements that apply to commercial occupancies.

- Most of the lighting for commercial locations is to be considered a **continuous load**. Examples of exceptions to this statement would be the sleeping rooms of hotels and motels, which will be addressed later in this unit, and temporary commercial storage facilities and warehouses. The definition of a **continuous load** is a load where the maximum current is expected to continue for **3 hours** or more. **[Article 100]**

- In general, branch circuit conductors shall have an allowable ampacity (current carrying capacity) of NOT less than **125%** of the **continuous load**, plus **100%** of the **non-continuous** load to be served. **[210.19(A)(1)(a)]**

EXAMPLE - A branch circuit conductor supplying a continuous load of 24 amperes, must have an ampacity of at least _____.

A. 24 amperes
B. 30 amperes
C. 19 amperes
D. 36 amperes

ANSWER - (B) 30 amperes

24 amperes x 125% = 30 amperes

- In general, overcurrent devices (fuses and circuit breakers) protecting branch circuits, shall have a rating of not less that **125%** of the **continuous load** to be served plus **100%** of the **non-continuous** load to be served. **[210.20(A)]** Another way to look at it is, fuses and circuit breakers protecting branch circuits are not permitted to be loaded more than **80%** of their rated value when protecting **continuous loads**.

EXAMPLE - When a 30 ampere rated circuit breaker is used to protect a branch circuit supplying a continuous load, the load shall not exceed_____.

A. 30 amperes
B. 38 amperes
C. 24 amperes
D. 36 amperes

ANSWER - (C) 24 amperes

30 amperes x 80% = 24 amperes

- If the overcurrent device is listed for **continuous operation**, it shall be permitted to have a rating of **100%** of the **continuous load(s)** to be supplied. **[210.20(A)EX.]** But, circuit breakers are **NOT** listed for continuous operation, unless they have a rating of at least **400 amperes** or more. The NEC® does not address this issue.

- This continuous load requirement also applies to feeders **[215.2(A)(1)]** & **[215.3]** and services. **[230.42(A)(1)&(2)]**

Lighting Loads

- In general, 15- or 20-ampere rated branch circuits are used to supply lighting loads. **[210.23(A)]**

- General lighting loads for specific occupancies shall be based on the unit load per square feet depending on the type of occupancy as shown on Table **220.12**, and calculated from the outside dimensions of the building. **[220.12]** This is a **MINIMUM** requirement.

- Most commercial occupancies now contain fluorescent and/or HID lighting systems. When the occupancies contain lighting systems of this category, the **larger** of either the area load of the VA per square foot of the facility, or the total connected load of the ampere ratings of the ballast or transformers of the luminaries (lighting fixtures) shall be used to size branch circuit, feeder, and service-entrance conductors. **[220.18(B)]**

EXAMPLE - A retail department store having dimensions of 100 feet by 150 feet is to be constructed. The store will have three-hundred (300) fluorescent luminaires (lighting fixtures) installed for general lighting. Each luminaire will contain two (2), 120-volt ballasts that draw 0.75 amperes each.

Determine the demand load, in VA, that must be applied to the service-entrance conductors for the general lighting.

A. 45,000 VA
B. 54,000 VA
C. 56,250 VA
D. 67,500 VA

ANSWER - (D) 67,500 VA

Compare the two methods and use the larger value.

Table 220.12
150 ft. x 100 ft. = 15,000 sq. ft.

15,000 sq. ft. x 1.9 VA = 28,500 VA
(continuous load x 125%
35,625 VA

220.18(B)
300 (fixt.) x 2 (ballast) x 120 volts x .75 amps = 54,000 VA
(continuous load) x 125%
67,500 VA

- Show window lighting for retail stores is commonly calculated at 200 volt-amperes per linear foot of show window. **[220.43(A)]** Such lighting is usually considered a **continuous load** because it is normally operated continuously for three (3) hours or more. Multiply **200 VA** per linear foot times **125%** to determine the load in VA.

EXAMPLE - A retail store is to have 125 feet of show window lighting, which will be operated continuously during the business day. Determine the demand load in VA.

A. 31,250 VA
B. 25,000 VA
C. 28,125 VA
D. 12,500 VA

ANSWER - (A) 31,250 VA

200 VA x 125 ft. x 125% = 31,250 VA

- When calculating the number of branch circuits required for lighting systems or receptacles, you can use the following formula:

$$\text{Number of circuits} = \frac{\text{Load VA}}{\text{circuit VA}}$$

EXAMPLE - The total demand load for the show window lighting of a retail store is determined to be 31,250 VA. Determine the MINIMUM number of 120 volt, 20 ampere branch circuits required to supply the show window lighting.

A. ten
B. twelve
C. thirteen
D. none of these

ANSWER - (C) thirteen

$$\# \text{ of circuits} = \frac{31{,}250 \text{ VA}}{120 \text{ volts} \times 20 \text{ amps}} = \frac{31{,}250 \text{ VA}}{2{,}400 \text{ VA}} = 13 \text{ circuits}$$

- In addition to the general lighting, many commercial occupancies, particularly retail stores, have track lighting mounted for display or accent lighting. Again, commercial lighting systems are usually considered as continuous use. For track lighting in non-dwelling occupancies a load of **150 volt-amperes** shall be included for every **two (2) feet** of track. **[220.43(B)]** Multiply **150 VA** per linear foot times **125%** and divide by **two (2)** to determine the load in VA.

EXAMPLE - A retail store is to have eighty (80) feet of accent track lighting installed and will be in use continuously during business hours. For the purpose of sizing branch-circuits, feeders and service-entrance conductors, determine the load in VA.

A. 15,000 VA
B. 10,000 VA
C. 12,500 VA
D. 7,500 VA

ANSWER - (D) 7,500 VA

$$\frac{150 \text{ VA} \times 80 \text{ ft.} \times 125\%}{2} = \frac{15{,}000}{2} = 7{,}500 \text{ VA}$$

- The general lighting and general-use receptacles for the guest rooms and suites of hotels and motels are permitted to be calculated by applying a demand load of **2 VA** per square foot **[Table 220.12]** and is permitted to be reduced by applying the demand factors as shown in **Table 220.42**. Even though this is a commercial occupancy, loads of this category are not considered as continuous use.

EXAMPLE - Determine the general lighting and general-use receptacle demand load, in VA, for the guest rooms of a twenty-four (24) unit motel. Each guest room has 600 square feet of living area.

A. 14,400 VA
B. 14,240 VA
C. 21,600 VA
D. 28,800 VA

ANSWER - (B) 14,240 VA

24 units x 600 x 1.7 VA **[Table 220.12]** = 24,480 VA

First 20,000 VA at 60% = 12,000 VA **[Table 220.42]**
4,800 VA at 50% = 2,240 VA
Demand Load = 14,240 VA

Electric Sign Loads

- The NEC® requires each commercial occupancy with grade level access to pedestrians to be provided with at least one (1) outlet for an exterior electric sign or outline lighting system. The outlet(s) is/are to be supplied by a branch-circuit rated at least 20 amperes. **[600.5(A)]**

- The branch-circuits that supply electric signs with incandescent and fluorescent lighting are not to exceed 20 amperes. **[600.5(B)(1)]**

- When calculating feeder and service-entrance conductors, each electric sign branch-circuit is to be calculated at a MINIMUM of **1,200 VA**. **[220.14(F)]** This VA rating is to be multiplied by **125%**; for the purpose of calculations electric signs are to be considered continuous loads. **[600.5(B)]**

EXAMPLE - A motel to be constructed will have two (2) 20 ampere, 120-volt branch-circuits provided for the exterior electric signs. Determine the minimum demand load, in VA, on the feeder and service-entrance conductors.

A. 2,400 VA
B. 3,000 VA
C. 4,800 VA
D. 6,000 VA

ANSWER - (B) 3,000 VA

1,200 VA x 2 (signs) x 125% = 3,000 VA

Receptacle Loads

- For non-dwelling occupancies each general-use receptacle outlet is to be calculated at **180 VA** for each single or duplex receptacle on one yoke or strap **[220.14(I)]**; receptacle loads are permitted to be made subject to the demand factors given in **Table 220.44** when calculating the demand loads on feeders and services. **[220.44]** General-use receptacle loads are generally not considered to be a continuous load.

Table 220.44 Demand Factors for Non-dwelling Receptacle Loads

Portion of Receptacle Load to Which Demand Factor Applies (Volt-Ampere)	Demand Factor (Percent)
First 10 kVA or less	100
Remainder over 10 kVA at	50

EXAMPLE – What is the service demand load, in VA, for one-hundred and fifty (150), 20 ampere, 120-volt general-use duplex receptacles installed in an office building?

A. 27,000 VA
B. 23,125 VA
C. 24,250 VA
D. 18,500 VA

ANSWER - (D) 18,500 VA

150 receptacles x 180 VA = 27,000 VA (connected load)

First 10 kVA at 100% = 10,000 VA
remainder (17,000 VA) at 50% = 8,500 VA
Total = 18,500 VA

- When the exact number of general-use receptacle outlets to be installed in a bank or an office building has not yet been determined, **one (1) VA** per square foot of interior space is to be applied when calculating feeders or services. **[Table 220.12, Note B]** and **[220.14(K)]** When this condition occurs, the receptacle loads are **not** permitted to be made subject to the demand factors given in **Table 220.44. [220.44]**

EXAMPLE - A 20,000 square foot bank building is to be constructed and the exact number of general-use receptacles to be installed in unknown. Determine the demand load, in VA, on the service-entrance conductors for the unknown receptacles.

A. 20,000 VA
B. 18,000 VA
C. 36,000 VA
D. 60,000 VA

ANSWER - (A) 20,000 VA

20,000 sq. ft. x 1 VA = 20,000 VA

- When calculating the service and/or feeder demand load for multioutlet assemblies installed in commercial, industrial and educational facilities, the calculation is to be based on the use of the supplied cord-connected equipment that is expected to be used at the same time. **[220.14(H)]** (1) Where the cord-connected equipment are **unlikely** to be used simultaneously, each **five (5) feet** or fraction thereof shall be considered as one (1) outlet of not less than **180 VA**. (2) Where the cord-connected equipment are **likely** to be used simultaneously each **one (1) foot** or fraction thereof shall be considered as one outlet of not less than **180 VA**.

- The demand factors shown on **Table 220.44** may also be applied to fixed multioutlet assemblies when located in non-dwelling occupancies. Multioutlet assembly receptacles are generally not to be considered a continuous load; if they are **continuous, multiply by 125%.**

EXAMPLE - What is the service demand load, in VA, for one-hundred (100), 20 ampere, 120-volt, general-use receptacles and one-hundred (100) feet of multioutlet assembly, installed in an office building, where the cord connected appliances are unlikely to be used simultaneously?

A. 21,600 VA
B. 15,800 VA
C. 10,800 VA
D. 8,100 VA

ANSWER - (B) 15,800 VA

Receptacles – 180 VA x 100 = 18,000 VA
Multioutlet assembly – 100 ft. / 5 = 20 x 180 VA = 3,600 VA
connected load = 21,600 VA

Apply demand factors **[Table 220.44]**

First 10 kVA at 100% = 10,000 VA
Remainder (11,600 VA) at 50% = 5,800 VA
demand load = 15,800 VA

EXAMPLE - Refer to the previous example and consider the cord-connected appliances are to be used simultaneously and determine the demand load.

A. 15,800 VA
B. 36,000 VA
C. 23,000 VA
D. 18,000 VA

ANSWER - (C) 23,000 VA

Receptacles – 180 VA x 100 = 18,000 VA
Multioutlet assembly – 100 ft. x 180 VA = 18,000 VA
Connected load = 36,000 VA

First 10 kVA at 100% = 10,000 VA
Remainder (26,000 VA) at 50% = 13,000 VA
Demand Load = 23,000 VA

Air Conditioning Loads

- When sizing overcurrent protection, branch-circuit, feeder and service conductors for air-conditioning equipment, you will find many air-conditioning condensing units are sized according to **TONS** and not horsepower. The NEC® does not address this issue. A useful and practical method to convert **tons** to **VA** is to consider **one (1) ton** of air-conditioning condensing load equals **2,400 VA**. To find the load, in amperes, simply apply the current formula I = P ÷ E. Multiply 2,400 VA times the tonage of the A/C unit and divide by the voltage. For the purpose of calculating loads in this text this is the method that will be used.

EXAMPLE - A 240-volt, single-phase, 3½ ton A/C condensing unit will draw_____ of current.

A. 30 amperes
B. 35 amperes
C. 40 amperes
D. 45 amperes

ANSWER - (B) 35 amperes

$$I = \frac{3.5 \times 2{,}400\ \text{VA}}{240\ \text{volts}} = \frac{8{,}400}{240} = 35\ \text{amperes}$$

- Branch-circuit conductors supplying a single air-conditioning condensing unit are required to have a current-carrying capacity (ampacity) of not less than **125 percent** of the rated-current of the air-conditioning unit supplied. **[440.32]**

EXAMPLE - Branch-circuit conductors supplying an air-conditioning condensing unit having a rated-current of 35 amperes, are required to have an ampacity of at LEAST _____.

A. 28 amperes
B. 35 amperes
C. 44 amperes
D. 53 amperes

ANSWER - (C) 44 amperes

35 amperes x 125% = 43.75 amperes

- A value of not less than **100%** of the rated-current of the air-conditioning equipment is to be applied to feeder and service equipment and conductors.

- Fuses and circuit breakers provided for the protection of air-conditioning equipment shall be capable of carrying the starting current of the motor. **[440.22(A)]** The overcurrent protection device is mandated to be sized between **175 percent** and no more than **225 percent** of the rated-current of the air-conditioning equipment.

EXAMPLE - A circuit breaker provided to protect an air-conditioning condensing unit with a rated current of 35 amperes is required to have a MAXIMUM ampere rating of no more than _____.

A. 60 amperes
B. 80 amperes
C. 75 amperes
D. 70 amperes

ANSWER - (D) 70 amperes

35 amperes x 225% = 78.75 amperes

*NOTE: Under this condition, you must go down to the next standard size circuit breaker, because you may not exceed **225%** of the rated-current of the A/C unit.

Electric Space-Heating Loads

- All fixed space heating equipment, including blower motors, shall be considered as **continuous load(s)**, when sizing branch-circuit conductors and overcurrent protection for the heating units. **[424.3(B)]** The branch-circuit conductors supplying electric space-heating equipment are required to have an ampacity of not less than **125 percent** of the current rating of the heating unit(s) to be served.**[210.19(A)(1)]** This rule does not apply when sizing feeders and/or services. The feeder and/or service demand load is calculated at **100 percent** of the total heating load. **[220.51]**

EXAMPLE - The branch-circuit conductors supplying a 240-volt, single-phase, 15 kW rated fixed electric space heater provided with a 10 ampere blower motor are required to have an ampacity of at LEAST _______.

A. 63 amperes
B. 78 amperes
C. 91 amperes
D. 109 amperes

ANSWER - (C) 91 amperes

First find the current rating of the heater.

$I = P \div E \quad I = \dfrac{15 \text{ kW} \times 1{,}000}{240 \text{ volts}} = 62.5 \text{ amperes}$

62.5 amperes (heater)
+10.0 amperes (blower)
72.5 amperes x 125% = 91 amperes

EXAMPLE - The overcurrent protection device for the above referenced heating unit is required to have a standard rating of not less than _______.

A. 75 amperes
B. 80 amperes
C. 90 amperes
D. 100 amperes

ANSWER - (D) 100 amperes

The next standard size overcurrent device has a rating of 100 amperes. **[240.6(A)]**

EXAMPLE - Determine the service demand load, in VA, for an office building that has three (3), 208-volt, three-phase, 10 kW fixed electric space heaters, provided with a 1,945 VA blower motor in each heating unit.

A. 35,835 VA
B. 44,794 VA
C. 53,585 VA
D. 55,583 VA

ANSWER - (A) 35,835 VA

10,000 VA + 1,945 VA = 11,945 x 3 units = 35,835 VA

- When determining the demand load on the service-entrance conductors for the fixed electric space heating or air-conditioning load, the smaller of the two loads is permitted to be omitted; because both loads are unlikely to be used at the same time. **[220.60]** Apply only the largest load(s) that will be used at one time for calculating the total load on feeder or service conductors.

EXAMPLE - A retail store is to have a ten (10) ton A/C unit and a thirty-five (35) kW electric heating unit installed. Both units are 240-volts, single-phase. Determine the demand load, in amperes on the service-entrance conductors for the A/C and heating equipment.

A. 100 amperes
B. 125 amperes
C. 146 amperes
D. 183 amperes

ANSWER - (C) 146 amperes

First compare the two loads.

A/C Unit
10 tons x 2,400 VA = 24,000 VA

$$I = \frac{24{,}000 \text{ VA}}{240 \text{ volts}} = 100 \text{ amperes}$$

Heating Unit

$$I = \frac{35 \text{ kW} \times 1{,}000}{240 \text{ volts}} = \frac{35{,}000}{240} = 146 \text{ amperes}$$

*NOTE: The heating unit is the larger load therefore, the A/C unit is permitted to be omitted.

- Today, many buildings are provided with roof-mounted heating and cooling systems that are in one complete unit in order to save space. The cooling capacity usually range from 5 tons up to 200 tons. Examples of good applications for roof-mounted heating and cooling systems are schools, office buildings, retail stores, super markets and manufacturing facilities.

Kitchen Equipment

- For electric kitchen equipment in commercial occupancies the branch circuits and overcurrent protection are sized according to the nameplate rating on the appliance. When sizing feeder and service conductors the demand factors shown on **Table 220.56** may be applied. However, the feeder or service demand load is **not** permitted to be **less** than the sum of the **two (2) largest** kitchen equipment loads. **[220.56]**

EXAMPLE - A catering service is to have the following cooking related equipment in the kitchen:

- water heater – 5.5 kW
- booster heater – 7.0 kW
- dishwasher – 2.0 kW
- sterilizer - 2.5 kW
- oven - 6.0 kW
- grill - 5.0 kW
- mixer - 3.0 kW
- freezer - 3.5 kW
- refrigerator - 2.5 kW

What is the demand load, in kW, on the service-entrance conductors for the appliances?

A. 37.00 kW
B. 25.90 kW
C. 13.00 kW
D. 24.05 kW

ANSWER - (D) 24.05 kW

water heater		- 5.5 kW
booster heater		- 7.0 kW
dishwasher		- 2.0 kW
sterilizer		- 2.5 kW
oven		- 6.0 kW
grill		- 5.0 kW
mixer		- 3.0 kW
freezer		- 3.5 kW
refrigerator		- 2.5 kW
(connected load)		37 kW
(demand)		x 65 % **[Table 220.56]**
Demand Load	=	24.05 kW

Laundry Equipment

- The branch-circuit conductors and overcurrent protection for laundry equipment in commercial occupancies are to be sized in accordance to the appliance **nameplate rating**. The NEC® does not permit a demand factor to be applied to service, feeder or branch-circuit conductors for commercial laundry equipment therefore, the laundry equipment demand load is to be calculated at **100%.**

EXAMPLE - The laundry room of a multi-family dwelling will have the following laundry equipment installed:

- two – clothes dryers - 7,000 VA each
- three – washing machines - 1,920 VA each
- three – washing machines - 1,500 VA each

What is the demand load, in VA, on the service and feeder conductors for the listed appliances?

A. 24,260 VA
B. 18,500 VA
C. 16,982 VA
D. 14,000 VA

ANSWER - (A) 24,260 VA

clothes dryers – 2 x 7,000 VA =	14,000 VA
washing machine – 3 x 1,920 VA =	5,760 VA
washing machine – 3 x 1,500 VA =	4,500 VA
TOTAL =	24,260 VA

Mobile Home and Manufactured Home Parks

- The distribution system to mobile home lots is required to be 120/240 volts, single-phase. **[550.30]** Because appliances, luminaries, and other equipment are installed in a mobile home when manufactured and are rated 120/240-volts single-phase; three-phase systems and systems of a different voltage would not be compatible to the loads to be supplied.

- Each mobile home lot is required to be calculated on the basis of the larger of (1) a minimum of not less than **16,000 VA** for each mobile home lot or (2) the calculated load of the largest typical mobile home the lot will accommodate. **[550.31]** However, for each mobile home to be served the service equipment is to be rated at least 100 amperes, **[550.32(C)]** and the mobile home lot feeder conductors shall have a current carrying capacity (ampacity) of not less than 100 amperes. **[550.33(B)]**

- When sizing service-entrance conductors for a mobile home park the demand factors, based on the number of mobile homes in the park, displayed in **Table 550.31** are permitted to be applied.

EXAMPLE - What is the MINIMUM demand load, in amperes, on the service conductors of a mobile home park consisting of fifteen (15) lots?

A. 250 amperes
B. 260 amperes
C. 400 amperes
D. 1,000 amperes

ANSWER - (B) 260 amperes

15 lots x 16,000 VA (MINIMUM) = 240,000 VA
demand = x .26 **[Tbl. 550.31]**
demand load = 62,400 VA

$I = P \div E$

$I = \frac{62{,}400\ \text{VA}}{240\ \text{volts}} = 260$ amperes

EXAMPLE - A twenty-five (25) lot mobile home park is to be constructed. Each lot in the park is capable of accommodating a mobile home with a rating of 24,000 VA. Determine the demand load, in amperes, on the park service conductors.

A. 1,000 amperes
B. 650 amperes
C. 400 amperes
D. 600 amperes

ANSWER - (D) 600 amperes

25 lots x 24,000 VA = 600,000 VA
x .24 **[Tbl.550.31]**
Demand load = 144,000 VA

$I = P \div E$

$I = \frac{144{,}000\ \text{VA}}{240\ \text{volts}} = 600$ amperes

Recreational Vehicle Parks

- For recreational vehicle parks the NEC® requires electrical equipment connected line-to-line shall have a voltage rating of 208-230 volts. **[551.40(A)]** Therefore, recreational vehicle parks are permitted to be provided with 120-volt, 120/240-volt, single-phase or 208Y/120-volt, three-phase electrical systems. Typically, most older recreational vehicle parks have 120/240-volt, single-phase distribution systems.

- When sizing service-entrance or feeder conductors for a recreational vehicle park, the demand factors, reflected in **Table 551.73(A)**, based on the number of sites in the park, are permitted to be applied.

- **Each RV site** supplied with electrical power is required to be provided with at least **one (1) 20 ampere**, 125-volt receptacle outlet. **[551.71(A)]** For the basis of calculation, 20 ampere, 120-volt sites are considered as **2,400 VA per site**. **[551.73(A)]**

- At least **20 percent** of existing and **40 percent** of new RV sites in the park supplied with electrical power are required to be provided with a **50 ampere**, 125/250-volt receptacle outlet. **[551.71(C)]** The 50 ampere sites are considered as **12,000 VA** per site, for the basis of calculation. **[551.73(A)]** Where the RV site has more than one (1) receptacle outlet, the calculated load shall only be calculated for the highest rated receptacle.

EXAMPLE - When a newly constructed forty (40) site RV park supplies all the RV sites with electrical power, the NEC® requires at LEAST _____ of the sites to be provided with a 50 ampere, 125/250-volt receptacle.

A. eight
B. ten
C. twelve
D. sixteen

ANSWER- (D) sixteen

40 sites x 40% = 16 sites

- At least **70 percent** of all RV sites in the park supplied with electrical power are required to be provided with a **30-ampere**, 125-volt receptacle. **[551.71(B)]** For the basis of calculation 30-ampere, 125-volt, RV sites are considered as **3,600 VA** per site. **[551.73(A)]**

EXAMPLE - Refer to the previous example. How many sites in the RV park are required to be provided with a 30-ampere, 125-volt receptacle outlet?

A. eight
B. twelve
C. twenty-eight
D. forty

ANSWER - (C) twenty-eight

40 sites x 70% = 28 sites

- Dedicated **tent sites** in a RV park that are provided with only 20 ampere, 125-volt receptacles are considered as **600 VA** per site, for the basis of calculation. Because these sites are not intended to accommodate recreational vehicles, the calculated load is permitted to be smaller. **[551.73(A)]**

- When determining the total load for a recreational vehicle park, you must take into consideration the loads required for the recreational buildings, swimming pools, stores, service buildings, etc. These amenities are to be considered commercial loads and are to be sized separately and then added to the value calculated for the RV sites, where they are all supplied by one service. **[551.73(B)**

- Typically, recreational vehicle parks are provided with one service and the RV sites are supplied from a common feeder through one or more sub-panel(s). The demand factors shown on **Table 551.73(A)** are to be applied when sizing RV site feeders and service-entrance conductors.

EXAMPLE - What is the feeder/service demand load, in amperes, for the RV sites of a recreational vehicle park that has twenty (20) sites provided with 50 ampere 125/250-volt receptacles, fifteen (15) sites provided with both 30 ampere and 20 ampere receptacles and five (5) RV site provided with 20 ampere, 125-volt receptacles? The electrical system is 120/240-volts, single-phase.

A. 392 amperes
B. 553 amperes
C. 441 amperes
D. 535 amperes

ANSWER - (B) 553 amperes

50 ampere sites	– 12,000 VA x 20 sites = 240,000 VA
30/20 ampere sites	– 3,600 VA x 15 sites = 54,000 VA
20 ampere sites	– 2,400 VA x 5 sites = 12,000 VA
	306,000 VA

Table 551.73(A) (demand) x .41
Demand Load = 125,460 VA

I = P ÷ E
I = 125,460 VA = 553 amperes
240 volts

Electric Welders

- The NEC® provides rules governing two general types of electric welding machines.
  1. Arc welders
     Non-motor generator – a transformer supplies current for an AC arc welder.
     Motor generator – A generator or rectifier supplies current for DC arc welder.
  2. Resistance welders, which are commonly referred to as "spot" welders which derive their power from an AC power source.

- The ampacity of the supply conductors to individual arc welders is determined by selecting the appropriate factor shown in **Table 630.11(A)** based on the type of welding machine and the duty cycle of the welder. **[630.11(A)]** An arc welder with a 60% duty cycle means the welding machine will be used approximately for 6 minutes out of every 10 minutes. The selected factor is then multiplied by the primary current rating displayed on the welder nameplate to determine the minimum current-carrying capacity (ampacity) of the circuit conductors. The actual size of the conductors are selected from **Table 310.16.**

EXAMPLE - The minimum ampacity of the branch-circuit conductors supplying a transformer arc welder with a 60 percent duty cycle and a primary current of 50 amperes indicated on the nameplate is ______.

A. 40 amperes
B. 44 amperes
C. 39 amperes
D. 50 amperes

ANSWER - (C) 39 amperes

50 amperes x .78 (multiplier) = 39 amperes

➢ When a feeder supplies more than one arc welding machine the conductor ampacity rating is based on the sum of the current ratings of the individual arc welders determined by applying **Table 630.11(A)** and multiplying by **100 percent** of the **two** largest welders, plus **85 percent** of the **third** largest welder, plus **70 percent** of the **fourth** largest welder, plus **60 percent** of **all remaining** welders in the group. **[630.11(B)]**

EXAMPLE - A feeder at a school welding shop is to supply the following listed transformer arc welders all with a 50 percent duty cycle.

- two (2) 60 ampere primary current
- two (2) 50 ampere primary current
- two (2) 40 ampere primary current

The feeder is required to have an ampacity of at LEAST _____.

A. 213 amperes
B. 196 amperes
C. 182 amperes
D. 176 amperes

ANSWER - (D) 176 amperes

60 amperes x .71 = 43 x 100% = 43 amperes
60 amperes x .71 = 43 x 100% = 43 amperes
50 amperes x .71 = 36 x 85% = 31 amperes
50 amperes x .71 = 36 x 70% = 25 amperes
40 amperes x .71 = 28 x 60% = 17 amperes
40 amperes x .71 = 28 x 60% = 17 amperes
176 amperes

➢ The ampacity of the supply conductors for a resistance type welder, when the primary current and duty cycle are known, shall not be less than the product of the actual primary current when welding and the multiplication factors shown in **Table 630.31(A).**

EXAMPLE - A resistance type (spot) welder with a duty cycle of 25 percent and with an actual primary current of 30 amperes is to be served. The conductors supplying the welder are required to have an ampacity of at LEAST ______.

A. 15 amperes
B. 20 amperes
C. 25 amperes
D. 30 amperes

ANSWER - (A) 15 amperes

30 amperes x .50 = 15 amperes

- When conductors supply two or more resistance type welding machines, the conductors ampacity rating is based on the sum of the primary current of the individual welders determined by applying **Table 630.31(A)** and multiplying by 100% of the largest welder, plus 60 percent of the values obtained for all remaining welders in the group. **[630.31(B)]**

EXAMPLE - Three (3) spot welders, each having a primary current of 30 amperes and a duty cycle of 10 percent are to be supplied by a common branch circuit. The branch-circuit conductors are required to have an ampacity of at LEAST_______.

A. 15 amperes
B. 22 amperes
C. 66 amperes
D. 99 amperes

ANSWER - (B) 22 amperes

30 amperes x .32 = 10 amperes x 100% = 10 amperes
30 amperes x .32 = 10 amperes x 60% = 6 amperes
30 amperes x .32 = 10 amperes x 60% = 6 amperes
22 amperes

Commercial Service and Feeder Sizing

➢ For the purpose of sizing the service for a commercial building, the following steps may be used to determine the demand load.

Step 1 — Determine the lighting load. Include:
(1) the **larger** of the area load of the VA per square foot of the facility **[Table 220.12]** or the connected loads of the lighting fixtures **[220.18(B)]** and apply **Table 220.42 if applicable**,
(2) sign lighting, **[220.14(F)]**
(3) show windows, **[220.43(A)]**
(4) track lighting **[220.43(B)]**

Step 2 — Calculate the receptacle load. Include:
(1) 180 VA per receptacle outlet **[220.14(I)]**
(2) fixed multi-outlet assemblies **[220.14(H)]** apply demand factors per **Table 220.44**

Step 3 — Compare the air-conditioning loads or the space heating loads. Use the **larger** of the two loads at **100%**.

Step 4 — Determine the kitchen equipment load. Apply **Table 220.56** for 3 or more units of kitchen equipment.

Step 5 — Calculate the laundry equipment at **100%**

Step 6 — Add any other miscellaneous loads not covered in the above steps. Examples: walk-in coolers, water heaters, frozen food display cases, welders, exhaust fans, motors, etc.

Step 7 — Add the value determined from the above listed steps together to find the volt ampere rating of the service. Next, apply the current formula (I = P ÷ E) and size the service-entrance conductors using 75°C conductors selected from **Table 310.16.**

EXAMPLE - A hair salon is 4,000 square feet; the service is 208Y/120-volts, three-phase. Determine the service demand load and the service conductor size for the hair salon which has the following equipment.

- 20 feet of show window lighting
- 150 feet of track lighting
- 120 feet of fixed multi-outlet assembly (appliances will be used simultaneously)
- 50 – 120-volt, 20 ampere duplex receptacles
- one – 12 ton A/C unit, 3-phase (gas heating)
- one – 5 kW cooktop, 208-volt, single-phase
- one – 4 kW oven, 208-volt, single-phase
- one – 1,200 VA, microwave oven
- one – 1,200 VA, refrigerator/freezer
- two – 1,800 VA, washing machines
- one – 5 kW, clothes dryer, 208-volt, single-phase
- one – electric sign circuit

SOLUTION -

LIGHTING

General lighting	- 4,000 sq. ft. x 1.9 VA*	= 7,600 VA	
Show Window	- 20 ft. x 200 VA x 125%	= 5,000 VA	
Track Lighting	- 150 ft.÷2 x 150 VA x 125%	= 14,063 VA	
Sign Circuits	- 1 x 1,200 VA x 125%	= 1,500 VA	
		28,163 VA	= 28,163 VA

RECEPTACLES

Multi-outlet Assembly –	- 120 ft. x 180 VA	= 21,600 VA
Receptacles	- 50 x 180 VA	= 9,000 VA
		30,600 VA

Table 220.44

1st 10 kVA @ 100%	= 10,000 VA	
20,600 VA @50%	= 10,300 VA	
	20,300 VA	= 20,300 VA

COMPARE A/C VERSUS HEATING

A/C – 12 ton x 2,400 VA per ton	= 28,800 VA	= 28,800 VA
HTG. – N/A	= N/A	

KITCHEN EQUIPMENT

Cooktop - 5 kW		= 5,000 VA	
Oven	- 4 kW	= 4,000 VA	
Microwave	- 1,200 VA	= 1,200 VA	
Refrigerator	- 1,200 VA	= 1,200 VA	
		11,400 VA	
	Table 220.56	x .8	
		9,120 VA	= 9,120 VA

LAUNDRY EQUIPMENT

Washing Machine – 2 x 1,800 VA	= 3,600 VA	
Clothes Dryer - 1 x 5,000 VA	= 5,000 VA	
	8,600 VA	= 8,600 VA

DEMAND LOAD = 94,983 VA

$$I = \frac{94{,}983\ \text{VA}}{208 \times 1.732} = 263.65 \text{ amperes}$$

Size 300 kcmil copper 75°C rated service-entrance conductors or size 500 kcmil aluminum 75°C rated service-entrance conductors should be selected from **Table 310.16.**

*NOTE – The 125 percent multiplier for a continuous load as specified in 210.20(A) is included when using the unit in this table for calculating the minimum lighting load for a specified occupancy.

COMMERCIAL CALCULATION (RETAIL)

1. LIGHTING: ***Table 220.12 or 220.18(B)***

General Lighting: ______ sq. ft. x _____ VA = ______ VA
220.18(B): _____ fixtures x _____ VA x 125% = _____ VA
Show Window: _____ ft. x 200 VA x 125% = _____ VA
Track Lighting: _____ ft. / 2 x 150 VA x 125% = _____ VA
Sign Ckts. _____ x 1,200 VA x 125% = _____ VA
Misc. Lighting: _____ VA
Total Lighting = (_____) VA [_____] VA

2. RECEPTACLES: 220.14(I) and/or 220.14(H)

Receptacles: 180 VA x _____ receptacles = _____ VA
Multi-outlet Assembly: 180 VA x _____ ft. = _____ VA
Total = (_____) VA

Table 220.44

First 10,000 VA x 100% = _____ VA
Remainder: _____ VA x 50% = _____ VA
Demand = (_____) VA [_____] VA

3. HEATING or A/C at 100% (largest):

Heating unit = _____ VA x _____ units = _____ VA
A/C unit = _____ VA x _____ units = _____ VA
Heat pump = _____ VA x _____ units = _____ VA
Largest Load = _____ VA x _____ units = _____ VA (_____) VA [_____] VA

4. KITCHEN EQUIPMENT: 220.56

Range _____ VA x _____ units = _____ VA
Cooktop _____ VA x _____ units = _____ VA
Oven _____ VA x _____ units = _____ VA
Dishwasher _____ VA x _____ units = _____ VA
Water Heater _____ VA x _____ units = _____ VA
______ _____ VA x _____ units = _____ VA
______ _____ VA x _____ units = _____ VA
Total = (_____) VA
Table 220.56 x____%
Demand = (_____) VA [_____] VA

5. LAUNDRY EQUIPMENT:

Washing Machine _____ VA x _____ units _____ VA
Clothes Dryer _____ VA x _____ units _____ VA
Water Heater _____ VA x _____ units _____ VA
_____ _____ VA x _____ units _____ VA
Total = (_____) VA [_____] VA

6. MISCELLANEOUS LOADS: ____ VA
_____ VA
Total = (_____) VA [____] VA

7. TOTAL _____ VA

Line I = _______ VA = _____ amperes
volts

Conductors are to be sized per Table 310.16

COMMERCIAL CALCULATION (RETAIL)

1. LIGHTING: ***Table 220.12 or 220.18(B)***

General Lighting: ***4,000*** sq. ft. x ***1.9*** VA = ***7,600*** VA

220.18(B): ____ fixtures x _____ VA x 125% = _____ VA

Show Window: ***20*** ft. x 200 VA x 125%= ***5,000*** VA

Track Lighting: ***150*** ft. / 2 x 150 VA x 125% = ***14,063*** VA

Sign Ckts. ***1*** x 1,200 VA x 125% = ***1,500*** VA

Total Lighting = (***35,563***) VA [***35,563***] VA

2. RECEPTACLES: 220.14(I) and/or 220.14(H)

Receptacles: 180 VA x ***50*** receptacles = ***9,000*** VA

Multi-outlet Assembly: 180 VA x ***120*** ft. = ***21,600*** VA

Total = (***30,600***) VA

Table 220.44

First 10,000 VA x 100% = ***10,000*** VA

Remainder: ***20,600*** VA x 50% = ***10,300*** VA

Demand = (***20,300***) VA [***20,300***] VA

3. HEATING or A/C at 100% (largest):

Heating unit = ***20,000*** VA x ***1*** units =***20,000*** VA

A/C unit = ***28,800*** VA x ***1*** units =***28,800*** VA

Heat pump = ______ VA x _____ units =______ VA

Largest Load = ***28,800*** VA x ***1*** units =***28,800*** VA (***28,800***) VA [***28,800***] VA

4. KITCHEN EQUIPMENT: 220.56

Range _____ VA x _____ units = _____ VA

Cooktop ***5,000*** VA x ***1*** units = ***5,000*** VA

Oven ***4,000*** VA x ***1*** units = ***4,000*** VA

Dishwasher _____ VA x _____ units = _____ VA

_______ _____ VA x _____ units = _____ VA

Microwave ***1,200*** VA x ***1*** units = ***1,200*** VA

Refrigerator ***1,200*** VA x ***1*** units = ***1,200*** VA

Total = (***11,400***) VA

Table 220.56 x ***80*** %

Demand = (***9,120***) VA [***9,120***] VA

5. LAUNDRY EQUIPMENT:

Washing Machine ***1,800*** VA x ***2*** units ***3,600*** VA

Clothes Dryer ***5,000*** VA x ***1*** units ***5,000*** VA

Water Heater _____ VA x _____ units _____ VA

_____ _____ VA x _____ units _____ VA

Total = (***8,600***) VA [***8,600***] VA

6. MISCELLANEOUS LOADS: ____ VA

_____ VA

Total = (_____) VA [____] VA

7. TOTAL ***94,983*** VA

Line $I = \dfrac{94{,}983 \text{ VA}}{208 \times 1.732} = 263.65$ amperes

Conductors are to be sized per Table 310.16.

JOURNEYMAN ELECTRICIAN'S EXAM PREP GUIDE
EXAM #1

The following questions are based on the 2020 edition of the National Electrical Code® and are typical of questions encountered on most Journeyman Electricians' Licensing Exams. On each question select the best answer from the choices given and review your answers with the answer key included in this book. Typically, the only material permitted for use on this type of exam is a calculator, scratch paper and a current edition of the NEC® book. Each question on this test has a value of 4 points; passing score is 70% therefore, in order to pass you need to get 18 of the 25 questions correct.

ALLOTTED TIME: 75 minutes

1. Where multiple driven ground rods are installed at a service, they shall be spaced NOT less than _____ apart.

A. 2 feet
B. 4 feet
C. 6 feet
D. 8 feet

2. Where a one-family dwelling has a 200 ampere, 120/240-volt, single-phase main service panel and is being supplied with size 2/0 AWG THW copper ungrounded (line) service-entrance conductors in rigid metal conduit (RMC), the MINIMUM required size of the bonding jumper for this service-entrance conduit is _____ copper.

A. 6 AWG
B. 4 AWG
C. 2 AWG
D. 1/0 AWG

3. A disconnect switch enclosure installed in a Class II, Division 2, hazardous location in an industrial establishment shall be _____.

A. dusttight
B. heavy-duty type
C. raintight
D. general-duty type

4. The interior of enclosures or raceways installed underground shall be considered to be a _____ location.

A. dry
B. damp
C. hazardous
D. wet

5. Determine the ampacity of four (4) size 1/0 AWG THW copper current-carrying conductors installed in a common raceway with an ambient temperature of 86 degrees F.

A. 150 amperes
B. 105 amperes
C. 112 amperes
D. 120 amperes

6. The NEC® defines a continuous load to be a load where the maximum current on the circuit is expected to continue for at LEAST____ hours or more.

A. three
B. four
C. six
D. eight

7. Determine the MINIMUM size THW copper branch-circuit conductors the NEC® requires to supply a 3-phase, continuous-duty, ac motor that draws 70 amperes per phase. Consider all terminations are rated for 75 deg. C.

A. 1 AWG
B. 2 AWG
C. 3 AWG
D. 4 AWG

8. Given: You have determined a conductor has a computed ampacity of 75 amperes. What is the MAXIMUM standard ampere rating of the overcurrent protection device the NEC® permits to protect this circuit here this is not a motor circuit or part of a multioutlet branch circuit supplying more than one receptacle?

A. 70 amperes
B. 75 amperes
C. 80 amperes
D. 85 amperes

9. A 208-volt, 3-phase, 50 hp, squirrel-cage, continuous-duty, ac motor has a full-load running current rating of _____.

A. 130 amperes
B. 143 amperes
C. 162 amperes
D. 195 amperes

10. What is the MAXIMUM distance that a disconnect switch is permitted to be located from the operator's station for a portable carnival ride?

A. 6 feet
B. 10 feet
C. 25 feet
D. 50 feet

11. Determine the MINIMUM trade size electrical metallic tubing (EMT) required to enclose eight (8) size 6 AWG copper conductors with THHW insulation, when installed in a 50-foot conduit run.

A. 1 in.
B. 1¼ in.
C. 1½ in.
D. 2 in.

12. Where exceptions are not applicable, when a feeder supplies a continuous load of 240 amperes, the overcurrent protection device protecting this feeder circuit shall have a rating of at LEAST _____.

A. 240 amperes
B. 300 amperes
C. 250 amperes
D. 275 amperes

13. Liquidtight flexible metal conduit (LFMC) shall be securely fastened in place WITHIN _____ of each box or other conduit termination.

A. 4½ feet
B. 3 feet
C. 12 inches
D. 18 inches

14. When a pull box or junction box contains conductors of size 4 AWG and larger and a straight pull of the conductors is to be made, the length of the box shall NOT be less than ____times the trade diameter of the largest conduit entering the pull box or junction box.

A. six
B. four
C. eight
D. twelve

15. Conduit nipples not over 24 inches long may be filled to a MAXIMUM of _____ of their cross-sectional area.

A. 30 percent
B. 40 percent
C. 54 percent
D. 60 percent

16. Determine the MAXIMUM number of size 14 AWG THHN conductors permitted to be installed in a trade size 3/8 in. flexible metal conduit (FMC) that contains a bare size 14 AWG grounding conductor, when the FMC has external fittings.

A. two
B. three
C. four
D. five

17. Which of the following listed conduits does the NEC® permit to enclose conductors supplying wet-niche underwater pool luminaires?

A. electrical metallic tubing (EMT)
B. electrical nonmetallic tubing (ENT)
C. galvanized rigid metal conduit (RMC)
D. Schedule 40 rigid polyvinyl chloride conduit (PVC)

18. Underground wiring is not permitted under a permanently installed swimming pool or within _____ of the pool, unless the wiring is supplying the associated pool equipment.

A. 10 feet
B. 6 fcct
C. 5 feet
D. 8 feet

19. Which of the following listed types of batteries is NOT permitted for use as a source of power for emergency systems?

A. automotive
B. lead acid type
C. alkali type
D. all of these

20. In new installations, the MINIMUM clear working space the NEC® requires between a 480Y/277-volt, switchboard and a 480-volt motor control center when facing each other is _____.

A. 3 feet
B. 3½ feet
C. 4 feet
D. 6 feet

21. In the guest rooms of hotels, motels, and sleeping rooms of dormitory units a MINIMUM of _____ 125-volt, 15- or 20-ampere, general purpose receptacles installed in the room is/are required to be readily accessible.

A. one
B. two
C. three
D. all

22. When branch circuit conductors are installed inside a ballast enclosure of a luminaire and are within three (3) inches of the ballast, the conductors shall have a temperature rating NOT lower than _____, unless supplying a luminaire marked as suitable for a different insulation temperature.

A. 105 deg. C
B. 90 deg. C
C. 75 deg. C
D. 60 deg. C

23. When size 4 AWG or larger conductors enter a panelboard, which of the following must be provided?

A. A bonding jumper.
B. A grounding clip.
C. An identified bushing or threaded hub.
D. An insulated grounding conductor.

24. Class _____ locations are those that are hazardous because of the presence of easily ignitible fibers or where materials producing combustible flyings are handled, but in which such fibers/flyings are not likely to be in suspension in the air in quantities sufficient to produce ignitible mixtures.

A. I
B. II
C. III
D. IV

25. A single-phase, 240-volt, 15 kVA standby generator may be loaded to a MAXIMUM of _____ per line.

A. 62.50 amperes
B. 31.25 amperes
C. 41.66 amperes
D. 52.50 amperes

END OF EXAM #1

JOURNEYMAN ELECTRICIAN'S EXAM PREP GUIDE
EXAM #2

The following questions are based on the 2020 edition of the National Electrical Code® and are typical of questions encountered on most Journeyman Electricians' Licensing Exams. On each question select the best answer from the choices given and review your answers with the answer key included in this book. Typically, the only material permitted for use on this type of exam is a calculator, scratch paper and a current edition of the NEC® book. Each question on this test has a value of 4 points; passing score is 70% therefore, in order to pass you need to get 18 of the 25 questions correct.

ALLOTTED TIME: 75 minutes

1. In general, for other than dwelling units, all 15- and 20-ampere, 125-volt, single-phase receptacles installed on rooftops must be provided with _____.

   I. GFCI protection
   II. AFCI protection

A. I only
B. II only
C. Both I and II
D. Neither I nor II

2. Where the motor controller also serves as a disconnecting means, it shall open all _____ conductors to the motor.

A. grounded
B. neutral
C. grounding
D. ungrounded

3. Before demand factors are taken into consideration for commercial occupancies, general-purpose receptacle loads are to be computed at NOT less than _____ per duplex or single receptacle outlet mounted on one yoke.

A. 100 VA
B. 120 VA
C. 150 VA
D. 180 VA

4. Conductors with ______ insulation have a greater ampacity when used in a dry location compared to when used in a wet location.

A. THW
B. RHW
C. THWN
D. THHW

5. Where a submersible pump is used in a metal well casing, the well casing shall be _____ the pump circuit equipment grounding conductor.

A. isolated from
B. connected to
C. exothermic welded to
D. none of these

6. In a health care facility, low voltage electrical equipment that is likely to become energized that is frequently in contact with the bodies of patients, shall operate on a voltage of _____ or less if the equipment is not approved as intrinsically safe, double insulated or moisture resistant.

A. 10 volts
B. 24 volts
C. 100 volts
D. 120 volts

7. When ambient temperature is not a factor, a size 8 AWG single copper conductor with type FEPB insulation, installed in free air, has an ampacity of _____.

A. 80 amperes
B. 55 amperes
C. 45 amperes
D. 83 amperes

8. For the purpose of determining conductor fill in a device box, a three-way toggle switch is counted as equal to _____ conductor(s), based on the largest conductor connected to the switch.

A. zero
B. one
C. two
D. three

9. When determining the required ampacity of the branch circuit conductors to supply a 3-phase, continuous duty ac motor, current values given on _____ shall be used.

A. the motors nameplate
B. Table 430.248 of the NEC®
C. Table 430.52 of the NEC®
D. Table 430.250 of the NEC®

10. When calculating the total load for a building or structure, what is the MINIMUM computed branch circuit load, in volt-amps, permitted by the NEC® for a branch circuit serving an exterior continuous-duty electric sign?

A. 1,200 volt-amps
B. 1,800 volt-amps
C. 1,500 volt-amps
D. 2,000 volt-amps

11. Determine the MAXIMUM number of size 1 AWG XHHW compact conductors permitted in a trade size 3 in., rigid Schedule 40 PVC conduit more than 24 inches long.

A. 21
B. 19
C. 14
D. 18

12. Infrared commercial and industrial heating appliances shall have overcurrent protection NOT exceeding _____.

A. 20 amperes
B. 40 amperes
C. 50 amperes
D. 60 amperes

13. Class _____ hazardous locations are those in which flammable liquid-produced vapors, or combustible liquid-produced vapors are or may be present in the air in quantities sufficient to produce explosive or ignitible mixtures.

A. I
B. II
C. III
D. IV

14. In indoor areas where walls are frequently washed, such as laundries or car washes, metallic conduit and metallic panelboards shall be mounted with a _____ space between the wall and conduit or panelboard when the equipment is installed exposed.

A. 3/4 in.
B. 1/2 in.
C. 1/8 in.
D. 1/4 in.

15. A branch circuit served by size 12 AWG conductors is a _____ rated branch circuit when protected by a 15-ampere circuit breaker.

A. 20 ampere
B. 25 ampere
C. 15 ampere
D. 10 ampere

16. What is the MAXIMUM overcurrent protection allowed for the protection of resistance-type fixed electric space heating equipment?

A. 30 amperes
B. 40 amperes
C. 48 amperes
D. 60 amperes

17. Information technology equipment shall be permitted to be connected to a branch circuit by a listed power-supply cord having a length NOT to exceed _____.

A. 10 feet
B. 15 feet
C. 12 feet
D. 20 feet

18. Type MI cable shall be supported and secured at intervals NOT exceeding _____ .

A. 2 feet
B. 4 feet
C. 6 feet
D. 10 feet

19. General use snap switches supplying inductive loads shall be loaded to NO more than _____ of the ampere rating of the switch at the applied voltage.

A. 50 percent
B. 60 percent
C. 75 percent
D. 80 percent

20. Direct-buried conductors emerging from grade shall be protected by raceways or covers up to at LEAST _____ above finished grade.

A. 8 feet
B. 10 feet
C. 12 feet
D. 15 feet

21. What is the required size copper equipment grounding conductor for a 50-ampere rated branch circuit where the conductors are installed in PVC conduit?

A. 12 AWG
B. 10 AWG
C. 8 AWG
D. 6 AWG

22. Disregarding exceptions, all 3-phase, 4-wire, 480Y/277-volt, electrical services, require ground-fault protection for each service disconnecting means, when rated for at LEAST _____ or more.

A. 400 amperes
B. 600 amperes
C. 1,000 amperes
D. 1,500 amperes

23. Determine the conductor ampacity given the following related information:

* conductors are size 500 kcmil copper
* conductor insulation is THWN
* eight (8) current-carrying conductors are in the raceway
* ambient temperature is 125 deg. F
* conduit length is 50 feet
* installation is a wet location

A. 178.2 amperes
B. 199.5 amperes
C. 294.6 amperes
D. 380.0 amperes

24. When connecting to luminaires, trade size 3/8 in. flexible metal conduit (FMC) is permitted to enclose tap conductors, provided the length of the FMC does NOT exceed _____ .

A. 3 feet
B. 4 feet
C. 6 feet
D. 8 feet

25. Where a trade size 1/2 in. rigid metal conduit (RMC) is installed in a Class I location and a 1/2 in. conduit seal is required, the MINIMUM thickness of the sealing compound shall NOT be less than _____.

A. 3/8 in.
B. 1/2 in.
C. 5/8 in.
D. 3/4 in.

END OF EXAM #2

JOURNEYMAN ELECTRICIAN'S EXAM PREP GUIDE
EXAM #3

The following questions are based on the 2020 edition of the National Electrical Code® and are typical of questions encountered on most Journeyman Electricians' Licensing Exams. On each question select the best answer from the choices given and review your answers with the answer key included in this book. Typically, the only material permitted for use on this type of exam is a calculator, scratch paper and a current edition of the NEC® book. Each question on this test has a value of 4 points; passing score is 70% therefore, in order to pass you need to get 18 of the 25 questions correct.

ALLOTTED TIME: 75 minutes

1. As a general rule in a dwelling, branch circuits provided to supply receptacle outlets in an attached garage shall have no other outlets. An exception to this rule is _____.

A. receptacle outlets in an adjacent laundry room
B. readily accessible outdoor receptacle outlets
C. receptacle outlets in the foyer
D. rooftop receptacle outlets

A. 300 volts
B. 450 volts
C. 500 volts
D. 600 volts

2. A 30 hp, 480-volt, 3-phase wound-rotor, ac motor has a full-load running current rating of _____.

A. 27 amperes
B. 32 amperes
C. 40 amperes
D. 50 amperes

3. The MAXIMUM ampacity rating of an individual branch circuit in a flat conductor cable (Type FCC) assembly shall be _____.

A. 10 amperes
B. 15 amperes
C. 20 amperes
D. 30 amperes

4. In dwelling units, GFCI protection is required for all 15-and 20-ampere, 125-volt receptacles located within at LEAST _____ of the outside edge of a bathtub or shower stall.

A. 4 feet
B. 6 feet
C. 8 feet
D. 10 feet

5. What MAXIMUM percent of a metal wireway cross-section may be occupied by splices, taps and conductors at any point?

A. 20 percent
B. 30 percent
C. 40 percent
D. 75 percent

6. In an underground rigid polyvinyl chloride conduit (PVC) system that consist of 50 feet length between pulling points, what is the MAXIMUM number of bends this run may have?

A. four (4) - 90 degree
B. six (6) - 90 degree
C. four (4) - 120 degree
D. two (2) - 90 degree

7. Grounding electrodes made of pipe or conduit shall NOT be smaller than _____ electrical trade size.

A. 1/2 in.
B. 3/4 in.
C. 1 in.
D. 1½ in.

8. Liquidtight flexible metallic conduit (LFMC) shall NOT be used:

A. in lengths in excess of 6 feet.
B. in concealed work.
C. in hazardous locations.
D. where subject to physical damage.

9. Determine the ampacity of a size 3 AWG THHN copper conductor where given the following related information.

* Two (2) current-carrying conductors are in the raceway.
* The ambient temperature is 35 deg. C.
* The terminations are rated at 60 deg. C.

A. 105.6 amperes
B. 85 amperes
C. 81.6 amperes
D. 110 amperes

10. As per a general NEC® rule, communications wires and cables shall have a vertical clearance of NOT less than _____ from all points above roofs which they pass.

A. 3 feet
B. 4 feet
C. 6 feet
D. 8 feet

11. Standard trade size 2 in. rigid Schedule 40 polyvinyl chloride conduit (PVC), shall be supported at LEAST every _____.

A. 3 feet
B. 5 feet
C. 6 feet
D. 8 feet

12. Where an ac system operating at less than 1000 volts is grounded at any point at the service, a main bonding jumper shall connect the grounded conductor(s) to _____.

A. each service disconnecting means enclosure
B. each meter base only
C. the grounding electrode
D. all sub-panels

13. In industrial establishments, where sizes 1/0 AWG through 4/0 AWG single conductor cables are installed in ladder type cable tray, the MAXIMUM allowable rung spacing for the cable tray shall be _____ .

A. 6 inches
B. 9 inches
C. 12 inches
D. 15 inches

14. The NEC® mandates the MAXIMUM length permitted for a flexible cord supplying a 208-volt, single-phase, room air-conditioner to be _____.

A. 4 feet
B. 6 feet
C. 8 feet
D. 10 feet

15. In general, which of the following receptacle outlets in a commercial kitchen are required by the NEC® to be GFCI protected?

A. All 125-volt, 15- or 20-ampere receptacles only.
B. All 125-volt, 15- or 20-ampere receptacles in wet locations only.
C. All 125-volt through 250-volt, single-phase, receptacles rated 50-amperes or less.
D. All 125-volt countertop receptacles only.

16. When installing pendant mounted luminaires, the pendant conductors LONGER than _____ shall be twisted together where not cabled in a listed assembly.

A. 18 inches
B. 24 inches
C. 30 inches
D. 36 inches

17. Branch-circuit conductors supplying more than one motor shall have an ampacity of at LEAST_____ of the FLC of the highest rated motor in the group, and 100 percent of the FLC of the other motor(s) in the group.

A. 25 percent
B. 80 percent
C. 100 percent
D. 125 percent

18. What is the MINIMUM size wire-type equipment grounding conductor required for a 5 hp, 3-phase, 208-volt motor having 20 ampere rated overload protection and branch-circuit, short-circuit and ground-fault protection rated 30 amperes?

A. 10 AWG
B. 14 AWG
C. 12 AWG
D. 8 AWG

19. Where a retail clothing store has dimensions of 100 ft. by 75 ft., what is the MINIMUM general lighting demand load, in VA, on the ungrounded (phase) service-entrance conductors?

A. 28,125 VA
B. 18,000 VA
C. 14,250 VA
D. 22,500 VA

20. For nonshielded conductors of over 1000 volts, the conductors shall not be bent to a radius of LESS than _____ times the overall conductor diameter.

A. six
B. eight
C. ten
D. twelve

21. Where an ac electrical service is supplied with four (4) parallel sets of size 500 kcmil aluminum ungrounded conductors, what is the MINIMUM size copper grounding electrode conductor required when connected to the concrete encased reinforcing building steel?
(Assume the grounding conductor does not extend to other types of electrodes.)

A. 4 AWG
B. 3/0 AWG
C. 250 kcmil
D. 2/0 AWG

22. Where an ac transformer arc welder has a 50 ampere rated primary current and a 60 percent duty cycle, the MINIMUM size 60 deg. C rated copper conductors the NEC® requires to supply this welder is _____ .

A. 6 AWG
B. 8 AWG
C. 10 AWG
D. 4 AWG

23. When installing wiring for sensitive electronic equipment, the MAXIMUM voltage to ground is required to be _____ .

A. 277 volts
B. 120 volts
C. 60 volts
D. 30 volts

24. In a health care facility, a patient bed location in a critical care area (Category 1) is required to have which of the following?

A. Four single receptacles or two duplex receptacles.
B. Fourteen single receptacles or seven duplex receptacles.
C. Six duplex receptacles or twelve single receptacles.
D. Eight single receptacles or four duplex receptacles.

25. Flexible cords and cables shall NOT be used ____ .

A. as elevator cables
B. when run through holes in walls
C. as data processing cables
D. to prevent transmission of vibration

END OF EXAM #3

JOURNEYMAN ELECTRICIAN'S EXAM PREP GUIDE
EXAM #4

The following questions are based on the 2020 edition of the National Electrical Code® and are typical of questions encountered on most Journeyman Electricians' Licensing Exams. On each question select the best answer from the choices given and review your answers with the answer key included in this book. Typically, the only material permitted for use on this type of exam is a calculator, scratch paper and a current edition of the NEC® book. Each question on this test has a value of 4 points; passing score is 70% therefore, in order to pass you need to get 18 of the 25 questions correct.

ALLOTTED TIME: 75 minutes

1. Conductors installed in electrically heated floors in bathrooms, kitchens, and in hydromassage bathtub locations shall be provided with____ protection.

A. ground-fault circuit interrupter (GFCI)
B. arc-fault circuit interrupter (AFCI)
C. heat-detecting circuit interrupter (HDCI)
D. all the above

2. Where large electrical equipment containing overcurrent devices, rated at LEAST ____ or more, is installed in an equipment room, personnel door(s) located less than 25 feet from the nearest edge of the working space must open in the direction of egress and have listed panic hardware.

A. 600 amperes
B. 800 amperes
C. 1000 amperes
D. 2000 amperes

3. What is the MAXIMUM length of a flexible cord that may be used for a recirculating water-pump motor on a swimming pool at a dwelling?

A. 3 feet
B. 4 feet
C. 6 feet
D. 8 feet

4. Plate grounding electrodes shall be installed NOT less than _____ below the surface of the earth.

A. 12 inches
B. 18 inches
C. 24 inches
D. 30 inches

5. A disconnecting means shall be provided on the supply side of all fuses in circuits having a voltage of at LEAST _____ to ground so that each circuit containing fuses can be independently disconnected from the source of power.

A. 120 volts
B. 250 volts
C. 150 volts
D. 277 volts

6. Where an 80-ampere, 240-volt, single-phase load is located 200 feet from a panelboard and is supplied with size 3 AWG copper conductors with THWN insulation, what is the approximate voltage-drop on the circuit?
(K = 12.9)

A. 6.0 volts
B. 4.0 volts
C. 9.2 volts
D. 7.84 volts

7. Enclosures in a Class I, Division 1 location containing components that have arcing devices must have an approved conduit seal located within at LEAST _____ of each conduit run entering or leaving such enclosures.

A. 12 inches
B. 18 inches
C. 24 inches
D. 4½ feet

8. The purpose of the NEC® is _____ .

A. to have an installation that is efficient
B. the practical safeguarding of persons and property
C. for future expansion of electrical use
D. to provide an installation that is adequate for good service

9. The NEC® considers the area around the outdoor motor fuel dispensing pumps of an automotive service station to be a hazardous location. This area extends a height of 18 inches above grade, and up to a horizontal distance of _____from the enclosure of the outdoor motor fuel dispensing pumps.

A. 5 feet
B. 10 feet
C. 16 feet
D. 20 feet

10. According to the National Electrical Code®, what are the three (3) separate branches of the essential electrical systems for hospitals?

A. The emergency branch, life safety branch and the standby branch.
B. The life safety branch, equipment branch and the critical branch.
C. The normal branch, life safety branch and the alternate branch.
D. The essential branch, the emergency branch and the equipment branch.

11. Type UF cable is NOT permitted to be used _____.

A. in an attic space
B. as a substitute for Type NM cable
C. as service-entrance cable
D. for solar photovoltaic systems

12. Where an office building has a 208Y/120-volt, 3-phase service with a balanced net computed load of 90 kVA, what is the current each ungrounded (phase) conductor will carry at full load?

A. 188 amperes
B. 250 amperes
C. 433 amperes
D. 750 amperes

13. When bonding the structural reinforcing steel of a swimming pool, what is the smallest size wire-type solid bare copper bonding conductor permitted for this installation?

A. 12 AWG
B. 10 AWG
C. 8 AWG
D. 6 AWG

14. For dwelling units, GFCI protection shall be provided for lighting outlets not exceeding 120 volts where installed in _____.

I. crawl spaces
II. bathrooms

A. I only
B. II only
C. both I and II
D. neither I nor II

15. Where a motor of more than 1 horsepower has a temperature rise of 50 deg. C indicated on the nameplate, for the purposes of selecting the overload device, this device shall be selected to trip at NO more than _____ of the motor's full-load ampere rating. (Assume modification of this value is not necessary.)

A. 100 percent
B. 115 percent
C. 125 percent
D. 130 percent

16. Where a size 14 AWG branch-circuit conductor protected by a 15 ampere rated circuit breaker supplies three (3) 20 ampere rated duplex receptacles, this branch circuit _____ .

A. would be in compliance with the NEC® if the wire was size 12 AWG
B. would be in compliance with the NEC® if the breaker was rated 20-amperes
C. is not in compliance with the NEC® because the receptacles have a 20 ampere rating
D. is in compliance with the NEC®

17. What is the MAXIMUM number of times a wire-type grounding electrode conductor is permitted to be spliced by use of listed split-bolt connectors?

A. one
B. two
C. three
D. none

18. Given: A metal junction box has a volume of 27 cubic inches and contains a total of six (6) size 12 AWG conductors, no grounding conductors,
devices or fittings are contained in the box. Additional wires of size 10 AWG need to be added in the box. What is the MAXIMUM number of size 10 AWG conductors may be added to this box?

A. two
B. five
C. six
D. eight

19. For enclosing a mobile home supply cord, what is the MAXIMUM trade
size conduit permitted between the branch circuit panelboard of a mobile home and the underside of a mobile home floor?

A. 1 in.
B. 1¼ in.
C. 1½ in.
D. 2 in.

20. Which of the following wiring methods is/are approved for use for
fixed wiring in an area above Class I locations in a commercial repair garage?

A. Type MI cable
B. Type TC cable
C. Type MC cable
D. all of the above

21. Class II locations are those that are hazardous because of the presence of _____ .

A. flammable gas
B. ignitible fibers
C. ignitible vapors
D. combustible dust

22. Branch-circuit conductors supplying a fixed storage-type electric water heater with a capacity of 120 gallons or less, shall have an ampacity of NOT less than _____ of the full-load current of the water heater.

A. 80 percent
B. 100 percent
C. 125 percent
D. 150 percent

23. Household-type appliances with surface heating elements having a MAXIMUM demand of more than _____ shall have its power supply subdivided into two (2) or more circuits.

A. 60 amperes
B. 50 amperes
C. 40 amperes
D. 30 amperes

24. When driving a ground rod and solid rock is encountered, the ground rod is permitted to be buried in a trench at LEAST _____ deep.

A. 3 feet
B. 4 feet
C. 24 inches
D. 30 inches

25. A total of ten (10) copper THW conductors are to be installed in a 20-foot run of intermediate metal conduit (IMC), five (5) size 1 AWG and five (5) size 3 AWG. What is the MINIMUM allowable trade size IMC required to contain these ten (10) conductors?

A. 1½ in.
B. 2 in.
C. 2½ in.
D. 3 in.

END OF EXAM #4

JOURNEYMAN ELECTRICIAN'S EXAM PREP GUIDE
EXAM #5

The following questions are based on the 2020 edition of the National Electrical Code® and are typical of questions encountered on most Journeyman Electricians' Licensing Exams. On each question select the best answer from the choices given and review your answers with the answer key included in this book. Typically, the only material permitted for use on this type of exam is a calculator, scratch paper and a current edition of the NEC® book. Each question on this test has a value of 4 points; passing score is 70% therefore, in order to pass you need to get 18 of the 25 questions correct.

ALLOTTED TIME: 75 minutes

1. Where flexible cord is used as the wiring method to supply ac motors, the MINIMUM size of the conductors shall be selected in accordance with _____ of the NEC®.

A. Table 310.16
B. Table 310.17
C. Table 310.16
D. Section 400.5

2. When an industrial control panel is supplied from a 3-phase, 4-wire, delta-connected electrical system, the phase having the higher voltage to ground is _____ .

A. required to be the "A" phase
B. required to be the "B" phase
C. required to be the "C" phase
D. permitted to be any phase

3. When used outdoors and ambient temperature is not a factor, size 6/3 w/g Type UF cable has an ampacity of _____.

A. 65 amperes
B. 60 amperes
C. 55 amperes
D. 50 amperes

4. Shore power for boats shall be provided by single "twist-lock" receptacles rated NOT less than ______ .

A. 20 amperes
B. 30 amperes
C. 50 amperes
D. 60 amperes

5. Where a mobile home has the main service disconnecting means installed outdoors, the disconnecting means shall be installed so the bottom of the enclosure is NOT less than _____ above finished grade.

A. two feet
B. three feet
C. four feet
D. six feet

6. Determine the ampacity of a 3-conductor size 6 AWG XHHW aluminum SER cable installed in the attic of a one-family dwelling where the ambient temperature is 110 degrees F.

A. 41.2 amperes
B. 52.2 amperes
C. 47.9 amperes
D. 56.2 amperes

7. Unless specifically identified for a higher percentage of fill, the cross-sectional area of the conductors in a conduit seal shall NOT exceed _____
of the cross-sectional area of a rigid metal conduit of the same trade size.

A. 25 percent
B. 40 percent
C. 50 percent
D. 60 percent

8. Where a transformer is installed to supply a 243 ampere, 208-volt, 3-phase load the transformer must have a kVA rating of at LEAST _____.

A. 300 kVA
B. 150 kVA
C. 112½ kVA
D. 90 kVA

9. Direct-buried cables or conductors located in a trench below two (2) inch thick concrete or equivalent shall have a MINIMUM cover requirement of _____.

A. 6 inches
B. 12 inches
C. 18 inches
D. 24 inches

10. The MAXIMUM unsupported length of Type MC cable used to supply a luminaire in an accessible ceiling is permitted to be NOT more than _____ in length.

A. 10 feet
B. 6 feet
C. 4½ feet
D. 18 inches

11. The MAXIMUM required distance between trade size 2 in. rigid metal conduit supports is ____.

A. 16 feet
B. 10 feet
C. 12 feet
D. 8 feet

12. Where a submersible pump is located in a pond of a water treatment plant, the on land service equipment for the pump shall be NO closer than _____ horizontally from the shoreline.

A. 6 feet
B. 10 feet
C. 5 feet
D. 3 feet

13. When splicing existing underground service conductors to extend to a new service location, the NEC® requires _____ .

I. the use of splice boxes
II. the conductors to be protected with a covering of at least two (2) inches of concrete

A. I only
B. II only
C. either I or II
D. neither I nor II

14. Equipment supplied by Class 1 circuits such as fire alarm, control, and signaling circuits shall be grounded, UNLESS operating at less than _____ .

A. 25 volts
B. 120 volts
C. 50 volts
D. 150 volts

15. A single-phase, 120/240-volt, 18 kW rated home standby generator has a full-load current rating of _____ .

A. 75 amperes
B. 87 amperes
C. 100 amperes
D. 150 amperes

16. A premises wiring system supplied by a grounded ac electrical service, shall have a grounding electrode conductor connected to _____ .

A. the grounded service conductor
B. the service disconnect enclosure
C. the equipment grounding conductor
D. the meter socket enclosure

17. Intrinsically safe apparatus, associated apparatus, and other equipment shall be installed _____, unless the equipment is a simple apparatus that does not interconnect intrinsically safe circuits.

A. in accordance with the control drawings
B. in the electrical equipment room
C. on a backboard of at least 3/4 in. thick plywood
D. in a dedicated enclosure

18. When a retail furniture store has 80 continuous linear feet of display show window, the NEC® mandates at LEAST _____ 125-volt, single-phase 15- or 20-ampere rated receptacle outlets shall be provided within 18 inches of the top of the show window for the show window lighting.

A. six
B. seven
C. eight
D. nine

19. Single grounding type receptacles, with GFCI protection that provide power for water pump circulation motors of permanently installed swimming pools shall be located at LEAST ___ from the inside walls of the pool.

A. 5 feet
B. 10 feet
C. 20 feet
D. 6 feet

20. What MINIMUM size 75°C copper feeder conductors are required to supply the following group of 3-phase, 230-volt motors?

* one (1) 15 hp wound-rotor
* one (1) 7½ hp induction-type
* one (1) 3 hp induction-type

A. 4 AWG THWN
B. 4 AWG THHN
C. C. 3 AWG THW
D. 2 AWG THW

21. Which of the following is NOT required to be marked on the nameplate of a transformer?

A. kVA rating
B. manufacturer
C. voltage
D. overcurrent protection

22. In general, when current-carrying conductors are installed in parallel, the paralleled conductors in each phase shall _____.

I. be the same size in circular mil area
II. have the same insulation type

A. I only
B. II only
C. both I and II
D. neither I nor II

23. In compliance with the rules set forth by the NEC®, conductors with type ______ insulation are not permitted for use in wet locations such as, where installed underground in a conduit or outdoors exposed to the weather.

A. TW
B. THWN
C. THHN
D. XHHW

24. Where transformer vaults are not protected with an automatic fire-suppression system, they shall be constructed of materials that have a MINIMUM fire-resistance rating of _____.

A. 1 hour
B. 2 hours
C. 3 hours
D. 4 hours

25. In regard to new outdoor installations of permanently installed swimming pools, luminaires installed above the pool or within 5 feet horizontally from the inside wall of the pool, shall be installed at a height of NOT less than _____ above the maximum water level of the pool.

A. 10 feet
B. 12 feet
C. 15 feet
D. 8 feet

END OF EXAM #5

JOURNEYMAN ELECTRICIANS EXAM PREP GUIDE
EXAM #6

The following questions are based on the 2020 edition of the National Electrical Code® and are typical of questions encountered on most Journeymen Electricians' Licensing Exams. On each question select the best answer from the choices given and review your answers with the answer key included in this book. Typically, the only material permitted for use on this type of exam is a calculator, scratch paper and a 2020 edition of the NEC® book. Each question on this test has a value of 4 points; passing score is 70% therefore, in order to pass you need to get 18 of the 25 questions correct.

ALLOTTED TIME: 75 minutes

1. According to Ohms Law, what is the electrical unit of current?
A. volt
B. ampere
C. ohm
D. watt

2. The NEC® definition of _____ is "connected to establish electrical continuity and conductivity".

A. bonded (bonding)
B. bonding jumper
C. Bonding jumper (main)
D. bonding jumper, equipment

3. In addition to the number of 120-volt, single-phase branch circuits required in other areas of a dwelling, at least one additional _____ branch circuit shall be provided to supply the laundry outlet in the laundry room.

A. 15-ampere
B. 20-ampere
C. 25-ampere
D. 30-ampere

4. Where rigid metal conduit (RMC) or intermediate metal conduit (IMC) is threaded in the field where corrosion protection is necessary, the threads shall be coated with a/an _____ compound.

A. oil and tar based
B. judged suitable-corrosion-resistant
C. corrosion-proof
D. approved electrically conductive, corrosion-resistant

5. In a straight run of rigid Type PVC conduit, expansion fittings are to be provided to compensate for thermal expansion and contraction where the length change is expected to be at least _____ or greater.

A. 1/2 in.
B. 3/8 in.
C. 1/4 in.
D. 3/4 in.

6. Which of the following shall be permitted in the dedicated electrical space above a panelboard?

A. air-conditioning ducts
B. leak protection
C. piping
D. sprinkler protection

7. For other than submersible types of motors, they shall be located so that adequate _____ is provided and so that maintenance, such as lubrication of bearings and replacing of brushes, can be readily accomplished.

A. ventilation
B. spacing
C. air-flow
D. dimensions

8. For bathtub and shower areas, no parts of cord-connected luminaires, lighting track or ceiling-suspended (paddle) fans shall be located within a zone measured _____ horizontally from the top of the bathtub rim or shower stall threshold.

A. 3 feet
B. 4 feet
C. 6 feet
D. 8 feet

9. Given: After all demand factors have been taken into consideration, a one-family dwelling with a 120/240-volt, single-phase electrical system has a demand load of 35,000 VA. The MINIMUM size THWN copper phase conductors required for an underground installed service is _____.

A. 2 AWG
B. 1/0 AWG
C. 1 AWG
D. 2 AWG

10. In general, when sizing the overcurrent protection, disconnect size and the supply circuit conductors for a motor used in a continuous-duty application, they shall be sized based on the:

A. full-load running current of the motor given in the Tables of the NEC.
B. actual current marked on the motor nameplate.
C. locked-rotor current.
D. starting current of the motor.

11. Continuous-duty motors, more than one hp, with a marked service factor less than 1.15 shall have the MINIMUM running overload protection sized at _____ of the nameplate rating of the motor, where modification of this value is not necessary.

A. 140 percent
B. 125 percent
C. 130 percent
D. 115 percent

12. Mobile home service equipment shall be located in sight from and NOT more than _____ from the exterior wall of the mobile home it serves.

A. 25 feet
B. 30 feet
C. 50 feet
D. 100 feet

13. As a general rule, switches or circuit breakers shall _____.

A. not disconnect the grounded conductor of a circuit
B. be marked by means of a printed tag
C. be of the externally operable type
D. disconnect the grounded conductor of a circuit

14. What is the MINIMUM number of 120-volt, 20-ampere, single phase branch-circuits that must be provided to supply receptacle outlets in dwelling units?

A. two
B. three
C. four
D. five

15. Small gage conductors such as a single size 16 AWG conductor is permitted to carry continuous loads up to _____, as long as the conductor is protected by a fuse or circuit breaker.

A. 20 amperes
B. 15 amperes
C. 12 amperes
D. 8 amperes

16. The accessible portion of abandoned supply circuits and interconnecting cables located in an information technology equipment room shall be removed, UNLESS ____.

A. tagged and identified as abandoned
B. identified as Type CMP
C. contained in a raceway
D. disconnected from their supply source

17. Generally, in dwelling units, where one or more lighting outlets are installed for interior stairways, there shall be a wall switch at each floor level, and landing level that includes an entryway, to control the lighting outlets where the stairway between floor levels has at LEAST _____ risers or more.

A. four
B. five
C. six
D. eight

18. A receptacle installed outdoors in a location protected from the weather or in other damp locations shall have an enclosure for the receptacle that is _____ when the receptacle is covered (attachment plug cap not inserted and receptacle covers closed).

A. waterproof
B. weatherproof
C. raintight
D. watertight

19. A fused disconnecting means for motor circuits rated 1000 volts or less, shall have an ampacity of at LEAST _____ of the full-load current rating of the motor it disconnects.

A. 100 percent
B. 115 percent
C. 125 percent
D. 150 percent

20. Determine the current, in amperes, on the circuit conductors for a 208Y/120-volt, 3-phase system where each phase is balanced with a 2,500 VA load and the total load is 7,500 VA.

A. 12.01 amperes
B. 20.82 amperes
C. 36.05 amperes
D. 40.00 amperes

21. No overcurrent device shall be connected in series with any conductor that is intentionally grounded, unless the overcurrent device or circuit breaker _____.

A. simultaneously opens all conductors of the circuit including the grounded conductor
B. is corner-grounded, wye voltage systems
C. is part of a listed assembly for motor short-circuit and ground-fault protection
D. is red in color

22. For temporary wiring installations that have an assured equipment grounding conductor program, all required tests shall be performed at intervals NOT exceeding.

A. 1 month
B. 2 months
C. 3 months
D. 6 months

23. For continuous-duty motors, the motor nameplate current rating is used to determine the size of the _____ required for the motor.

A. short-circuit protection
B. branch-circuit conductors
C. disconnecting means
D. motor overload protection

24. GFCI protection for personnel is required where a 125-volt, single-phase, receptacle is located on a wet bar countertop if within _____ from the top inside edge of the bowl of the sink.

A. 6 feet
B. 10 feet
C. 12 feet
D. 15 feet

25. Boxes shall be closed by suitable covers securely fastened in place. An underground metal box cover that weighs over ______ shall be considered meeting this requirement.

A. 75 pounds
B. 80 pounds
C. 90 pounds
D. 100 pounds

END OF EXAM #6

JOURNEYMAN ELECTRICIANS EXAM PREP GUIDE
EXAM #7

The following questions are based on the 2020 edition of the National Electrical Code® and are typical of questions encountered on most Journeymen Electricians' Licensing Exams. On each question select the best answer from the choices given and review your answers with the answer key included in this book. Typically, the only material permitted for use on this type of exam is a calculator, scratch paper and a 2020 edition of the NEC® book. Each question on this test has a value of 4 points; passing score is 70% therefore, in order to pass you need to get 18 of the 25 questions correct.

ALLOTTED TIME: 75 minutes

1. The branch-circuit conductors supplying a continuous-duty ac motor shall have an ampacity of NOT less than what percent of the motors full-load current rating?
A. 115 percent
B. 125 percent
C. 100 percent
D. 150 percent

2. Luminaires installed under metal-corrugated sheet roofing decking shall be installed and supported so there is NOT less than _____ clearance from the roof decking to the top of the luminaires.

A. 1 inch
B. 1¼ inches
C. 1½ inches
D. 1¾inches

3. For the purpose of calculating the general lighting load for a dwelling unit, the floor area should include all the following EXCEPT _____.

A. kitchens
B. bathrooms
C. an unfinished basement intended for future living space
D. an open porch not adaptable for future use

4. Where flexible cord is approved for use and used with a specific listed appliance, it shall be considered to be protected _____.

A. at 125% of the branch circuit rating
B. at 80% of the branch circuit rating
C. at 100% of the branch circuit rating
D. when applied within the appliance listing requirements

5. Electrical equipment, such as distribution panelboards, motor controllers, and motor control centers that are located in other than dwelling units, and are likely to require examination, adjustment, servicing, or maintenance while energized shall be field or factory marked to warn qualified persons of _____.

A. potential electric arc flash hazards
B. arcing parts
C. shock hazard warning
D. conductor ampacity corrections

6. Determine the MINIMUM required ampacity of the branch-circuit conductors to supply a continuous-duty, Design B, 3-phase, 208-volt, 10 hp, ac motor.

A. 30.8 amperes
B. 46.2 amperes
C. 38.5 amperes
D. 32.2 amperes

7. What is the MAXIMUM ampere rating permitted for a 125-volt, single-phase, receptacle having a cord-and-plug connected motor-load that does NOT have overload protection?

A. 10 amperes
B. 15 amperes
C. 20 amperes
D. 25 amperes

8. Which of the following 125-volt, single-phase, 15- and 20-ampere rated dwelling unit receptacles do NOT require GFCI protection for personnel?

A. A receptacle located outdoors.
B. A receptacle installed in a crawl space.
C. A receptacle behind the refrigerator in the kitchen, where more than 6 ft. from the sink.
D. A receptacle in the garage for a garage-door opener.

9. Fastened in place utilization equipment, other than luminaires, that is connected to a branch circuit with other loads shall NOT exceed _____ of the branch circuit rating.

A. 50 percent
B. 75 percent
C. 80 percent
D. 100 percent

10. In compliance with the NEC®, a 3 in. x 2 in. x 1½ in. metal device box may contain NO more than _____ size 12 AWG conductors.

A. three
B. four
C. five
D. six

11. The workspace in front of electrical equipment such as panelboards, switchboards and motor control centers rated 1000 volts or less, shall be at LEAST _____ wide or the width of the equipment, whichever is greater.

A. 12 inches
B. 15 inches
C. 18 inches
D. 30 inches

12. Each receptacle of dc plugging boxes in motion picture studios shall be rated at NOT less than _____.

A. 50 amperes
B. 30 amperes
C. 15 amperes
D. 20 amperes

13. Where a retail clothing store has an actual connected fluorescent general lighting load of 14,000 VA how many 120-volt, singe phase branch-circuits are required for the general lighting? Given: The lighting loads will be used continuously throughout the business day.

A. ten
B. seven
C. eight
D. nine

14. The NEC® mandates specific branch-circuits, receptacle outlets and utilization equipment to be provided with a ground-fault circuit interrupter (GFCI); this device is intended _____.

A. to prevent overloading the conductors
B. to prevent overloading the circuit breakers
C. for the protection of equipment from overloads
D. for the protection of personnel

15. For a grounded electrical system, the equipment grounding conductor shall be sized in accordance with the _____.

A. ungrounded circuit conductors
B. overcurrent protective device
C. size of the service entrance conductors
D. grounding electrode length

16. Determine the MINIMUM size 75°C copper conductors permitted to supply a 30 hp, 230-volt, 3-phase, induction-type, continuous-duty motor.

A. 4 AWG THHN
B. 2 AWG THW
C. 4 AWG THWN
D. 3 AWG THW

17. Given: A rigid metal conduit (RMC) originates from a panelboard in an area that is unclassified, then passes through a Class I, Division 1 area, and then terminates in equipment that is also in an unclassified area. The RMC is without any connections or fittings except at the terminations. How many seal-off fittings are required in the RMC?

A. none
B. one
C. two
D. three

18. What is the MAXIMUM distance between conduit supports for trade size 1 in. Schedule 40 rigid PVC conduit?

A. 10 feet
B. 3 feet
C. 5 feet
D. 6 feet

19. Receptacles supplying power to freestanding-type office furnishings shall be located NOT more than _____ from the furnishing that is connected to it.

A. 6 feet
B. 3 feet
C. 1 foot
D. 8 feet

20. For the purpose of determining conductor fill in a device box, the NEC® mandates a switch to be counted as equal to two (2) conductors. The volume allowance for the two (2) conductors shall be based on the:

A. largest size wire in the box.
B. largest grounding conductor in the box.
C. largest size wire connect to the switch.
D. the number of clamps in the box.

21. A device or group of devices that serves to govern, in some predetermined manner, the electric power delivered to the apparatus to which it is connected is a _____.

A. panelboard
B. governor
C. generator
D. controller

22. Which of the following type motors are NOT approved for use in a Class, I Division 1 location?

A. Totally enclosed fan cooled motors.
B. Submerged motors in a liquid that is flammable only when vaporized.
C. Totally enclosed motors with positive-pressure ventilation.
D. Totally enclosed motors filled with inert gas.

23. Unless listed and identified otherwise, terminations and conductors of circuits rated 100 amperes or larger, shall be rated for _____.

A. 60°C
B. 75°C
C. 90°C
D. 100°C

24. Determine the conductor ampacity where given the following related information:

- conductors are size 500 kcmil THWN copper
- ambient temperature is 125°F
- eight (8) current-carrying conductors are in the raceway

A. 178.2 amperes
B. 199.5 amperes
C. 294.6 amperes
D. 380.0 amperes

25. Receptacles incorporating an isolated grounding conductor connection intended for the reduction of electrical noise, shall be identified by a/an _____ located on the face of the receptacle.

A. red dot
B. orange dot
C. yellow happy face
D. orange triangle

END OF EXAM #7

JOURNEYMAN ELECTRICIANS EXAM PREP GUIDE
EXAM #8

The following questions are based on the 2020 edition of the National Electrical Code® and are typical of questions encountered on most Journeymen Electricians' Licensing Exams. On each question select the best answer from the choices given and review your answers with the answer key included in this book. Typically, the only material permitted for use on this type of exam is a calculator, scratch paper and a 2020 edition of the NEC® book. Each question on this test has a value of 4 points; passing score is 70% therefore, in order to pass you need to get 18 of the 25 questions correct.

ALLOTTED TIME: 75 minutes

1. When determining the initial standard size time-delay fuses for branch-circuit, short-circuit and ground-fault protection for a three-phase, continuous-duty, squirrel cage, ac motor, the fuses shall have a rating of _____ of the full-load current rating of the motor. When the value determined does not correspond to a standard ampere rating, the next higher standard rating shall be permitted.
A. 175 percent
B. 150 percent
C. 225 percent
D. 250 percent

2. A junction box to be installed will contain five (5) size 12 AWG conductors and six (6) size 10 AWG conductors. The junction box is required to have a volume of at LEAST _____.

A. 21.00 cu.in.
B. 22.75 cu. in.
C. 24.75 cu. in.
D. 26.25 cu. in.

3. Neon sign equipment having an open circuit voltage exceeding how many volts shall NOT be installed in or on dwelling occupancies?

A. 1000 volts
B. 300 volts
C. 250 volts
D. 125 volts

4. What MINIMUM size equipment grounding conductor is required for a 240-volt, single-phase, 10 kW residential electric range?

A. 10 AWG
B. 8 AWG
C. 12 AWG
D. 6 AWG

5. Where the NEC® specifies that one equipment shall be within sight of another equipment, the specified equipment is to be visible and NOT more than _____ distant from the other.

A. 100 feet
B. 50 feet
C. 10 feet
D. 25 feet

6. All 125-volt, single-phase, 15- and 20-ampere receptacle outlets in a dwelling must be installed in habitable rooms so that no point along the floor line is further from an outlet than _____.

A. 5 feet
B. 4½ feet
C. 6 feet
D. 12 feet

7. Luminaires mounted in walls of permanently installed swimming pools shall be installed with the top of the luminaire lens NOT less than _____ below the normal water level of the pool, unless the luminaire is listed and identified for use at lesser depths.

A. 18 inches
B. 6 inches
C. 24 inches
D. 12 inches

8. Where there is no overcurrent protection on the secondary side of a 480-volt transformer with a primary current of 100 amperes, the rating of the primary overcurrent protective device should NOT exceed _____.

A. 100 amperes
B. 250 amperes
C. 125 amperes
D. 80 amperes

9. For the purpose of maintaining and servicing a 3-phase, 208Y/120-volt switchboard, a MINIMUM clear working depth distance of _____ must be maintained in front of the switchboard.

A. 4 feet
B. 3½ feet
C. 2 feet
D. 3 feet

10. Where a permanently installed generator is installed as a separately derived system, which of the following must be provided?

A. main bonding jumper
B. system bonding jumper
C. one grounding electrode only
D. multiple grounding electrodes

11. Type AC cable shall provide an adequate path for _____.

A. water drainage
B. a grounding electrode
C. fault-current
D. grounding conductors

12. Mandatory rules of the NEC® are those that identify actions that are specifically required or prohibited are characterized by the use of the terms _____.

A. shall or shall not
B. may or may not
C. will or will not
D. all of these terms apply

13. For a direct burial feeder cable to a water well pump located 50 feet from a dwelling, which of the following listed wiring methods is approved for such use?

A. Type NM cable
B. Type AC cable
C. Type TC cable
D. Type UF cable

14. All of the following wiring methods are permitted in a ceiling space used as a return-air plenum EXCEPT:

A. Type AC cable.
B. rigid PVC conduit.
C. intermediate metal conduit (IMC).
D. Type MI cable.

15. A 240-volt, single-phase 10 kW commercial dishwasher will draw _____ of current.

A. 21 amperes
B. 24 amperes
C. 42 amperes
D. 30 amperes

16. A type of fuse NOT permitted for new installations and shall be used only for replacements in existing installations is a/an _____ fuse.

A. Edison-base
B. Class K
C. Class CC
D. time-delay

17. Which of the following listed flexible cords shall be permitted to be immersed in water to supply a permanently installed fountain located at an amusement park?

A. Type SJOW
B. Type SOO
C. Type SJ
D. Type SOW

18. Where cord-and-plug connected appliances are likely to be used simultaneously, each _____ or fraction thereof of fixed multioutlet assemblies used in other than dwelling units, shall be considered as an outlet of not less than 180 volt-amperes.

A. 24 inches
B. 6 inches
C. 48 inches
D. 12 inches

19. All 15- and 20-ampere, single-phase, 125-volt receptacles located within at LEAST _____ of the inside walls of a permanently installed swimming pool must be protected by a Class A ground-fault interrupter.

A. 10 feet
B. 15 feet
C. 25 feet
D. 20 feet

20. A point on a wiring system at which current is taken to supply luminaires, appliances, heaters, motors and similar current-consuming equipment is considered a/an _____.

A. outlet
B. service
C. receptacle
D. circuit breaker

21. The MINIMUM number of 120-volt, 15-ampere, general lighting branch circuits required for a dwelling with 70 feet by 30 feet of livable space is _____.

A. two
B. three
C. four
D. five

22. Given: A branch circuit supplies a single hermetic refrigerant motor-compressor, with a FLC rating of 18 amperes, for an air conditioning unit on a dwelling unit. If 30-ampere fuses used as overcurrent protection will not carry the starting current of the unit, the rating of the fuses may be increased to a MAXIMUM value of ____.

A. 35 amperes
B. 40 amperes
C. 45 amperes
D. 50 amperes

23. The NEC® requires branch circuits be rated in accordance with the overcurrent protective device. Therefore, which of the following combinations of loads are permitted for lighting branch-circuits?

A. 20, 30, 40, 50 and 70 amperes
B. 20, 30, 40, 50 and 60 amperes
C. 15, 25, 35, 45 and 50 amperes
D. 15, 20, 30, 40 and 50 amperes

24. As a general rule, outside open conductors on insulators must be covered or insulated when they are within _____ of a building or structure, other than supporting poles or towers.

A. 10 feet
B. 12 feet
C. 15 feet
D. 25 feet

25. Metal wireways shall be securely supported where run horizontally at each end and at intervals not to exceed to exceed _____.

A. 6 feet
B. 5 feet
C. 8 feet
D. 4 feet

END OF EXAM #8

JOURNEYMAN ELECTRICIANS EXAM PREP GUIDE
EXAM #9

The following questions are based on the 2020 edition of the National Electrical Code® and are typical of questions encountered on most Journeymen Electricians' Licensing Exams. On each question select the best answer from the choices given and review your answers with the answer key included in this book. Typically, the only material permitted for use on this type of exam is a calculator, scratch paper and a 2020 edition of the NEC® book. Each question on this test has a value of 4 points; passing score is 70% therefore, in order to pass you need to get 18 of the 25 questions correct.

ALLOTTED TIME: 75 minutes

1. Every panelboard circuit and circuit modification shall be:

A. legibly identified at the panelboard or adjacent to the panelboard.
B. copper conductors only.
C. marked before insulating.
D. identified by orange in color.

2. Installation of direct-buried cables in an area that is subject to movement by frost or settlement shall be _____.

A. prohibited
B. pre-tensioned prior to cover
C. placed with "S" loops or adequate allowance for movement
D. placed on running boards of pressure-treated wood or PVC type boards

3. As a general rule, the disconnecting means for an air-conditioning or refrigerating equipment is required to be a MINIMUM rating of _____ of its nameplate rated-load current.

A. 100%
B. 115%
C. 125%
D. 150%

4. Electrical equipment rooms or enclosures housing electrical apparatus that are controlled by a lock(s) shall be considered accessible to _____.

A. qualified persons only
B. electricians only
C. the building management
D. the authority having jurisdiction

5. What MINIMUM size copper THW conductors are required to supply a single-phase, 240-volt, 5 hp motor and a single-phase, 240-volt, 1kW, non-continuous non-motor load?

A. 10 AWG
B. 6 AWG
C. 4 AWG
D. 8 AWG

6. When buried under a driveway of a dwelling, rigid metal conduit shall have a MINIMUM ground cover of _____.

A. 24 inches
B. 18 inches
C. 12 inches
D. 6 inches

7. Cable splices made and insulated by approved methods shall be permitted to be located within a cable tray, provided they are _____.

A. well insulated from physical damage
B. performed with only copper conductors
C. accessible
D. non-accessible

8. Metallic surface-type cabinets for electrical equipment in damp or wet locations shall be mounted so there is at LEAST _____ air space between the cabinet and the wall or other supporting surface.

A. 1/8 in.
B. 1/4 in.
C. 3/8 in.
D. 1/2 in.

9. Given: An equipment disconnecting means is mounted at a height of 6 feet on a remote wall in an aircraft storage and maintenance hangar. The disconnect switch is 10 feet horizontally away from any aircraft fuel tanks. The disconnect switch is located in a/an _____ area.

A. Class II, Division 1
B. Class I, Division 2
C. Class I, Division 1
D. unclassified

10. The size of an equipment grounding conductor is most dependent upon _____.

A. line voltage
B. line resistance
C. line inductance
D. available fault-current

11. Busways shall be securely supported at intervals NOT exceeding _____ unless the raceway is otherwise designed and marked.

A. 6 feet
B. 5 feet
C. 8 feet
D. 4 feet

12. Given: You are to install an underground 50 ft. run of Schedule 40 PVC conduit that will contain three (3) size 2 AWG THWN circuit conductors and one (1) size 8 AWG THWN equipment grounding conductor. In compliance with the NEC®, what is the MINIMUM trade size PVC required for this installation?

A. 2 in.
B. 1 in.
C. 1¼ in.
D. 1½ in.

13. A single-phase, 125-volt, 15- or 20-ampere receptacle outlet shall be installed at each residential kitchen countertop and work surface that is at LEAST _____ or wider.

A. 48 inches
B. 23 inches
C. 24 inches
D. 12 inches

14. The short-circuit and ground-fault protective device protecting an air-conditioner motor-compressor branch circuit shall have sufficient _____ to permit the motor-compressor and other motors to start and accelerate their loads.

A. time delay
B. overcurrent protection
C. load
D. rating

15. Non-heating leads of heating cables, if any, of electric space-heating cables shall be at least _____ in length.

A. 7 feet
B. 10 feet
C. 8 feet
D. 6 feet

16. At least one 15-volt, single-phase, 15- or 20-ampere-rated receptacle outlet is required to be installed within 18 in. of the top of a show window for each ____ linear feet or major fraction thereof of horizontal show window area.

A. 10 feet
B. 12 feet
C. 15 feet
D. 18 feet

17. Where junction or pull boxes enclose conductors of size 4 AWG or larger the boxes are to be sized by the raceway(s) entering the box and not by the size of the conductors contained in the box. Where splices, angle or U-pulls are made, the distance between each raceway entry in the box and opposite wall of the box shall NOT be less than _____ times the largest raceway in a row plus the sum of the additional raceways in the row.

A. eight
B. ten
C. six
D. seven

18. Circuit protection must be designed and capable of disconnecting motors and their controllers from the circuit. The disconnecting means of motors and their controllers shall open _____ supply conductor(s) of the circuit.

A. the neutral
B. the A phase
C. the B phase
D. simultaneously all ungrounded phase

19. A feeder tap less than 25 feet long does not require overcurrent protection at the tap if the ampacity of the tap conductor is at LEAST _____ of the rating of the overcurrent device protecting the feeder conductor.

A. one-half
B. 40%
C. one-third
D. 25%

20. As a general rule, overhead spans of open conductors and multiconductor cables, of not over 1000 volts, shall have a vertical clearance of NOT less than _____ above the roof surface of a building or structure.

A. 8 feet
B. 10 feet
C. 6 feet
D. 8½ feet

21. Given: A 75 kVA transformer will supply a 225 ampere rated panelboard with size 4/0 AWG THWN copper conductors. What MINIMUM size copper system bonding jumper is required for the transformer?

A. 1/0 AWG
B. 2 AWG
C. 4 AWG
D. 6 AWG

22. In a Class I, Division 1 location, each conduit entry into an explosionproof enclosure shall have a conduit seal installed within _____ from the enclosure.

A. 24 inches
B. 30 inches
C. 36 inches
D. 18 inches

23. Each commercial building accessible to pedestrians shall have an outside electric sign circuit rated at LEAST _____ that supplies no other load.

A. 15 amperes
B. 20 amperes
C. 25 amperes
D. 30 amperes

24. As a general rule, overhead service conductors, installed as open conductors, must have a clearance of at LEAST _____ laterally (to the side) from windows that are designed to be opened, doors, ladders, stairs and porches.

A. 3 feet
B. 4 feet
C. 6 feet
D. 8 feet

25. Given: A 240-volt, single-phase motor has the following marked on the nameplate:
FLA 18 amperes
Temperature rise 40°C
Service factor 1.15

The overloads have a setting of 22.5 amperes however, the overload devices trip and do not allow the motor to start. The NEC® allows modification of this value and a higher setting of NOT larger than _____ is permitted for the overloads.

A. 26.4 amperes
B. 23.4 amperes
C. 25.2 amperes
D. 28.6 amperes

END OF EXAM #9

JOURNEYMAN ELECTRICIANS EXAM PREP GUIDE
EXAM #10

The following questions are based on the 2020 edition of the National Electrical Code® and are typical of questions encountered on most Journeymen Electricians' Licensing Exams. On each question select the best answer from the choices given and review your answers with the answer key included in this book. Typically, the only material permitted for use on this type of exam is a calculator, scratch paper and a 2020 edition of the NEC® book. Each question on this test has a value of 4 points; passing score is 70% therefore, in order to pass you need to get 18 of the 25 questions correct.

ALLOTTED TIME: 75 minutes

1. Where exceptions are not applicable, when a metal pole supports a luminaire, the pole shall be provided with an accessible handhole of NOT less than ____ near the base of the pole.
A. 2 in. x 6 in.
B. 3 in. x 4 in.
C. 2 in. x 4 in.
D. 4 in. x 6 in.

2. What is the MINIMUM wire bending space required at the top and bottom of a panelboard that has one (1) size 3/0 AWG conductor connected to each busbar in the panelboard?

A. 6½ inches
B. 8 inches
C. 7½ inches
D. 6 inches

3. A type of conductor insulation approved for use in both dry and wet locations is _____.

A. TFE
B. THHN
C. THWN
D. SA

4. Equipment or materials to which has been attached a symbol or other identifying mark of an organization that is acceptable to the authority having jurisdiction is defined as _____.

A. listed
B. labeled
C. approved
D. acceptable

5. Disregarding exceptions, the MAXIMUM distance permitted for seven (7) current-carrying multiconductor cables to be bundled together without requiring the ampacity of the conductors to be derated and adjustment factors be applied is _____.

A. 6 inches
B. 12 inches
C. 18 inches
D. 24 inches

6. On the job-site the cut ends of electrical metallic tubing (EMT) are required to be _____.

I. reamed
II. threaded

A. I only
B. II only
C. both I and II
D. neither I nor II

7. Unless permitted by local code regulations, Type AC cable shall be secured within _____ of every box, cabinet, or fitting and at intervals not exceeding 4½ feet where installed on or across framing members.

A. 12 inches
B. 18 inches
C. 24 inches
D. 30 inches

8. Given: A 120/240-volt, single-phase, one-family dwelling service has a metal chain link fence opposite exposed live parts of the service equipment. The required depth of the clear working space in front of the service equipment must be at LEAST _____.

A. 2 ft. 6 in.
B. 3 ft.
C. 3 ft. 6 in.
D. 4 ft.

9. Branch circuits serving patient bed locations in the general care (category 2) spaces of hospitals shall _____.

A. provide a minimum of 4 receptacles
B. have isolated-ground receptacles
C. have GFCI protected receptacles
D. not be part of a multiwire branch circuit

10. What MINIMUM size ungrounded (phase) THWN copper service-entrance conductors are required for a 208Y/120-volt, three-phase commercial service with a demand load 72,000 VA?

A. 250 kcmil
B. 2/0 AWG
C. 3/0 AWG
D. 4/0 AWG

11. Given: A retail jewelry store has two (2) large show windows having a length of 15 feet each. One show window is on each side of the front entry/exit door. How many single-phase, 125-volt, 15- or 20-ampere rated receptacles must be provided for the show window lighting?

A. one per window
B. two per window
C. three per window
D. four per window

12. Type NM cable is permitted to be used under all the following conditions or locations EXCEPT:

A. as a feeder.
B. in Type V construction.
C. in a wet or damp location.
D. in multifamily dwellings.

13. What size copper grounding electrode conductor is required for a service where size 350 kcmil copper conductors are used as the service entrance conductors?

A. 3 AWG
B. 1/0 AWG
C. 4 AWG
D. 2 AWG

14. In kitchens of dwelling units, receptacle outlets serving each wall countertop and work surface shall be installed so that no point along the wall line is more than ______ measured horizontally from a receptacle outlet in that space.

A. 24 inches
B. 6 feet
C. 4 feet
D. 8 feet

15. Where portions of a raceway are known to be subjected to different temperatures and where condensation is known to be a problem, the raceway shall be ______.

A. protected by enamel
B. of nonmetallic material
C. coated with an approved corrosion-resistant material
D. filled with an approved material to prevent the circulation of air

16. Determine the ampacity of six (6) current-carrying size 4/0 AWG XHHW aluminum conductors where installed underground in a PVC conduit.

A. 135 amperes
B. 144 amperes
C. 185 amperes
D. 210 amperes

17. Given: A six (6) foot high chain-link fence topped with razor-wire, used to deter access by persons who are not qualified, encloses an outdoor installation of electrical apparatus rated 12 kV. The razor-wire above the chain-link fence shall be at LEAST ______ in height to comply with the NEC® standards.

A. 12 inches
B. 18 inches
C. 6 inches
D. 24 inches

18. Where electrical metallic tubing (EMT) is installed under metal-corrugated sheet roof decking, the EMT shall be installed so there is NOT less than ______ clearance from the lowest surface of the roof decking to the top of the EMT.

A. 1 in.
B. 1¼ in.
C. 1½ in.
D. 2 in.

19. Remote disconnecting controls shall not be required for critical operations data systems when _____.

A. an approved fire suppression system suitable for the application is in place
B. wiring is grouped and identified
C. wiring is in metal raceways
D. wiring is under raised floors

20. Unless listed and identified otherwise, terminations and conductors of circuits rated 100 amperes or less, or marked for conductor sizes 14 AWG through 1 AWG, shall be considered rated for _____.

A. 60°C
B. 75°C
C. 90°C
D. 30°C

21. In a dwelling, which of the following receptacles, if any, require GFCI protection?

I. 240-volt, 30-ampere clothes dryer receptacle
II. 240-volt, 50-ampere electric range receptacle

A. I only
B. II only
C. Neither I nor II
D. Both I and II

22. The NEC® requires a MAXIMUM spacing between supports for trade size 4 in. rigid polyvinyl chloride conduit (PVC) to be _____

A. 4 feet
B. 6 feet
C. 10 feet
D. 7 feet

23. Determine the MINIMUM size copper branch-circuit conductors required to supply a 5.0 kW, 240-volt, single-phase storage-type residential electric water heater. Use Type NM cable and consider all terminations to be rated 60°C.

A. 12 AWG
B. 10 AWG
C. 8 AWG
D. 6 AWG

24. As indicated in the NEC®, all of the following listed locations of dwelling units require AFCI protection on the 120-volt, single-phase, 15- and 20-ampere branch circuits supplying outlets or devices EXCEPT _____.

A. parlor, library and den
B. sunroom, closet and hallway
C. bathrooms and garages
D. dining room, living room and multimedia room

25. Where a 240-volt, single-phase residential branch-circuit using copper Type NM cable, supplies a 8 kW rated counter-mounted cooking unit and a wall-mounted oven rated 6 kW, what MINIMUM size NM cable is required?

A. 6/3 AWG with ground
B. 8/3 AWG with ground
C. 4/3 AWG with ground
D. 10/3 AWG with ground

END OF EXAM #10

JOURNEYMAN ELECTRICIANS EXAM PREP GUIDE
EXAM #11

The following questions are based on the 2020 edition of the National Electrical Code® and are typical of questions encountered on most Journeymen Electricians' Licensing Exams. On each question select the best answer from the choices given and review your answers with the answer key included in this book. Typically, the only material permitted for use on this type of exam is a calculator, scratch paper and a 2020 edition of the NEC® book. Each question on this test has a value of 4 points; passing score is 70% therefore, in order to pass you need to get 18 of the 25 questions correct.

ALLOTTED TIME: 75 minutes

1. Where used outdoors, aluminum or copper-clad aluminum grounding conductors shall NOT be installed or terminated within _____ of the earth.

A. 36 inches
B. 24 inches
C. 18 inches
D. 12 inches

2. A wall-mounted central vacuum assembly connected to a single receptacle located in an attached garage of a dwelling unit shall be provided with _____ protection.

A. AFCI
B. GFCI
C. LCDI
D. both AFCI and GFCI

3. Where a building or structure is supplied by more than one service:

A. a fire pump shall be installed.
B. an emergency system shall be installed.
C. an optional standby system shall be installed.
D. a permanent plaque shall be installed at each service disconnect.

4. Direct and alternating current differ in that alternating current _____.

A. reverses at intervals
B. travels in one direction
C. is intermittent
D. is asynchronous

5. As a general rule and under normal operating conditions, regardless of the type of insulation, size 12 AWG copper conductors are permitted to be protected by an overcurrent protective device with a standard rating of NOT more than _____.

A. 15 amperes
B. 20 amperes
C. 25 amperes
D. 30 amperes

6. For the purpose of service load calculations in dwelling units, each two (2) wire small appliance branch circuit shall be calculated at _____.

A. 1,000 VA
B. 1,200 VA
C. 1,500 VA
D. 2,000 VA

7. The disconnecting means for a permanently connected appliance, rated not over 300 VA or _____, is permitted to be the branch circuit overcurrent protective device where the switch or circuit breaker is within sight from the appliance or is lockable.

A. 1/8 hp
B. 1/16 hp
C. 1/4 hp
D. 1/2 hp

8. Where a straight run of trade size 4 in. conduit containing size 2/0 AWG conductors enters and exits a pull-box and no terminations or splices are made, what is the MINIMUM required length of the pull-box?

A. 20 inches
B. 24 inches
C. 32 inches
D. 36 inches

9. Where the design and operation of a generator does not prevent overloading, the ampacity of the conductors from the generator terminals to the first overcurrent protection device shall NOT be less than _____ of the nameplate current rating of the generator.

A. 115 percent
B. 125 percent
C. 130 percent
D. 150 percent

10. All single-phase cord-and-pug connected room air conditioners shall be provided with _____.

A. a cord not more than 6 ft. in length
B. a cord with conductors not smaller than 12 AWG
C. factory-installed GFCI protection
D. factory-installed AFCI, HCDI, or LCDI protection

11. The NEC® requires an equipment bonding jumper to be _____.

A. insulated
B. non-insulated
C. continuous
D. reliable

12. For Type MI cable with an outer sheath made of steel, a separate _____ shall be provided.

A. steel conductor
B. grounded conductor
C. ungrounded conductor
D. equipment grounding conductor

13. Luminaires shall be installed or constructed so that adjacent combustible materials will not be subject to temperatures in excess of _____.

A. 130°F
B. 194°F
C. 162°F
D. 100°F

14. Luminaires containing a metal halide lamp (other than a thick-glass PAR lamp) shall be provided with a containment barrier that encloses the lamp, or shall be provided with a physical means that only allow the use of a _____.

A. lamp that is Type O
B. mogul base lamp
C. lamp that is Type CB
D. lamp that is listed as explosion proof

15. Unless GFCI protection is provided, luminaires and ceiling fans located over or within 5 ft. horizontally from the inside walls of an indoor installed spa or hot tub shall have a mounting height of NOT less than _____ above the maximum water level of the spa or hot tub.

A. 6 feet
B. 8 feet
C. 10 feet
D. 12 feet

16. Which of the following wiring methods is approved for use under the accessible raised floor area of an information technology equipment room?

A. Type AC cable
B. rigid nonmetallic conduit
C. Type MC cable
D. all of these

17. The ampacity adjustment factors for conductors addressed in Section 310.15(C)(1) of the NEC® are not required to be applied when the conductors are installed in a metal wireway unless, the number of current-carrying conductors within the wireway exceeds _____ at any cross section of the wireway.

A. 20
B. 30
C. 40
D. 50

18. The voltage at the line terminals of a fire pump motor controller shall NOT drop more than _____ below the controller's nominal rated voltage under motor-starting conditions. This limitation shall not apply for emergency run mechanical starting.

A. 5 percent
B. 10 percent
C. 15 percent
D. 20 percent

19. Where a size 1/0 AWG THWN aluminum conductor is installed outdoors in a raceway with two (2) other current-carrying conductors of the same size and the ambient temperature reaches 110°F, the conductor has an ampacity of _____.

A. 100 amperes
B. 90 amperes
C. 98 amperes
C. 104 amperes

20. Ceiling suspended (paddle) fans weighing MORE than _____ shall be supported independently of the outlet box.

A. 35 pounds
B. 50 pounds
C. 30 pounds
D. 70 pounds

21. Inverse-time circuit breakers rated at _____ or less and 1000 volts or less shall have the ampere rating molded, stamped, etched or similarly marked into their handles or escutcheon areas.

A. 200 amperes
B. 100 amperes
C. 400 amperes
D. 600 amperes

22. Where the service of a building is provided with ground-fault protection, the MAXIMUM trip time delay shall be _____ for ground-fault currents equal to or greater than 3,000 amperes.

A. one second
B. five seconds
C. 30 seconds
D. 60 seconds

23. Conductor ampacity adjustment factors shall not apply to conductors in raceways having a length NOT exceeding _____.

A. 12 inches
B. 24 inches
C. 18 inches
D. 36 inches

24. The connection between the grounded circuit conductor and the equipment grounding conductor, or the supply-side bonding jumper, or both, at the electrical service of a building or structure is recognized as the _____ in the NEC®.

A. main bonding jumper
B. grounding electrode conductor
C. equipment bonding jumper
D. neutral conductor

25. Appliances require a separate disconnecting means or a unit switch with a marked "OFF" position, that is part of the appliance and will disconnect all _____.

A. circuit conductors
B. grounded conductors
C. ungrounded conductors
D. conductors including the grounding conductor

END OF EXAM #11

JOURNEYMAN ELECTRICIANS EXAM PREP GUIDE
EXAM #12

The following questions are based on the 2020 edition of the National Electrical Code® and are typical of questions encountered on most Journeymen Electricians' Licensing Exams. On each question select the best answer from the choices given and review your answers with the answer key included in this book. Typically, the only material permitted for use on this type of exam is a calculator, scratch paper and a 2020 edition of the NEC® book. Each question on this test has a value of 4 points; passing score is 70% therefore, in order to pass you need to get 18 of the 25 questions correct.
ALLOTTED TIME: 75 minutes

1. Which of the following statements is a correct NEC® provision for an equipment bonding jumper?

A. An equipment bonding jumper is permitted to be a wire, bus, or screw.
B. The bonding jumper shall be of the same size and of the same material as the ungrounded conductors in the raceway.
C. The size of an equipment bonding jumper on the load side of the service is based on the size of the largest ungrounded service-entrance conductor.
D. The maximum length of an equipment bonding jumper is 10 feet.

2. Where a 15- or 20-ampere rated branch circuit supplies three (3) 15-ampere rated receptacles, the MAXIMUM load any one receptacle is permitted to carry is _____.

A. 10 amperes
B. 15 ampere
C. 12 amperes
D. 8 amperes

3. Where a surface-mounted luminaire containing a ballast or transformer is to be located on combustible low-density cellulose fiberboard, the ballast or transformer shall be marked for this condition or shall be spaced NOT less than _____ from the surface of the fiberboard.

A. 1 in.
B. 1½ in.
C. 1¾ in.
D. 1¼ in.

4. A metal device box to be installed will contain one (1) duplex receptacle, two (2) internal cable clamps and two (2) size 12/2 with ground nonmetallic sheathed cables. To comply with NEC® standards the device box must have a volume, in cubic inches, of at LEAST _____.

A. 13.50 cubic inches
B. 15.75 cubic inches
C. 16.00 cubic inches
D. 18.00 cubic inches

5. On a 4-wire delta-connected system, the conductor having the higher phase voltage to ground shall be durably and permanently marked by an outer finish that is _____ in color or by other effective means if the grounded conductor is also present.

A. red
B. black
C. white
D. orange

6. Resistance-type hating elements in fixed electric space heating equipment shall be subdivided into loads NOT exceeding _____.

A. 60 amperes
B. 50 amperes
C. 48 amperes
D. 40 amperes

7. When a receptacle outlet is removed from an underfloor raceway, the conductors supplying the outlet _____.

A. shall be capped with an approved insulating material
B. shall be taped off and identified with red colored phase tape
C. are permitted to be marked, identified and remain in the raceway
D. shall be removed from the raceway

8. For other than listed low-voltage luminaires not requiring grounding, wet-niche luminaires installed in permanently installed swimming pools shall be connected to an insulated copper equipment grounding conductor NOT smaller than _____.

A. 12 AWG
B. 10 AWG
C. 14 AWG
D. 8 AWG

9. Disregarding exceptions, the MINIMUM size grounded or ungrounded conductors permitted to be connected in parallel (electrically joined at both ends) is _____.

A. 6 AWG
B. 1 AWG
C. 1/0 AWG
D. 2/0 AWG

10. For track lighting located in other than dwelling units, or guest rooms or suites of hotels or motels, a load of _____ shall be calculated for every two (2) feet of lighting track or fraction thereof.

A. 150 VA
B. 180 VA
C. 120 VA
D. 200 VA

11. Branch circuits supplying one or more information technology units or data processing units shall have an ampacity (current-carrying capacity) of NOT less than ______ of the total connected load.

A. 115%
B. 125%
C. 100%
D. 150%

12. Where installed in an ambient temperature of not more than 86°F, Type SRD multiconductor flexible cable consisting of size 8 AWG conductors and only two (2) conductors in the cable are current-carrying, the ampacity of the conductors is _____.

A. 25 amperes
B. 30 amperes
C. 40 amperes
D. 35 amperes

13. A fifty (50) ft. run of Schedule 40 PVC conduit is to contain the following copper conductors:

- four (4) size 1 AWG XHHW
- one (1) size 6 AWG bare

Determine the MINIMUM trade size Schedule 40 PVC required as per the NEC®.

A. 2 in.
B. 1½in.
C. 1¼ in.
D. 1 in.

14. For circuits over _____ to ground, the electrical continuity of rigid metal conduit (RMC) that contain any conductor, other than service conductors, shall be insured with two (2) locknuts, one inside and one outside of boxes and cabinets.

A. 120 volts
B. 150 volts
C. 240 volts
D. 250 volts

15. In regard to dwelling units, at LEAST _______ branch circuit(s) shall be provided to supply the laundry equipment receptacle outlet(s).

A. one 15-ampere
B. one 20-ampere
C. two-20-ampere
D. one 20-ampere and one 30-ampere

16. Given: An 18 cubic inch Type FS device box that contains a receptacle is supported only by two (2) underground installed rigid metal conduits that are made-up wrench-tight into the box. Each conduit shall be secured within at LEAST _____ of the box.

A. 18 inches
B. 12 inches
C. 24 inches
D. 8 inches

17. Where a conductor is marked *RHW-2* on the insulation, what does the *-2* represent?

A. The cable has two conductors.
B. The conductor is double insulated.
C. The conductor has a nylon outer jacket.
D. The conductor has a maximum operating temperature of 90°C.

18. Drywall or plasterboard surfaces that are damaged around boxes having a flush-type cover or faceplate shall be repaired so there will be no gaps greater than _____ at the edge of the box.

A. 1/8 in.
B. 1/4 in.
C. 3/8 in.
D. 1/2 in.

19. All electrical equipment including boxes, cabinets and raceways installed in Class I, Division 1 or 2 locations shall be _____ equipment.

A. explosion resistant
B. dust-tight
C. dust-proof
D. explosionproof

20. Where the service-entrance conductors for a commercial occupancy are size 350 kcmil aluminum, what size copper grounding electrode conductor would be required? (Assume the grounding electrode conductor extends to multiple electrodes.)

A. 6 AWG
B. 4 AWG
C. 2 AWG
D. 1/0 AWG

21. Single-conductor cable in exposed outdoor locations in solar photovoltaic (PV) systems dc circuits within the PV array, shall be permitted to be Type _____.

A. USE-2
B. RHW
C. THWN
D. all of these

22. What is the approximate horsepower rating of a 240-volt, single-phase motor that draws 18.5 amperes of current, with an efficiency of 85 percent?

A. 3½ hp
B. 5 hp
C. 10 hp
D. 7½ hp

23. Where exposed Type NM cable passes through a floor, the cable shall be protected from physical damage by an approved means extending at LEAST _____ above the floor.

A. 4 inches
B. 6 inches
C. 8 inches
D. 10 inches

24. Branch circuit outlets supplying 120-volt or 240-volt, single phase, swimming pool pump motors of 60-amperes or less, for a permanently installed swimming pool shall be provided with Class A GFCI protection for personnel when ____.

I. cord-and-plug connected to a receptacle
II. direct connected (hard-wired)

A. I only
B. II only
C. either I or II
D. neither I nor II

25. Recessed luminaires installed in suspended ceilings shall:

A. be supported independently of the ceiling grid.
B. not be attached to the ceiling framing members.
C. be attached to the building structural support framing members.
D. be attached to the ceiling framing members by clips, screws or rivets listed and identified for use with the luminaire and ceiling framing members.

END OF EXAM 12

JOURNEYMAN ELECTRICIAN'S EXAM PREP GUIDE
FINAL EXAM #1

The following questions are based on the 2020 edition of the National Electrical Code® and are typical of questions encountered on most Journeyman Electricians' Licensing Exams. Select the best answer from the choices given and review your answers with the answer key included in this book. Passing score on this exam is 70%. The exam consists of 80 questions valued at 1.25 points each, therefore you must answer 56 questions correct for a passing score. If you do not score at least 70%, try again and keep studying. GOOD LUCK.

ALLOTTED TIME: 4 hours

1. Where not in excess of 1000 volts, the MINIMUM permitted height of service-drop conductors installed over an apple orchard or orange grove is _____ above ground.

A. 12 feet
B. 15 feet
C. 21 feet
D. 18 feet

2. The purpose of the NEC® is _____.

A. to have an installation that is efficient
B. the practical safeguarding of persons and property
C. for future expansion of electrical use
D. to provide an installation that is adequate for good service

3. For the purpose of maintaining electrical equipment such as panelboards, switchboards, motor control centers and switchgear of 1000 volts or less, the width of the working space in front of the equipment shall be the width of the equipment or NOT less than _____, whichever is greater.

A. 24 inches
B. 48 inches
C. 30 inches
D. 36 inches

4. All 15- and 20-ampere 125-volt, single-phase straight blade-type receptacles located in _____ shall be listed as tamper-resistant.

A. dormitories
B. waiting rooms of dental offices
C. elementary schools
D. all of these

5. When wiring motor fuel dispensing pumps, the first fitting that should be installed in the raceway that emerges from below ground or concrete into
the base of the gasoline dispenser is a/an:

A. automatic cut-off breakaway valve.
B. disconnect.
C. sealing fitting.
D. no fittings of any kind are permitted in this location.

6. One kVA is equal to _____.

A. one hundred watts
B. one thousand volt-amps
C. one hundred kilo-watts
D. one hundred volt-amps

7. A 15 kW, 208-volt, single-phase heat-pump has a full-load current rating of _____.

A. 42 amperes
B. 125 amperes
C. 65 amperes
D. 72 amperes

8. When sizing the overcurrent protection for a single non-motor operated appliance such as a storage-type water heater, cooktop or range, which of the following need NOT to be taken into consideration?

A. The length of time the appliance operates.
B. The full-load current marked on the appliance.
C. The voltage rating of the appliance.
D. Where the overcurrent protection device selected is not a standard size.

9. When installed, a metal junction box will contain the following conductors:

* three - 6 AWG wires, 2 ungrounded & 1 grounded
* one - 8 AWG equipment grounding conductor
* two - internal clamps
* one - pigtail

Determine the MINIMUM size box, in cubic inches, the NEC® requires.

A. 16 cubic inches
B. 18 cubic inches
C. 20 cubic inches
D. 23 cubic inches

10. As a general rule, round access openings in a manhole shall NOT be less than _____ in diameter.

A. 24 inches
B. 26 inches
C. 30 inches
D. 36 inches

11. Strut-type channel raceways shall be permitted to be suspension mounted in air with identified methods at intervals NOT to exceed _____.

A. 6 feet
B. 10 feet
C. 12 feet
D. 8 feet

12. One- and two-family dwelling unit services are required to be provided with:

I. an emergency service disconnect.
II. a surge-protective device (SPD).

A. I only
B. II only
C. Both I and II
D. Neither I nor II

13. Determine the MINIMUM size 75 deg. C rated copper conductors required to supply a fixed electric space heating unit with heating elements having a full-load current rating of 125 amperes and a blower motor having a full-load current rating of 2.5 amperes.

A. 1 AWG
B. 2 AWG
C. 2/0 AWG
D. 3/0 AWG

14. Where a thermal protector is integral with the motor, the ultimate trip current of a thermally protected 2 horsepower, single-phase, 240-volt motor shall NOT exceed _____ of the full-load current of the motor.

A. 115 percent
B. 125 percent
C. 140 percent
D. 156 percent

15. Under which one of the following conditions are you required to use an approved electrically conductive corrosion resistance compound on metal conduit threads?

A. In Class I Division 1 locations.
B. In Class II Division 1 locations.
C. On field cut threads for indoor locations.
D. On field cut threads in corrosive locations.

16. Disregarding exceptions, each patient bed location in general care (category 2) spaces of hospitals shall be provided with a MINIMUM of _____ "hospital grade" receptacles.

A. eight
B. ten
C. twelve
D. fourteen

17. Where a receptacle outlet is installed for a specific appliance, such as a washing machine located in a laundry room, the outlet shall be installed within at LEAST _____ of the intended location of the appliance.

A. 4 feet
B. 6 feet
C. 5 feet
D. 8 feet

18. In general, overhead service-drop conductors shall NOT be smaller than size _____.

A. 8 AWG copper
B. 6 AWG copper
C. 8 AWG aluminum
D. 2 AWG aluminum

19. What MINIMUM size wire-type bonding conductor must bond all metal parts associated with a hot tub?

A. 12 AWG
B. 10 AWG
C. 8 AWG
D. 6 AWG

20. When installing galvanized rigid metal conduit (RMC), where structural members readily permit fastening, the conduit is required to be fastened within at LEAST _____ of a junction box, panelboard or cabinet.

A. 3 feet
B. 5 feet
C. 6 feet
D. 10 feet

21. A ground ring is permitted for use as a grounding electrode where consisting of at least _____ of bare copper conductor not smaller than _____ and buried not less than _____ below the surface of the earth.

A. 20 feet, 6 AWG, 24 inches
B. 20 feet, 2 AWG, 30 inches
C. 10 feet, 4 AWG, 24 inches
D. 10 feet, 6 AWG, 30 inches

22. Given: A 240-volt wye-connected motor derives power from a converted single-phase source. It is desired to connect a 120/240-volt transformer for control of the motor on the load side of the converter. The control transformer must _____ .

A. be connected to the manufactured phase
B. be disconnected after start-up of the motor
C. have separate overcurrent protection
D. not be connected to the manufactured phase

23. What is the MAXIMUM size overcurrent protection device required to protect size 14 AWG conductors used for the pump motor control-circuit that is protected by the motor branch circuit protection device and extends beyond the enclosure?

A. 15 amperes
B. 20 amperes
C. 45 amperes
D. 100 amperes

24. Where raceways are installed above grade outdoors and exposed to the weather, the interior of these raceways shall be considered to be a _____ location.

A. damp
B. moist
C. dry
D. wet

25. In dwelling units, hallways of at LEAST _____ or more in length shall be provided with at least one 125-volt, 15- or 20-ampere rated receptacle.

A. 10 feet
B. 12 feet
C. 15 feet
D. 20 feet

26. A motor overload device functions in direct response to _____.

A. voltage
B. motor current
C. temperature rise of the motor
D. ambient temperature

27. When a cord-and-plug connected water softener is wired to a 20-ampere rated branch-circuit, the SMALLEST size flexible cord to supply the water softener as permitted by the NEC® is size _____.

A. 18 AWG
B. 16 AWG
C. 14 AWG
D. 20 AWG

28. When twenty (20) size 10 AWG copper current-carrying conductors with THHN insulation are installed in a 50-feet run of trade size 1½ in. electrical metallic tubing (EMT), what is the ampacity rating of each of the size 10 AWG conductors?

A. 15 amperes
B. 20 amperes
C. 25 amperes
D. 30 amperes

29. Flexible metal conduit (FMC) is permitted for use in wet locations _____.

A. when the conductors within the FMC have a temperature rating of not less than 90 deg. C
B. when the conductors contained within the FMC are approved for use in wet locations
C. where the length of the FMC is not more than six (6) feet
D. under no circumstances

30. The MINIMUM size copper wire that may be used for grounding the secondary of an instrument transformer is _____.

A. 6 AWG
B. 8 AWG
C. 10 AWG
D. 12 AWG

31. In general, which one of the following statements is TRUE regarding the required disconnecting means for a fluorescent luminaire.

A. Only the ungrounded conductor to the ballast is required to be disconnected when connected to multiwire branch circuits.
B. The disconnecting means shall not be external to the luminaire.
C. The disconnecting means shall simultaneously break all supply conductors to the ballast, including the grounded conductor, when connected to a multiwire branch circuit.
D. The disconnecting means shall be external to the luminaire.

32. Class 1 control-circuit conductors and motor branch-circuits are permitted by the NEC® to occupy the same raceway, if the control circuit conductors _______.

A. carry no more than 24 volts
B. have a voltage to ground not to exceed 150 volts
C. have a voltage to ground not to exceed 277 volts
D. are functionally associated with the motor system

33. As confirmed by the NEC®, where a flat cable assembly, Type FC, is installed less than _____ above the floor or fixed working platform, where not subject to physical damage, it shall be protected by a cover identified for the use.

A. six feet
B. eight feet
C. three feet
D. four feet

34. A feeder supplying two (2) continuous-duty, 208-volt, 3-phase motors, one 10 hp and one 7½ hp shall have a MINIMUM ampacity of _____ amperes.

A. 55.00
B. 68.75
C. 62.70
D. 38.50

35. The reason the NEC® requires all phase conductors of the same circuit to be in the same ferrous metal raceway is to reduce ______ .

A. expense
B. inductive heat
C. voltage drop
D. resistance

36. Which of the following conductor insulation types, if any, is/are acceptable for wiring in a fluorescent luminaire when the branch circuit conductor passes within three (3) inches of the ballast?

I. THW
II. THWN

A. I only
B. II only
C. both I and II
D. neither I nor II

37. Where practicable, a separation of at LEAST _____ shall be maintained between communications wires and cables on buildings and lightning conductors.

A. 18 inches
B. 24 inches
C. 4 feet
D. 6 feet

38. A fluorescent luminaire shall be permitted to be cord connected _____ .

A. where the flexible cord is contained in an approved raceway
B. except at terminations, where the flexible cord is visible for its entire length
C. where the flexible cord is at least size 12 AWG
D. never

39. Wiring located above heated ceilings shall be spaced at not less than 2 inches above the heated ceiling and shall be considered as operating at an assumed ambient temperature of not less than _____.

A. 50°C
B. 99°F
C. 60°C
D. 75°C

40. An equipotential bonding grid must be installed in the deck around a permanently installed swimming pool; the bonding grid shall extend for at LEAST ____ horizontally beyond the inside walls of the pool.

A. 3 feet
B. 5 feet
C. 6 feet
D. 10 feet

41. Where not in excess of 1000 volts, open overhead service conductors over public driveways are required to maintain a vertical clearance of NOT less than _____ from final grade.

A. 10 feet
B. 12 feet
C. 15 feet
D. 18 feet

42. All permanently installed spa and hot tub equipment located in non-dwelling occupancies shall be provided with an emergency shutoff or control switch within sight of the unit(s), and located NOT less than _____ from the inside wall of the spa or hot tub.

A. 6 feet
B. 10 feet
C. 5 feet
D. 12 feet

43. Feeders to floating buildings and piers are permitted to be installed in _____ where flexible connections are required.

A. MC cable
B. AC cable
C. NMC cable
D. extra-hard usage portable power cable

44. Where a building or structure is supplied with a 3-phase, 480Y/277 volt service, each disconnecting means rated at LEAST _____ or more shall be provided with ground-fault protection.

A. 1000 amperes
B. 1200 amperes
C. 1500 amperes
D. 2000 amperes

45. In a marina, receptacles intended to supply shore power for boats shall be mounted not less than _____ above the deck surface of the pier and not below the electrical datum plane on a fixed pier.

A. 12 inches
B. 18 inches
C. 24 inches
D. 30 inches

46. Branch circuit conductors supplying a varying duty motor with a 30-minute and/or 60-minute rating shall have an ampacity of at LEAST ____ of the nameplate rating of the motor to be supplied.

A. 85 percent
B. 110 percent
C. 120 percent
D. 150 percent

47. Cablebus shall be installed only for _____ locations.

A. exposed
B. commercial
C. concealed
D. hazardous

48. Solar photovoltaic system dc circuits on or in one- and two-family dwellings shall be permitted to have a voltage of no greater than _____ .

A. 120 volts
B. 250 volts
C. 600 volts
D. 50 volts

49. A hospital conference room is considered to be an assembly occupancy when designed for the assembly of at LEAST _____ or more persons.

A. 25
B. 50
C. 75
D. 100

50. Determine the MINIMUM required size 75 deg. C rated copper conductors to supply a demand load of 200 amperes where installed in an area with an expected ambient temperature of 120 deg. F.

A. 3/0 AWG
B. 4/0 AWG
C. 300 kcmil
D. 250 kcmil

51. Where concrete encased, raceways approved for burial only shall require a concrete envelope NOT less than _____ thick.

A. 2 inches
B. 4 inches
C. 6 inches
D. 8 inches

52. Overhead communications wires and cables shall have a separation of at LEAST ____ from supply service-drops of 0-750 volts at any point in the span.

A. 30 inches
B. 24 inches
C. 12 inches
D. 18 inches

53. In general, electrical nonmetallic tubing (ENT) shall be securely fastened in place within at LEAST _____ of each outlet box, junction box, or panelboard.

A. 12 inches
B. 18 inches
C. 24 inches
D. 36 inches

54. Where flexible cord has one conductor identified by a ridge on the exterior of the cord, this conductor is identified as a/an _____ conductor.

A. ungrounded
B. grounded
C. phase
D. equipment grounding

55. Where a raceway enters a building or structure from an outside underground distribution system, it shall be _____.

A. sealed
B. marked
C. Schedule 40 PVC only
D. provided with a drain hole

56. Equipment grounding conductors used for systems over 1 kV that are not an integral part of a cable assembly shall NOT be smaller than _____ copper.

A. 8 AWG
B. 6 AWG
C. 4 AWG
D. 2 AWG

57. What is the MAXIMUM number of size 4 AWG THHN copper conductors permitted to be installed in a trade size 1¼ in. electrical metallic tubing (EMT) having a length of 18 inches?

A. 10
B. 11
C. 12
D. 13

58. What is the MINIMUM size 75 deg. C copper ungrounded (phase) service entrance conductors permitted for a 200-ampere rated commercial service?

A. 4/0 THW
B. 2/0 THW
C. 3/0 THHN
D. 3/0 THW

59. Where a surfaced-mounted luminaire containing a ballast, transformer, LED driver, or power supply is to be installed on combustible low-density cellulose fiberboard, it shall be marked for this condition or shall be spaced NOT less than _____ from the surface of the fiberboard.

A. 3/4 in.
B. 1 in.
C. 1¼ in.
D. 1½ in.

60. Which of the following listed cables have an overall covering that is fungus resistant?

A. Type NM
B. Type NMS
C. Type NMC
D. Type MI

61. The conductors in multiconductor portable cables of over 600 volts, used to connect mobile equipment and machinery, shall be at LEAST size _____ copper or larger and employ flexible stranding.

A. 14 AWG
B. 12 AWG
C. 10 AWG
D. 8 AWG

62. Where installed for a temporary electrical service in a wet location at a construction site, all _____ receptacles shall be listed as weather-resistant.

A. 125-volt, 30-ampere, straight-blade
B. 250-volt, 20-ampere, straight-blade
C. 125-volt, 30-ampere, twist-lock
D. 250-volt, 15-ampere, twist-lock

63. Given: Conductors of not over 25 ft. long are to be tapped from a service where two (2) parallel size 500 kcmil copper conductors per phase are protected by an 800 ampere overcurrent protection device. The tap conductors will terminate in a single circuit breaker. What MINIMUM size THW copper conductors are required for the tap conductors?

A. 500 kcmil
B. 400 kcmil
C. 300 kcmil
D. 250 kcmil

64. Disregarding exceptions, the MINIMUM size grounded or ungrounded conductors permitted to be connected in parallel (electrically joined at both ends) is _____.

A. 1/0 AWG
B. 1 AWG
C. 6 AWG
D. 2 AWG

65. Given: A 12 unit condo will have an 8 kW electric range in each unit;
apply the optional method of calculation for multifamily dwellings and calculate the demand load, in kW, on the ungrounded (line) service entrance conductors for the electric ranges.

A. 39.4 kW
B. 30.7 kW
C. 25.9 kW
D. 32.0 kW

66. Information technology equipment shall be permitted to be connected to a branch circuit by a power-supply cord having a length NOT to exceed _____ .

A. 6 feet
B. 8 feet
C. 10 feet
D. 15 feet

67. The classification of hazardous areas and zones is to be determined by _____ .

A. engineers
B. licensed electricians
C. qualified persons
D. the local authority having jurisdiction

68. When installing border lighting for stages in theaters, the luminaires shall be arranged so that no branch circuit will carry a load to exceed _____ .

A. 10 amperes
B. 20 amperes
C. 15 amperes
D. 30 amperes

69. Where a single device wider than two (2) inches is installed in a 2-gang device box, the device is to be counted as equal to _____ conductor(s).

A. one
B. two
C. three
D. four

70. When counting the number of circuit breakers in a panelboard, a 3-pole circuit breaker shall be considered as _____ overcurrent protective device(s).

A. two
B. three
C. one
D. four

71. Type AC cable shall be permitted _____ .

A. for feeders
B. in wet locations
C. in damp locations
D. where exposed to physical damage

72. Where conductors carrying alternating current are installed in ferrous metal raceways, _____ .

A. all phase conductors, and where used, the grounded conductor and equipment grounding conductor shall be grouped together
B. the phase conductors shall not be grouped with the grounded conductor
C. the grounding and grounded conductors shall be connected together at the terminations
D. the equipment grounding conductor is not permitted to be installed in a common raceway with the grounded conductors

73. Where a run of electrical metallic tubing (EMT) with compression-type fittings is installed _____ a wire-type equipment grounding conductor is required to be installed in the EMT with the circuit conductors.

A. along a bar joist supplying high-bay luminaires in a warehouse
B. within a metal stud wall supplying receptacles
C. outdoors on a roof supplying a roof top HVAC unit
D. exposed on the surface of a masonry wall

74. A neutral conductor is always _____ .

A. a grounded conductor not intended to carry current
B. an ungrounded conductor
C. green in color
D. the conductor connected to the neutral point of a system that is intended to carry current under normal conditions

75. Given: A one-family dwelling supplied by a single-phase, 120/240-volt system has a calculated demand load of 42,000 VA. What MINIMUM size XHHW aluminum conductors are required for the ungrounded (line) service-entrance conductors?

A. 1/0 AWG
B. 2/0 AWG
C. 3/0 AWG
D. 4/0 AWG

76. The ungrounded, grounded and equipment grounding conductors of Type TC cables shall be in sizes _____ to 1000 kcmil copper, nickel, or nickel-coated copper.

A. 18 AWG
B. 16 AWG
C. 14 AWG
D. 12 AWG

77. In general, all panelboards are required to have overcurrent protection, an EXCEPTION to this rule is _____ .

A. panelboards containing less than 42 overcurrent devices
B. panelboards containing only single-pole overcurrent devices
C. panelboards that supply a second bus structure within the same panelboard
D. for existing panelboards used as service equipment in an individual residential occupancy

78. Where a motor controller that is not an inverse time circuit breaker or molded case switch, controls a 120 hp, continuous-duty, ac motor of not over 600 volts, the controller shall have a horsepower rating of NOT less than _____ .

A. 120 hp
B. 150 hp
C. 175 hp
D. 200 hp

79. Overload relays and other devices for motor overload protection that are NOT capable of opening short-circuits or ground-faults shall be protected by a motor short-circuit protector or by _____.

A. an instantaneous trip circuit breaker only
B. fuses or circuit breakers
C. Class CC fuses only
D. a ground-fault circuit interrupter

80. An electrical system comprised of multiple power sources is known as a/an _____ .

A. emergency system
B. optional standby system
C. hybrid system
D. legally required standby system

END OF JOURNEYMAN ELECTRICIANS FINAL EXAM #1

JOURNEYMAN ELECTRICIAN'S EXAM PREP GUIDE
FINAL EXAM #2

The following questions are based on the 2020 edition of the National Electrical Code® and are typical of questions encountered on most Journeyman Electricians' Licensing Exams. Select the best answer from the choices given and review your answers with the answer key included in this book. Passing score on this exam is 70%. The exam consists of 80 questions valued at 1.25 points each, therefore you must answer 56 questions correct for a passing score. If you do not score at least 70%, try again and keep studying. GOOD LUCK.

ALLOTTED TIME: 4 hours

1. All single-phase, 125-volt 15- and 20-ampere rated receptacles located within _____ of the inside walls of a storable pool, storable spa, or storable hot tub
shall be provided with GFCI protection.

A. 8 feet
B. 10 feet
C. 15 feet
D. 20 feet

2. What is the MAXIMUM length permitted for flexible cord used to supply an electrically operated in-sink kitchen waste disposer?

A. 18 inches
B. 24 inches
C. 36 inches
D. 48 inches

3. Type AC cable installed horizontally through wooden or metal framing members is considered supported and secured where such support doesn't exceed _____ intervals.

A. 2 feet
B. 3 feet
C. 4½ feet
D. 6 feet

4. At least one 15- or 20-ampere, 125-volt, single-phase receptacle outlet NOT more than _____ above a balcony, deck, or porch walking surface shall be installed at each balcony, deck, or porch that is within 4 in. horizontally or attached to a dwelling and accessible from the dwelling unit.

A. 3 feet
B. 6½ feet
C. 8 feet
D. 5½ feet

5. Where raceways contain _____ or larger insulated circuit conductors and these conductors enter a raceway in a cabinet, the conductors shall be protected from abrasion by a smoothly rounded insulating surface such as a bushing.

A. 1 AWG
B. 2 AWG
C. 3 AWG
D. 4 AWG

6. The lightning protection system ground terminals shall be bonded to the building or structure grounding electrode system. The bonding shall be _____ and to all raceways, boxes, and enclosures between the cabinets or equipment and the grounding electrode.

A. insulated at both ends
B. insulated from one end
C. bonded at both ends
D. bonded at only one end

7. Where the initial protection specified in the NEC® is not sufficient for the starting current of an air-conditioner motor-compressor, the rating or setting shall be permitted to be increased, but shall NOT exceed _____ of the motor-compressor rated load current or branch circuit selection.

A. 225%
B. 175%
C. 200%
D. 125%

8. The service conductors between the terminals of the service equipment and a point usually outside the building, clear of building walls, where joined by splice or tap to the service drop or overhead service conductors are recognized as _____.

A. service-drop conductors
B. service lateral conductors
C. service entrance conductors
D. none of these

9. What is the ampacity (current-carrying capacity) of a size 10 AWG, THHN CU conductor when there are a total of four (4) current-carrying conductors in a raceway? Assume all terminations are rated 75°C.

A. 40 amperes
B. 32 amperes
C. 28 amperes
D. 30 amperes

10. Additional services shall be permitted for a single building or other structure sufficiently large to make two (2) or more services necessary if permitted by _____.

A. the registered design professional
B. qualified personnel
C. the engineer of record
D. special permission

11. Branch circuits that supply electric signs shall be considered _____ loads for the purposes of calculations.

A. continuous
B. non-continuous
C. full-current
D. readily accessible

12. Where a ground ring is used as a grounding electrode consisting of a size 2 AWG bare copper conductor encircling a building, buried 36 in. deep, in direct contact with the earth, the conductor is required to have a MINIMUM length of _____.

A. 15 feet
B. 20 feet
C. 25 feet
D. 50 feet

13. For low voltage lighting systems operating at 30 volts or less, the output circuits of the power supply are to be rated for NOT more than ____ under all load conditions.

A. 15 amperes
B. 20 amperes
C. 25 amperes
D. 30 amperes

14. Any connections or splices in an underground installation shall be approved for such locations, and the NEC® defines an underground installation, such as the interior surface of enclosures or raceways that are installed underground are considered a _____ location.

A. wet
B. damp
C. dry
D. approved

15. What is the horsepower rating of a single-phase, 120-volt ac motor that draws 9.8 amperes of current?

A. 1 hp
B. ¾ hp
C. ¼ hp
D. ½ hp

16. For installations of resistors and reactors, a thermal barrier shall be required if the space between them and any combustible material is LESS than _____.

A. 2 inches
B. 3 inches
C. 6 inches
D. 12 inches

17. Given: A trade size 3 in. electrical metallic tubing (EMT) will enter the bottom of a pull box and a trade size 3 in. flexible metal conduit (FMC) will enter the side of the box; the raceways will contain conductors of size 4 AWG or larger. What MINIMUM size pull box is required for this installation?

A. 12 in. x 12 in.
B. 18 in. x 18 in.
C. 24 in. x 30 in.
D. 24 in. x 18 in.

18. The service equipment for a mobile home is not permitted to be located in or on the exterior wall of the mobile home however, the service equipment shall be located in sight and NOT more than _____ from the exterior wall of the mobile home it serves.

A. 30 feet
B. 20 feet
C. 50 feet
D. 100 feet

19. Individual unit equipment for legally required standby illumination systems are permitted to have flexible cord-and-plug connections, provided the flexible cord does NOT exceed _____ in length.

A. 2 feet
B. 3 feet
C. 4 feet
D. 6 feet

20. A size 10 AWG flexible Type SJ cord shall be permitted for:

A. locations where oil-resistant insulation is required.
B. wet and damp locations.
C. a maximum of 600 volts.
D. a maximum of 300 volts.

21. All hydromassage bathtub metal piping systems and all grounded metal parts in contact with the circulating water associated with the bathtub shall be bonded together using a solid copper bonding jumper NOT smaller than _____.

A. 10 AWG
B. 6 AWG
C. 8 AWG
D. 12 AWG

22. Where a 125-volt, single-phase, 20-ampere receptacle is install in a residential laundry area, designated for the washing machine, the receptacle must be provided with _____.

A. AFCI protection only
B. GFCI protection only
C. neither AFCI nor GFCI protection
D. both AFCI and GFCI protection

23. According to the NEC® the required MINIMUM burial depth of a direct burial cable run of a GFCI protected, 15-ampere, 120-volt circuit, where the cable passes directly under the residential driveway is _____.

A. 12 inches
B. 16 inches
C. 18 inches
D. 24 inches

24. Where practical, conductors of dissimilar metals shall ____ in a terminal or splicing connector.

A. be listed.
B. be marked.
C. not be intermixed.
D. be for current-carrying conductors only.

25. Branch circuits that supply electric signs, other than neon signs, shall be rated NOT to exceed _____ .

A. 15 amperes
B. 30 amperes
C. 20 amperes
D. 40 amperes

26. Where the design and operation of a generator does not prevent overloading, the ampacity of the conductors from the generator terminals to the first overcurrent protection device shall NOT be less than _____ of the nameplate rating of the generator.

A. 115 percent
B. 125 percent
C. 130 percent
D. 150 percent

27. What is the primary full-load current rating of a 3-phase, 75 kVA, transformer that is 90% efficient, with a 480-volt primary and a 208Y/120-volt secondary?

A. 156.3 amperes
B. 208.3 amperes
C. 100.2 amperes
D. 360.6 amperes

28. Cable splices are permitted in a cable tray, provided _____.

A. the splices are contained in a junction box
B. the splices are accessible
C. the conductors are size 1/0 AWG or larger
D. the splices are made with compression type fittings

29. Where conduit or tubing nipples having length NOT to exceed 24 inches between boxes or enclosures, the nipples shall be permitted to be filled to _____ of their total cross-sectional area.

A. 53 percent
B. 31 percent
C. 40 percent
D. 60 percent

30. Polyvinyl chloride conduit (PVC) larger than trade size _____ shall not be used.

A. 4 inches
B. 5 inches
C. 4½ inches
D. 6 inches

31. Given: A 100 kVA, dry-type transformer with a 4,160-volt primary, which may be subject to be close to combustible material, is to be installed indoors. The transformer must have a clearance of at LEAST _____ from the combustible material.

A. 12 inches
B. 18 inches
C. 20 inches
D. 24 inches

32. Underground service conductors that are not encased in concrete and are buried 18 inches or more below grade shall have their location identified by a warning ribbon placed at LEAST _____ above the underground installation.

A. 6 inches
B. 12 inches
C. 10 inches
D. 8 inches

33. Electric signs shall be at LEAST _____ above areas accessible to vehicles unless protected from physical damage.

A. 12 feet
B. 14 feet
C. 16 feet
D. 18 feet

34. For a one-family dwelling unit, the service disconnecting means shall have a rating of NOT less than _____ when provided with a 240/240-volt, single-phase electrical system.

A. 60 amperes
B. 100 amperes
C. 150 amperes
D. 200 amperes

35. Unless adequate protection such as a steel plate is provided where a cable or raceway is installed through bored holes in wood members, holes shall be bored so that the edge of the hole is NOT less than _____ from the nearest edge of the wood member.

A. 1 inch
B. 1½ inches
C. 1¾ inches
D. 1¼ inches

36. Where a conduit longer than 24 inches contains two (2) ungrounded conductors, one (1) grounded conductor and one (1) equipment grounding conductor, the conduit may be filled to a MAXIMUM of _____ of its cross-sectional area.

A. 40 percent
B. 31 percent
C. 53 percent
D. 40 percent

37. Given: Four (4) size 2/0 AWG conductors contained in a trade size 2 in. conduit enter a pull box on the "east" side. The conductors then make a U turn and exit in a trade size 2½ in. conduit on the same side. What is the MINIMUM distance required, in inches, from the "east" side of the box to the opposite "west" side of the box?

A. 12 inches
B. 15 inches
C. 17 inches
D. 18 inches

38. At LEAST _____ of free conductor, measured from the point in the box where it emerges from its raceway, shall be left at each junction box or outlet box for splices or connection to devices.

A. 4 inches
B. 6 inches
C. 8 inches
D. 12 inches

39. Where heating elements of electric space-heating cables are installed in ceilings they shall be separated at LEAST _____ from the edge of outlet boxes and junction boxes that are to be used for mounting surface luminaires.

A. 2 in.
B. 6 in.
C. 8 in.
D. 10 in.

40. A metal underground water pipe is permitted for use as a grounding electrode where the water pipe is in direct contact with the earth for at LEAST _____ or more.

A. 5 feet
B. 8 feet
C. 20 feet
D. 10 feet

41. Overhead spans of open conductors of not over 300 volts to ground shall have a clearance of NOT less than _____ over residential driveways.

A. 12 feet
B. 10 feet
C. 15 feet
D. 18 feet

42. Single-phase, 125-volt, 15- and 20-ampere, receptacle outlets installed in floors of dwelling units shall not be counted as part of the required number of receptacle outlets, if they are MORE than _____ from the wall.

A. 18 inches
B. 12 inches
C. 30 inches
D. 24 inches

43. Where applying the general method of calculation for dwelling units, the load for household electric clothes dryer shall be a MINIMUM of _____ or the nameplate rating, whichever is larger, for each dryer served.

A. 4000 watts
B. 5000 watts
C. 7000 watts
D. 6000 watts

44. A transformer vault is required to be provided with a door sill or curb with a height of NOT less than _____.

A. 6 inches
B. 8 inches
C. 2 inches
D. 4 inches

45. A hazardous location where easily ignitible fibers or materials producing combustible flyings are handled, manufactured, or used, but where they are not likely to be in suspension in the air in quantities sufficient to produce ignitible mixtures is a _____ location.

A. Class I
B. Class II
C. Class III
D. Class IV

46. Given: A dairy farm with a 120/240-volt, single-phase electrical system will have the following three (3) loads supplied by a common service: one 18,000 VA, one 16,000 VA and one 10,000 VA. What is the demand load, in amperes, on the ungrounded (phase) service-entrance conductors?

A. 183 amperes
B. 152 amperes
C. 304 amperes
D. 114 amperes

47. What is the MINIMUM general lighting demand load, in VA, of an office building consisting of four (4) offices having a floor space of 20 feet x 30 feet each?

A. 780 VA
B. 3,900 VA
C. 4,800 VA
D. 3,120 VA

48. A circuit breaker protecting a single non-motor-operated appliance shall not exceed 20 amperes if the overcurrent rating is not marked and the appliance is rated _____ or less.

A. 13.3 amperes
B. 15.3 amperes
C. 16.0 amperes
D. 14.3 amperes

49. Where two (2) or more single-phase household electric ranges used in an instructional program, are supplied by a 3-phase, 4-wire feeder or service, the total load shall be calculated on the basis of _____ the MAXIMUM number connected between any two (2) phases.

A. one-third
B. twice
C. one-half
D. three times

50. As a general rule, receptacle outlets provided for the small appliance countertop circuits in the kitchen of a dwelling, shall be located above the countertop or work surface, but NOT more than _____ above the countertop or work surface.

A. 6 inches
B. 12 inches
C. 20 inches
D. 18 inches

51. Outside open overhead individual conductors over 1000 volts shall be a MINIMUM size of _____ copper where not supported by a messenger wire when the conductor span is 60 feet in length.

A. 10 AWG
B. 8 AWG
C. 6 AWG
D. 4 AWG

52. A hermetic motor-compressor that is protected against overloads by an inverse-time circuit breaker, shall be rated at NOT more than _____ of the motor-compressor full-load current.

A. 80%
B. 110%
C. 115%
D. 125%

53. What is the MAXIMUM standard size inverse-time circuit breaker that may be used for overcurrent protection for a branch-circuit supplying a 4.5 kW, 240-volt, single phase, 30 gallon storage-type water heater?

A. 40 amperes
B. 25 amperes
C. 30 amperes
D. 20 amperes

54. For 120-volt, 15- and 20 ampere branch circuits, the rating of any one (1) cord-and-plug connected utilization equipment not fastened in place shall NOT exceed _____ of the branch circuit ampere rating.

A. 80 percent
B. 70 percent
C. 60 percent
D. 50 percent

55. Generally, where installed on the outside of a raceway, the length of the equipment bonding jumper shall NOT exceed _____ and shall be routed with the raceway.

A. 4 feet
B. 6 feet
C. 5 feet
D. 8 feet

56. Where abandoned communications cables are identified for future use with a tag, the tag shall be _____.

A. red in color
B. orange in color
C. located outside of the junction box
D. of sufficient durability to withstand the environment involved

57. When exceptions to the NEC® are not a consideration, battery back-up exit luminaires (unit equipment) of emergency systems shall receive power from _____.

A. the branch circuit that supplies normal power circuits
B. a separate dedicated lighting branch circuit
C. a 3 ft. pig-tail fed from the emergency circuit
D. the same branch circuit serving the normal lighting in the area

58. Unless approved for a higher voltage, surface nonmetallic raceways are NOT approved for use where the voltage is ____ or more between conductors.

A. 300 volts
B. 240 volts
C. 125 volts
D. 150 volts

59. Circuit breakers shall be permitted to be connected in parallel _____.

A. never
B. where factory assembled
C. where the load to be supplied is not greater than 100 amperes
D. where the nominal voltage to ground is not more than 300 volts

60. All services supplying dwelling units shall be provided with:

I. a surge-protective device (SPD)
II. ground-fault circuit interrupter (GFCI) protection

A. I only
B. II only
C. Either I or II
D. Neither I nor II

61. Where a device box having dimensions of 3 in. x 2 in. x 2¾ in. contains a receptacle outlet, how may size 12 AWG conductors are permitted to be installed in the box?

A. six
B. five
C. four
D. seven

62. Given: An underground run of PVC with size 6 AWG conductors is the wiring method used to supply an air-conditioning unit that is protected by an overcurrent protective device rated 60 amperes. What is the MINIMUM size wire-type copper equipment grounding conductor that must be installed in the conduit?

A. 10 AWG
B. 12 AWG
C. 6 AWG
D. 8 AWG

63. In compliance with the NEC®, a trade size 1¼ in. electrical metallic tubing (EMT) may contain a MAXIMUM of _____ size 4 AWG copper THWN conductors where the tubing is more than 24 inches in length.

A. four
B. seven
C. six
D. ten

64. A one-family dwelling unit is to have the following fastened in place appliances installed:

1,200 VA dishwasher
4,000 VA water heater
1,150 VA garbage disposer
700 VA attic fan
1,920 VA garage door opener

The demand load, in VA, on the ungrounded service-entrance conductors for the listed appliances is _____ when using the general method of calculations for dwelling units.

A. 7,728 VA
B. 6,728 VA
C. 6,276 VA
D. 8,970 VA

65. Generally, where switches or circuit breakers are used as the main disconnecting means for a building service, they shall be installed such that the center of the grip of the operating handle of the switch or circuit breaker, when in its highest position, is NOT more than _____ above the floor or working platform.

A. 6 feet
B. 7 feet
C. 6 feet, 6 inches
D. 6 feet, 7 inches

66. A single-phase, 125-volt, 15- or 20-ampere receptacle outlet shall be installed at each residential kitchen countertop and work surface that is at LEAST _____ or wider.

A. 12 inches
B. 24 inches
C. 36 inches
D. 20 inches

67. What is the MAXIMUM standard size overcurrent protection permitted for the protection of resistance-type fixed electric space heating equipment?

A. 40 amperes
B. 50 amperes
C. 60 amperes
D. 70 amperes

68. Where exceptions are not a consideration, a multiwire branch circuit may supply only ____

A. 3-phase loads
B. line to line loads
C. line to ground
D. line to neutral

69. Which of the following is NOT a requirement for an intersystem bonding termination?

A. Consist of not less than three terminals.
B. Connected to the meter enclosure only with a minimum size 8 AWG conductor.
C. Terminals shall be listed for grounding and bonding.
D. Be accessible for connection and inspection.

70. The service equipment for a mobile home shall have an ampere rating of NOT less than _____ at 120/240-volts, single-phase.

A. 100 amperes
B. 50 amperes
C. 60 amperes
D. 150 amperes

71. Given: A commercial building provided with a 208Y/120-volt, 3-phase, electrical system has a calculated demand load of 72,000 VA; the ungrounded service-entrance conductors must have an ampacity of at LEAST _____.

A. 200 amperes
B. 350 amperes
C. 300 amperes
D. 250 amperes

72. For emergency systems, where internal combustion engines are used as the prime mover, an on-site fuel supply shall be provided with an on-premises fuel supply sufficient for NOT less than _____ full-demand operation of the system.

A. 8 hours
B. 4 hours
C. 6 hours
D. 2 hours

73. Which one of the following wiring methods is NOT approved for use in assembly locations, unless encased in concrete?

A. EMT
B. Schedule 80 PVC
C. Type MC cable
D. Type AC cable

74. In an industrial establishment, what is the MAXIMUM length of 200 ampere rated busway that may be tapped to 600 ampere rated busway, without additional overcurrent protection?

A. 10 feet
B. 25 feet
C. 50 feet
D. 75 feet

75. Thermal insulation shall not be installed above a recessed luminaire or within _____ of the recessed luminaire's enclosure unless, the luminaire is identified as Type IC for insulation contact.

A. 3 in.
B. 2 in.
C. 1 in.
D. 1/2 in.

76. Which of the following listed is considered a Class III, Division 2 location?

A. A grain storage silo.
B. A petroleum tank farm.
C. The area of a textile mill where cotton is processed.
D. A warehouse where cotton is stored.

77. Where the heating, air-conditioning or refrigeration equipment is installed on the roof of a commercial, industrial, or an apartment building, a single-phase, 125-volt, 15- or 20-ampere receptacle outlet _____.

A. is required to be within at least 100 ft. from the equipment
B. may be connected to the line side of the equipment disconnecting means, provided the receptacle is of the GFCI type
C. shall be located on the same level and within 25 ft. of the equipment
D. is permitted to be connected to the load side of the equipment disconnecting means, if within 10 ft. of the equipment and GFCI protected.

78. In Class II, Division 1 locations, where pendant mounted luminaires are suspended by rigid metal conduit (RMC) or intermediate metal conduit (IMC) and a means for flexibility is not provided, the conduit stems shall have a length of NOT more than _____.

A. 12 inches
B. 18 inches
C. 24 inches
D. 30 inches

79. In a dwelling unit bedroom, any wall space that is at LEAST _____ or more in width must be provided with a general-use 15- or 20-ampere, 125-volt, single-phase receptacle outlet.

A. 2 feet
B. 4 feet
C. 6 feet
D. 10 feet

80. Where a receptacle outlet is installed on an island in the kitchen of a dwelling unit, the receptacle is required to be located NOT more than _____below the work surface of the island.

A. 24 inches
B. 12 inches
C. 20 inches
D. 18 inches

END OF JOURNEYMAN FINAL EXAM #2

JOURNEYMAN ELECTRICIAN'S EXAM PREP GUIDE
PRACTICE EXAM #1
ANSWER KEY

ANSWER	REFERENCE	NEC PG. #
1. C	250.53(B)	pg. 121
2. B	250.102(C)(1) Table 250.102(C)(1)	pg. 127 pg. 127
3. A	502.10(B)(4)	pg. 379
4. D	300.5(B)	pg. 142
5. D	Table 310.16 Table 310.15(C)(1)	pg. 161 pg. 160

Size 1/0 AWG THW ampacity = 150 amperes before adjusting
150 amperes x 80% (adjustment factor) = 120 amperes

6. A	Article 100	pg. 34
7. C	430.22 Table 310.16	pg. 313 pg. 161

FLC of motor = 70 amperes x 125% = 87.5 amperes
Size 3 AWG THW with an ampacity of 100 amperes should be selected.

8. C	240.4(B)(1),(2)&(3) Table 240.6(A)	pg. 98 pg. 100
9. B	Table 430.250	pg. 333
10. A	525.21(A)	pg. 463
11. B	Annex C, Table C.1	pg. 730
12. B	215.3	pg. 72

240 amperes x 125% = 300 amperes

13. C	350.30(A)	pg. 209
14. C	314.28(A)(1)	pg. 188

15. D	Chapter 9, Note 4 to Tables	pg. 695
16. C	Table 348.22	pg. 208
17. D	680.23(B)(2)	pg. 569
18. C	680.11(A)	pg. 566
19. A	700.12(C)	pg. 609
20. C	Table 110.26(A)(1) Condition 3	pg. 50
21. B	210.60(B)	pg. 70
22. B	410.68	pg. 281
23. C	300.4(G)	pg. 142
24. C	500.5(D)	pg. 363
25. A	Single-Phase Current Formula I = P ÷ E	

$$\frac{15\text{ kVA} \times 1{,}000}{240\text{ volts}} = \frac{15{,}000}{240} = 62.50\text{ amperes}$$

##

JOURNEYMAN ELECTRICIAN'S EXAM PREP GUIDE
PRACTICE EXAM #2
ANSWER KEY

ANSWER	REFERENCE	NEC. PG. #
1. A	210.8(B)(3)	pg. 63
2. D	430.84, Exception	pg. 323
3. D	220.14(I)	pg. 75
4. D	Table 310.4(A) Table 310.16	pg. 153 pg. 161
5. B	250.112(M)	pg. 129
6. A	517.64(A)(1),(2)&(3)	pg. 449
7. A	Table 310.17	pg. 162
8. C	314.16(B)(4)	pg. 183
9. D	430.6(A)(1)	pg. 309
10. C	220.14(F) 600.5(C) 210.19(A)(1)(a)	pg. 75 pg. 509 pg. 65

1,200 VA x 125% = 1,500 VA

ANSWER	REFERENCE	NEC. PG. #
11. A	Annex C, Table C.11(A)	pg. 794
12. C	422.11(C)	pg. 287
13. A	500.5(B)	pg. 362
14. D	300.6(D)	pg. 144
15. C	210.18	pg. 65
16. D	424.22(B)	pg. 293
17. B	645.5(B)(1)	pg. 547
18. C	332.30	pg. 197
19. A	404.14(B)(2)	pg. 266
20. A	300.5(D)(1)	pg. 142

21. B	Table 250.122	pg. 133
22. C	230.95	pg. 96
23. A	Table 310.16 Table 310.15(B)(1) Table 310.15(C)(1)	pg. 161 pg. 159 pg. 160

Size 500 KCMIL THWN copper ampacity before derating = 380 amperes
380 amperes x .67 (temp. correction) x .7 (adjustment factor) = 178.22 amperes

24. C	348.20(A)(2)c. 410.117(C)	pg. 208 pg. 283
25. C	501.15(C)(3)	pg. 371

##

JOURNEYMAN ELECTRICIAN'S EXAM PREP GUIDE
PRACTICE EXAM #3
ANSWER KEY

ANSWER	REFERENCE	NEC PG. #
1. B	210.11(C)(4), Exception	pg. 64
2. C	Table 430.250	pg. 333
3. D	324.10(B)(2)	pg. 193
4. B	210.8(A)(9)	pg. 62
5. D	376.56(A)	pg. 229
6. A	352.26	pg. 211
7. B	250.52(A)(5)(a)	pg. 120
8. D	350.12	pg. 209
9. B	110.14(C) Table 310.16 Table 310.15(B)(1)	pg. 48 pg. 161 pg. 159

Size 3 AWG THHN ampacity before derating = 110 amperes (90ºC Column)
110 amperes x .96 (temperature correction) = 105.6 amperes

*NOTE: Size 3 AWG (60ºC Column) with an ampacity of 85 amperes should be selected from Table 310.16.

10. D	800.44(B)	pg. 665
11. B	Table 352.30	pg. 211
12. A	250.24(C)	pg. 115
13. B	392.10(B)(1)(a)	pg. 237
14. B	440.64	pg. 340
15. C	210.8(B)(2)	pg. 62
16. D	410.54(C)	pg. 280
17. D	430.24(1)&(2)	pg. 314

18. A	Table 250.122	pg. 133
19. C	220.12(A) Table 220.12 210.20(A) Article 100 Definitions	pg. 74 pg. 75 pg. 66 pg. 34

100 ft. x 75 ft. = 7,500 sq. ft. x 1.9 VA = 14,250 VA

*NOTE: The Note directly below Table 220.12 clarifies that the 125% multiplier for a continuous load as specified in 210.20(A) is already included in the unit load values in the table when calculating the minimum lighting load for a specified non-dwelling occupancy.

20. B	300.34	pg. 149
21. A	250.66(B)	pg. 124
22. B	Table 630.11(A) Table 310.16	pg. 540 pg. 161

.78 (duty cycle) x 50 amperes (primary current) = 39 amperes
*NOTE: Tbl. 310.16 indicates size 8 AWG conductors should be selected.

23. C	647.1	pg. 553
24. B	517.19(B)(1)&(2)	pg. 439
25. B	400.10 400.12(2)	pg. 258 pg. 259

##

JOURNEYMAN ELECTRICIAN'S EXAM PREP GUIDE
PRACTICE EXAM #4
ANSWER KEY

ANSWER	REFERENCE	NEC PG. #
1. A	424.44(E)	pg. 294
2. B	110.26(C)(3)	pg. 51
3. A	680.21(A)(3)	pg. 567
4. D	250.53(A)(5)	pg. 121
5. C	240.40	pg. 104
6. D	Chapter 9, Table 8 Voltage-drop formula	pg. 705

$$VD = \frac{2KID}{CM} \quad VD = \frac{2 \times 12.9 \times 80 \text{ amps} \times 200 \text{ ft.}}{52,620 \text{ CM}} = 7.84 \text{ volts}$$

ANSWER	REFERENCE	NEC PG. #
7. B	501.15(A)(1)	pg. 370
8. B	90.1(A)	pg. 29
9. D	Table 514.3(B)(1)	pg. 416
10. B	517.31(A)	pg. 441
11. C	340.12(1)	pg. 204
12. B	Trade & General Knowledge 3-Phase Current Formula	

$$I = \frac{kVA \times 1,000}{E \times 1.732} \quad I = \frac{90 \times 1,000}{208 \times 1.732} = \frac{90,000}{360.25} = 250 \text{ amperes}$$

ANSWER	REFERENCE	NEC PG. #
13. C	680.26(B) 680.26(B)(1)(a)	pg. 579 pg. 579
14. A	210.8(E)	pg. 63
15. B	430.32(A)(1)	pg. 316
16. C	Table 210.21(B)(3)	pg. 67
17. D	250.64(C)(1)	pg. 122

18. B	Table 314.16(B)	pg. 184

Size 12 AWG = 2.25 cu. in. x 6 (existing wire in box) = 13.5 cu. in.

27.0 cu. in. (allowable fill of box)
-13.5 cu. in. (existing wire in box)
13.5 cu. in. (remaining space available)

$\frac{\text{13.5 cu. in. (remaining space)}}{\text{2.5 cu. in. (\#10)}}$ = 5.4 = 5 size 10 AWG wires may be added

19. B	550.10(G)	pg. 474
20. D	511.7(A)(1)	pg. 409
21. D	500.5(C)	pg. 363
22. C	422.10(A) 422.13	pg. 287 pg. 288
23. A	422.11(B)	pg. 287
24. D	250.53(A)(4)	pg. 121
25. C	Chapter 9, Table 4 Chapter 9, Table 5	pg. 696 pg. 701

Size 1 AWG THW = .1901 sq. in. x 5 = .9505 sq. in.
Size 3 AWG THW = .1134 sq. in. x 5 = .567 sq. in.
Total = 1.5175 sq. in.

*NOTE: A trade size 2½ in. IMC with an allowable 40% fill of 2.054 sq. in. should be selected from Table 4 of Chapter 9.

##

JOURNEYMAN ELECTRICIAN'S EXAM PREP GUIDE
PRACTICE EXAM #5
ANSWER KEY

ANSWER	REFERENCE	NEC PG. #
1. D	430.6	pg. 308
2. B	409.102(B)	pg. 276
3. C	334.80 Table 310.16	pg. 204 pg. 161
4. B	555.33(A)(4)	pg. 502
5. A	550.32(F)	pg. 480
6. C	Table 310.4(A) Table 310.16 Table 310.15(B)(1)	pg. 154 pg. 161 pg. 159

Size 6 AWG AL XHHW ampacity before correction = 55 amperes
55 amperes x .87 (temperature correction) = 47.85 amperes

ANSWER	REFERENCE	NEC PG. #
7. A	501.15(C)(6)	pg. 371
8. D	3-phase Power Formula	

First find the VA: 208 volts x 1.732 x 243 amperes = 87,542 VA
87,542 ÷ 1000 = 87.5 kVA

ANSWER	REFERENCE	NEC PG. #
9. C	Table 300.5, Column 1	pg. 143
10. B	330.30(D)(2)	pg. 196
11. A	Table 344.30(B)(2)	pg. 207
12. C	682.11	pg. 580
13. D	300.5(E)	pg. 142
14. C	250.112(I)	pg. 129
15. A	Single-Phase Current Formula	

$I = \frac{\text{power}}{\text{volts}} \quad I = \frac{18 \text{ kW} \times 1{,}000}{240 \text{ volts}} = \frac{18{,}000}{240} = 75 \text{ amperes}$

16. A	250.24(A)	pg. 114
17. A	504.10(A)	pg. 386
18. B	210.62	pg. 70

$$\frac{\text{80 ft. (show window)}}{\text{12 ft. (per receptacle)}} = 6.7 = 7 \text{ receptacles}$$

19. D	680.22(A)(2)	pg. 567
20. A	430.24(1)&(2) Table 430.250 Table 310.16	pg. 314 pg. 333 pg. 161

15 hp FLC - 42 amperes x 125% = 52.5 amperes
7½ hp FLC - 22 amperes x 100% = 22.0 amperes
3 hp FLC – 9.6 amperes x 100% = 9.6 amperes
Total = 84.1 amperes

*NOTE: Size 4 AWG THWN conductors with an ampacity of 85 amperes should be selected from Table 310.16.

21. D	450.11(A)	pg. 346
22. C	310.10(G)(2)-(4)	pg. 156
23. C	300.5(B) 310.10(B)&(C) Table 310.4(A)	pg. 142 pg. 156 pg. 153
24. C	450.42	pg. 348
25. B	680.22(B)(1)	pg. 567

###

JOURNEYMAN ELECTRICIAN'S EXAM PREP GUIDE
PRACTICE EXAM #6
ANSWER KEY

ANSWER	REFERENCE	NEC PG. #
1. B	Ohms Law I = voltage ÷ ohms = amperes	
2. A	Article 100 - Definitions	pg. 33
3. B	210.11(C)(2)	pg. 64
4. D	300.6(A)	pg. 144
5. C	352.44	pg. 211
6. D	110.26(E)(1)(a)&(c)	pg. 51
7. A	430.14(A)	pg. 313
8. A	410.10(D)	pg. 278
9. D	Single-phase Current Formula I = P ÷ E 310.12(A) Table 310.12	 pg. 157 pg. 157

$$I = \frac{36{,}000\ VA}{240\ volts} = 145.8 \text{ amperes} \times .83 = 121 \text{ amperes}$$

Size 2 AWG copper conductors with an ampacity of 125 amperes should be selected from Table 310.12.

ANSWER	REFERENCE	NEC PG. #
10. A	430.6(A)(1)	pg. 309
11. D	430.32(A)(1)	pg. 316
12. B	550.32(A)	pg. 479
13. A	404.2(B)	pg. 263
14. D	210.11(C)(1)-(4)	pg. 64
15. D	240.4(D)(2)(1)	pg. 99
16. C	645.5(G)	pg. 548
17. C	210.70(A)(2)(3)	pg. 71

18. B 406.9(A) pg. 269

19. B 430.110(A) pg. 326

20. B 3-phase current formula

$I = VA \div volts \times 1.732$

$I = \frac{7,500\ VA}{208 \times 1.732} = \frac{7,500}{360.25} = 20.82$ amperes

21. A 240.22(1) pg. 103

22. C 590.6(B)(2)(3)d. pg. 506

23. D 430.6(A)(2) pg. 309

24. A 210.8(A)(7) pg. 62

25. D 314.72(E) pg. 190

###

JOURNEYMAN ELECTRICIAN'S EXAM PREP GUIDE
PRACTICE EXAM #7
ANSWER KEY

ANSWER	REFERENCE	NEC PG. #
1. B	430.22	pg. 313
2. C	410.10(F)	pg. 278
3. D	220.11	pg. 74
4. D	240.5(B)(1)	pg. 100
5. A	110.16	pg. 48
6. C	Table 430.250 430.22	pg. 333 pg. 313

FLC of motor = 30.8 amperes amperes x 125% = 38.5 amperes

ANSWER	REFERENCE	NEC PG. #
7. B	430.42(C)	pg. 318
8. C	210.8(A)(1)-(7)	pg. 62
9. A	210.23(A)(2)	pg. 67
10. A	Table 314.16(A)	pg. 184
11. D	110.26(A)(2)	pg. 50
12. B	530.14	pg. 465
13. C	Article 100 - Definitions 210.19(A)(1)(a)	pg. 34 pg. 65

14,000 VA (continuous load) x 125%= 17,500 VA

120 volts x 20 amperes = 2,400 VA of 1 circuit

$\frac{\text{17,500 VA (load)}}{\text{2,400 VA (circuit)}}$ = 7.29 = 8 – 120 volt, 20-ampere lighting circuits

ANSWER	REFERENCE	NEC PG. #
14. D	Article 100 - Definitions	pg. 37
15. B	250.32(B)(1) Table 250.122	pg. 118 pg. 133

16. D	Table 430.250 430.22 Table 310.16	pg. 333 pg. 313 pg. 161

FLC of motor – 80 amperes x 125% = 100 amperes
Size 3 AWG 75°C rated CU conductors with an ampacity of 100 amperes should be selected from Table 310.16.

17. A	501.15(A)(4), Exception 1	pg. 370
18. B	Table 352.30	pg. 211
19. C	605.9(B)	pg. 516
20. C	314.16(B)(4)	pg. 183
21. D	Article 100 – Definitions	pg. 34
22. A	501.125(A)(1)-(4)	pg. 375
23. B	110.14(C)(1)(b)(1)	pg. 48
24. A	Table 310.16 Table 310.15(B)(1) Table 310.15(C)(1)	pg. 161 pg. 159 pg. 160

500 kcmil THWN copper ampacity before derating = 380 amperes
380 amps x .67 (temp. correction) x .7 adj. factor = 178.22 amperes

25. D	406.3(D)	pg. 267

##

JOURNEYMAN ELECTRICIAN'S EXAM PREP GUIDE
PRACTICE EXAM #8
ANSWER KEY

ANSWER	REFERENCE	NEC PG. #
1. A	Table 430.52 430.52(C)(1), Exception 1	pg. 319 pg. 318
2. D	Table 314.16(B)	pg. 184

Size 12 AWG – 2.25 cu. in x 5 wires = 11.25 cu. in.
Size 10 AWG - 2.50 cu. in. x 6 wires = 15.00 cu. in.
TOTAL = 26.25 cu. in.

ANSWER	REFERENCE	NEC PG. #
3. A	600.32(I)	pg. 572
4. A	Table 220.55, Column C 210.19(A)(3) Table 250.122	pg. 78 pg. 65 pg. 133
5. B	Article 100 - Definitions	pg. 37
6. C	210.52(A)(1)	pg. 68
7. A	680.23(A)(5)	pg. 568
8. C	450.3(B) Table 450.3(B)	pg. 343 pg. 344

100 amperes x 125% = 125 amperes

ANSWER	REFERENCE	NEC PG. #
9. D	Table 110.26(A)(1)	pg. 51
10. B	250.35(A) 250.30(A)(1)	pg. 119 pg. 116
11. C	320.108	pg. 191
12. A	90.5(A)	pg. 30
13. D	340.10(1)	pg. 204
14. B	300.22(C)(1)	pg. 148

15. C Single-phase current formula

I = power ÷ volts

$$I = \frac{10{,}000 \text{ watts}}{240 \text{ volts}} = 41.6 \text{ amperes}$$

16. A 240.51(B) pg. 105

17. D 680.56(B) pg. 577
Table 400.4 pg. 254

18. D 220.14(H)(2) pg. 75

19. D 680.22(A)(4) pg. 567

20. A Article 100 – Definitions pg. 38

21. C 220.14(J) pg. 75

70 ft. x 30 ft. = 2100 sq. ft. x 3 VA = 6300 VA (house load)
120 volts x 15 amperes = 1800 VA (one circuit)

$$\frac{6300 \text{ VA (load)}}{1800 \text{ VA (circuit)}} = 3.5 = 4 \text{ general lighting circuits}$$

22. B 440.22(A) pg. 338

18 amperes x 225 % = 40.5 amperes

23. D 210.18 pg. 65

24. A 225.4 pg. 82

25. B 376.30(A) pg. 229

##

JOURNEYMAN ELECTRICIAN'S EXAM PREP GUIDE
PRACTICE EXAM #9
ANSWER KEY

ANSWER	REFERENCE	NEC PG. #
1. A	408.4(A)	pg. 272
2. C	300.5(J)(IN)	pg. 144
3. B	440.12(A)(1)	pg. 336
4. A	110.26(F)	pg. 52
5. D	Table 430.248	pg. 332
	430.24(1)&(3)	pg. 314
	Single-phase current formula	
	Table 310.16	pg. 161

FLC of motor = 28 amperes x 125% = 35.0 amperes
Non-motor load I = P÷E I = 1000 ÷ 240 = 4.1 amperes
Total load = 39.1 amperes

Size 8 AWG THW CU conductors with an ampacity of 50 amperes should be selected from Table 310.16.

ANSWER	REFERENCE	NEC PG. #
6. B	Table 300.5, Column 2	pg. 143
7. C	392.56	pg. 242
8. B	312.2	pg. 179
9. D	513.3(C)(1)	pg. 412
10. D	250.4(A)(5)	pg. 111
11. B	368.30	pg. 225
12. C	Chapter 9, Table 5	pg. 701
	Chapter 9, Table 4	pg. 699

Size 2 AWG THWN = 0.1158 sq. in. x 3 wires = 0.3474 sq. in.
Size 8 AWG THWN = 0.0366 sq. in. x 1 wire = 0.0366 sq. in.
Total = 0.3840 sq. in.

The 40% Column of Table 4 shows a trade size 1¼ in. PVC with a permitted fill of 0.581 sq. in. should be selected.

13. D	210.52(C)(1)	pg. 68
14. A	440.54(B)	pg. 340
15. A	424.34	pg. 293
16. B	210.62	pg. 70
17. C	314.28(A)(2)	pg. 188
18. D	430.103	pg. 325
19. C	240.21(B)(2)(1)	pg. 101
20. D	225.19(A)	pg. 84
21. B	250.30(A)(1) 250.28(D)(1) Table 250.102(C)(1)	pg. 116 pg. 115 pg. 127
22. D	501.15(A)(1)	pg. 370
23. B	600.5(A)	pg. 509
24. A	230.9(A)	pg. 89
25. C	430.32(A)(1) 430.32(C)	pg. 316 pg. 316

18 amperes x 140% = 25.2 amperes

##

JOURNEYMAN ELECTRICIAN'S EXAM PREP GUIDE
PRACTICE EXAM #10
ANSWER KEY

ANSWER	REFERENCE	NEC PG. #
1. C	410.30(B)(1)	pg. 279
2. A	Table 312.6(B), Column 1	pg. 185
3. C	Table 310.4(A) 310.10(B)&(C)(2)	pg. 153 pg. 156
4. B	Article 100 - Definitions	pg. 38
5. D	310.15(C)(1)	pg. 158
6. A	358.28(A)&(B)	pg. 219
7. A	320.30(B)	pg. 191
8. B	Table 110.26(A)(1)	pg. 50
9. D	517.18(A) 517.21	pg. 438 pg. 440
10. C	3-phase current formula Table 310.16	 pg. 161

$I = P \div E \times 1.732 \quad I = \frac{72{,}000 \text{ VA}}{208 \times 1.732} = \frac{72{,}000}{360.25} = 199.8$ amperes

Size 3/0 AWG THWN conductors with an ampacity of 200 amperes should be selected from Table 310.16.

ANSWER	REFERENCE	NEC PG. #
11. B	210.62	pg. 70

One receptacle is required for each 12 ft. of show window or major fraction thereof therefore, 2 receptacles are required for each 15 ft. show window.

ANSWER	REFERENCE	NEC PG. #
12. C	334.12(B)(4)	pg. 199
13. D	250.66 Table 250.66	pg. 123 pg. 123
14. A	210.52(C)(1)	pg. 69
15. D	300.7(A)	pg. 145

16. B	Table 310.4(A)	pg. 154
	Table 310.16	pg. 161
	Table 310.15(C)(1)	pg. 160

Size 4/0 AWG XHHW AL – (75°C ampacity, wet location) = 180 amperes
180 amperes x .8 (adjustment factor) = 144 amperes

17. A	110.31	pg. 52
18. C	300.4(E)	pg. 141
19. A	645.10(B)(4)	pg. 548
20. A	110.14(C)(1)(a)	pg. 48
21. D	210.8(A)(6)&(10)	pg. 62
22. D	Table 352.30	pg. 211
23. B	422.13	pg. 288
	344.80	pg. 200
	Single-phase current formula	
	Table 310.16	pg. 161

$I = P \div E \quad I = \frac{5 \text{ kW} \times 1000}{240 \text{ volts}} = \frac{5000}{240} = 20.8 \text{ amperes} \times 1.25 = 26 \text{ amperes}$

Size 10 AWG NM cable with an ampacity of 30 amperes should be selected.

24. C	210.12(A)	pg. 64
25. B	334.80	pg. 200
	Table 220.55, Notes 1 & 4	pg. 78
	Single-phase current formula	
	Table 310.16(B)	pg. 161

8 kW + 6 kW = 14 kW (treat as one range)
14 kW – 12 kW = 2 kW x 5% = 10% increase in Column C
8 kW (column C) x 110% = 8.8 kW

$I = P \div E \quad I = \frac{8.8 \text{ kW} \times 1000}{240 \text{ volts}} = \frac{8800}{240} = 36.7 \text{ amperes}$

Size 8 AWG NM cable with an ampacity of 40 amperes should be selected from the 60°C column of Table 310.16.

##

JOURNEYMAN ELECTRICIAN'S EXAM PREP GUIDE
PRACTICE EXAM #11
ANSWER KEY

ANSWER	REFERENCE	NEC PG. #
1. C	250.64(A)(3)	pg. 122
2. B	210.8(A)(2)	pg. 62
3. D	230.2(E)	pg. 89
4. A	Trade knowledge	
5. B	240.4(D)(5)	pg. 99
6. C	220.52(A)	pg. 77
7. A	422.31(A)	pg. 289
8. C	314.28(A)(1)	pg. 188
	4 in. (conduit) x 8 = 32 inches	
9. A	445.13	pg. 341
10. D	440.65	pg. 340
11. C	250.102(D)	pg. 127
12. D	332.108	pg. 198
13. B	410.11	pg. 278
14. A	410.130(F)(5)	pg. 283
15. D	680.43(B)(1)(a)	pg. 575
16. D	645.5(E)(1)(b)	pg. 547
17. B	376.22(B)	pg. 229
18. C	695.7(A)	pg. 604

19. C	Table 310.16 Table 310.15(B)(1)	pg. 161 pg. 159

1/0 AWG AL ampacity before correcting = 120 amperes
120 amperes x .82 (temperature correction factor) = 98.4 amperes

20. D	314.27(C)	pg. 187
21. B	240.83(B)	pg. 105
22. A	230.95(A)	pg. 96
23. B	310.15(C)(1)(b)	pg. 158
24. A	Article 100 – Definitions	pg. 33
25. C	422.34	pg. 290

##

JOURNEYMAN ELECTRICIAN'S EXAM PREP GUIDE
PRACTICE EXAM #12
ANSWER KEY

ANSWER	REFERENCE	NEC PG. #
1. A	250.102(A)	pg. 126
2. C	Table. 210.21(B)(2)	pg. 66
3. B	410.136(B)	pg. 284
4. D	314.16(B)(1),(2),(4)&(5) Table 314.16(B)	pg. 183 pg. 184

2 ungrounded conductors = 2 x 2.25 cu. in. = 4.50 cubic inches
2 grounded conductors = 2 x 2.25 cu. in. = 4.50 cubic inches
2 grounding conductors = 1 x 2.25 cu. in. = 2.25 cubic inches
2 cable clamps = 1 x 2.25 cu. in. = 2.25 cubic inches
1 device = 2 x 2.25 cu. in. = 4.50 cubic inches
Total = 18.00 cubic inches

ANSWER	REFERENCE	NEC PG. #
5. D	110.15	pg. 48
6. C	424.22(B)	pg. 293
7. D	390.57	pg. 237
8. A	680.23(F)(2)	pg. 569
9. C	310.10(G)(1)	pg. 156
10. A	220.43(B)	pg. 76
11. B	645.5(A)	pg. 547
12. C	Table 400.5(A)(1), Column B	pg. 257

13. B	Chapter 9, Table 5	pg. 703
	Chapter 9, Table 8	pg. 705
	Chapter 9, Table 4	pg. 699

Size 1 AWG XHHW = .1534 sq. in. x 4 wires = .6136 sq. in.
Size 6 AWG bare = .0270 sq. in.
Total = .6406 sq. in.

A trade size 1½ in. Schedule 40 PVC with an allowable fill of .794 sq. in. should be selected from Table 4 of Chapter 9.

14. D	250.97, Exception 2	pg. 126
15. B	210.11(C)(2)	pg. 64
16. A	314.23(F)	pg. 186
17. D	Table 310.4(A)	pg. 152
18. A	314.21	pg. 185
19. D	500.7(A)	pg. 364
20. C	Table 250.66	pg. 123
21. A	690.31(C)(1)(2)	pg. 589
22. B	horsepower formula	

$$HP = \frac{I \times E \times Eff.}{746 \text{ watts}}$$ *NOTE – 1 hp = 746 watts

$$HP = \frac{18.5 \text{ amps} \times 240 \text{ volts} \times .85 \text{ eff.}}{746 \text{ watts}} = \frac{3{,}774}{746} = 5.05 \text{ hp}$$

23. B	334.15(B)	pg. 199
24. C	680.21(C)	pg. 567
25. D	410.36(B)	pg. 279

##

JOURNEYMAN ELECTRICIAN'S EXAM PREP GUIDE
FINAL EXAM #1
ANSWER KEY

ANSWER	REFERENCE	NEC PG. #
1. D	230.24(B)(4)	pg. 90
2. B	90.1(A)	pg. 29
3. C	110.26(A)(2)	pg. 50
4. D	406.12(1)-(7)	pg. 271
5. C	514.9(A)	pg. 419
6. B	Trade Knowledge	
7. D	Single-Phase Current Formula	

$I = \frac{\text{Power}}{\text{volts}}$ $I = \frac{15 \text{ kW} \times 1{,}000}{240 \text{ volts}} = \frac{15{,}000}{240} = 72.1$ amperes

8. A	422.11(E)(3)	pg. 287
9. D	314.16(B) 314.16(B)(1),(2)&(5) Table 314.16(B)	pg. 183 pg. 183 pg. 184

2 - 6 AWG ungrounded conductors = 2 x 5.00 cu. in. = 10 cu. in.
1 - 6 AWG grounded conductor = 1 x 5.00 cu. in. = 5 cu. in.
1 - 8 AWG equipt. grounding = 1 x 3.00 cu. in. = 3 cu. in.
2 - internal clamps = 1 x 5.00 cu. in. = 5 cu. in.
1 - pigtail = -0- = 0 cu. in.
TOTAL = 23 cu. in.

10. B	110.75(A)	pg. 57
11. B	384.30(B)	pg. 234
12. C	230.67(A) 230.85	pg. 93 pg. 95

13. C	424.4(B) Table 310.16	pg. 291 pg. 161

[125 amperes + 2.5 amperes] x 125% = 159 amperes

*NOTE: Size 2/0 AWG conductors with an ampacity of 175 amperes should be selected from Table 310.16.

14. D	Table 430.248 430.32(A)(2)	pg. 332 pg. 316
15. D	300.6(A)	pg. 144
16. A	517.18(B)(1)	pg. 438
17. B	210.50(C)	pg. 68
18. A	230.23(B)	pg. 89
19. C	680.43(E)(3)	pg. 575
20. A	344.30(A)(1)	pg. 207
21. B	250.52(G)(4) 250.53(F)	pg. 120 pg. 121
22. D	455.9	pg. 350
23. C	430.72(B)(2) Table 430.72, Column B	pg. 322 pg. 322
24. D	300.9	pg. 145
25. A	210.52(H)	pg. 70
26. B	430.32(A)(1)	pg. 316
27. B	240.5(B)(4)	pg. 100
28. B	Table 310.16 Table 310.15(C)(1)	pg. 161 pg. 160

Size 10 AWG THHN ampacity (before adjusting) = 40 amperes
40 amps x 50% (adjustment factor for 20 wires) = 20 amperes

29. D	348.12(1)	pg. 208
30. D	250.178	pg. 137
31. C	410.130(G)(1)(2)&(3)	pg. 283
32. D	725.48(B)(1) 300.3(C)(1)	pg. 634 pg. 140

33. B	322.10(3)	pg. 192
34. C	Table 430.250 430.24(1)&(2)	pg. 333 pg. 314

10 hp - FLC = 30.8 amps x 125% = 38.5 amperes
7½ hp - FLC = 24.2 amps x 100% = <u>24.2 amperes</u>
TOTAL = 62.7 amperes

35. B	300.20(A)	pg. 147
36. A	410.68 Table 310.4(A)	pg. 281 pg. 153
37. D	800.53	pg. 665
38. B	410.62(C)(1)	pg. 281
39. A	424.36	pg. 293
40. A	680.26(B)(2)	pg. 571
41. D	230.24(B)(4)	pg. 90
42. C	680.41	pg. 574
43. D	555.34(A)(2)	pg. 502
44. A	230.95	pg. 96
45. A	555.33	pg. 502
46. D	Table 430.22(E)	pg. 314
47. A	370.10(1)	pg. 226
48. C	690.7	pg. 583 & 584
49. D	518.1	pg. 452
50. C	Table 310.16 Table 310.15(B)(1)	pg. 161 pg. 159

$\frac{200 \text{ amperes (load)}}{.75 \text{ (temp. correction)}} = 266.6$ amperes

*NOTE: Size 300 kcmil 75° rated CU conductors with an ampacity of 285 amperes should be selected from Table 310.16

51. A	Table 300.5, Note 2	pg. 143
52. C	800.44(A)(4)	pg. 665
53. D	362.30(A)	pg. 221

54. B	400.22 & 22(F)	pgs. 259 & 260
55. A	225.27	pg. 85
56. B	250.190(C)(1)	pg. 139
57. B	Chapter 9, Table 4 Chapter 9, Table 5 Note 7 to Chapter 9 Tables	pg. 696 pg. 701 pg. 695

$\frac{\text{0.897 sq. in. (conduit)}}{\text{0.0824 sq. in. (wire)}}$ = 10.8 = 11 #4 AWG THHN conductors permitted

58. D	Table 310.16	pg. 161
59. D	410.136(B)	pg. 284
60. C	334.116(B)	pg. 200
61. B	400.31(A)	pg. 260
62. B	406.9(B)(1)	pg. 270
63. C	240.21(B)(2)(1) Table 310.16	pg. 101 pg. 161

800 amperes ÷ 3 = 266.6 amperes
*NOTE: Size 300 kcmil THW CU conductors with an ampacity of 285amperes should be selected from Table 310.16.

64. A	310.10(G)(1)	pg. 156
65. A	220.84(C)(3)a. Table 220.84	pg. 81 pg. 80

8 kW x 12 = 96 kW x 41% (demand factor) = 39.36 kW demand

66. D	645.5(B)(1)	pg. 547
67. C	505.7(A)	pg. 390
68. B	520.41(A)	pg. 455
69. D	314.16(B)(4)	pg. 183
70. B	408.36, Exception 1	pgs. 273 & 274
71. A	320.10(1) 320.12(1)&(2)	pg. 190 pg. 190
72. A	300.20(A)	pg. 147
73. C	440.9	pg. 336
74. D	Article 100 Definitions	pg. 38

75. B	Single-phase Current Formula	
	310.12(A)	pg. 157
	Table 310.12	pg. 157

I = VA ÷ E   I = 42,000 VA ÷ 240 volts = 175 amperes
175 amperes x .83 = 145.25 amperes

Size 2/0 AWG XHHW aluminum conductors with an ampacity of 150 amperes should be selected from Table 310.12.

76. C	336.104	pg. 201
77. D	408.36, Exception 2	pg. 274
78. A	430.83(A)(1)	pg. 323
79. B	430.40	pg. 318
80. C	Article 100 Definitions	pg. 37

##

JOURNEYMAN ELECTRICIAN'S EXAM PREP GUIDE
FINAL EXAM #2
ANSWER KEY

ANSWER	REFERENCE	NEC PG. #
1. D	680.32	pg. 573
2. C	422.16(B)(1)(1)	pg. 288
3. C	320.30(C)	pg. 191
4. B	210.52(E)(3)	pg. 69
5. D	300.4(G)	pg. 142
6. C	250.64(E)(1) 250.106	pg. 123 pg. 129
7. A	440.22(A)	pg. 338
8. C	Article 100 – Definitions	pg. 40
9. B	110.14(C) Table 310.16 Table 310.15(C)(1)	pg. 48 pg. 161 pg. 160

10 AWG THHN ampacity before adjusting (90°C column) = 40 amperes
40 amperes x .8 (adjustment factor) = 32 amperes ampacity
However, according to 240.4(D)(7) the overcurrent protection is limited to 30 amperes.

ANSWER	REFERENCE	NEC PG. #
10. D	230.2(B)(2)	pg. 88
11. A	600.5(B)	pg. 509
12. B	250.52(A)(4)	pg. 120
13. C	411.3	pg. 286
14. A	300.5(B)	pg. 142
15. D	Table 430.248	pg. 332
16. D	470.3	pg. 352

17. B	314.28(A)(2)	pg. 188

3 inches (raceway) x 6 = 18 inches

18. A	550.32(A)	pg. 479
19. B	701.12(J)	pg. 614
20. D	Table 400.4	pg. 253
21. C	680.74(B)	pg. 579
22. D	210.8(A)(10) 210.12(A)	pg. 62 pg. 64
23. A	Table 300.5, Column 4	pg. 143
24. C	110.14	pg. 47
25. C	600.5(C)(2)	pg. 509
26. A	445.13(A)	pg. 341
27. C	Three-phase current formula	

$$\frac{75 \text{ kVA x } 1{,}000}{480 \text{ x } 1.732 \text{ x } .9} = \frac{75{,}000}{748.22} = 100.2 \text{ amperes}$$

28. B	392.56	pg. 242
29. D	Chapter 9, Note 4	pg. 695
30. D	352.20(B)	pg. 211
31. A	450.21(A)	pg. 346
32. B	300.5(D)(3)	pg. 142
33. B	600.9(A)	pg. 510
34. B	230.79(C)	pg. 94
35. D	300.4(A)(1)	pg. 141
36. A	Chapter 9, Table 1	pg. 695
37. C	314.28(A)(2)	pg. 188

2.5 in. (largest conduit) x 6 = 15 in. + 2 in. (additional conduit) = 17 inches

38. B	300.14	pg. 146
39. C	424.39	pg. 294
40. D	250.52(A)(1)	pg. 120
41. A	225.18(2)	pg. 84

42. A	210.52(A)(3)	pg. 68
43. B	220.54	pg. 77
44. D	450.43(B)	pg. 348
45. C	500.5(D)	pg. 363
46. B	220.103 Table 220.103 Single phase current formula	pg. 81 pg. 82

18,000 VA x 100% = 18,000 VA
16,000 VA x 75% = 12,000 VA
10,000 VA x 65% = 6,500 VA
Total = 36,500 VA

$I = VA \div volts$ $I = \frac{36,500}{240} = 152$ amperes

47. D	Table 220.12	pg. 75

20 ft. x 30 ft. = 600 sq. ft. per office x 1.3 VA = 780 VA
780 VA x 4 offices = 3,120 VA demand load

Comment: The note directly below Table 220.12 clarifies that the 125% multiplier for a continuous load as specified in Section 210.20(A) is already included in the unit load values in the table when calculating the minimum lighting load for a specified non-dwelling occupancy.

48. A	422.11(E)(2)	pg. 287
49. B	220.55	pg. 77
50. C	210.52(C)(3)(1)	pg. 69
51. C	225.6(A)(2)	pg. 82
52. D	440.52(A)(3)	pg. 339
53. C	422.11(E)(3) Table 240.6(A) Single-phase current formula $I = P \div E$	pg. 287 pg. 100

$I = \frac{4.5 \text{ kW} \times 1000}{240 \text{ volts}}$ $I = \frac{4,500}{240} = 18.75$ amperes x 150% = 28 amperes

The next standard size OCP with a rating of 30 amperes should be selected.

54. A	210.23(A)(1)	pg. 67
55. B	250.102(E)(2)	pg. 127
56. D	800.25	pg. 665

57. D 700.12(I)(2)(3)a. pg. 610

58. A 388.12(3) pg. 235

59. B 240.8 pg. 100

60. A 230.67(A) pg. 93

61. C 314.16(B)(4) pg. 183
Table 314.16(A) pg. 184

6 size 12 AWG permitted in the box – 2 (device) = 4 size 12 AWG permitted

62. A 250.122(A) pg. 132
Table 250.122 pg. 133

63. B Table C.1 of Annex C pg. 731

64. B 220.53 pg. 77

1,200 VA dishwasher
4,000 VA water heater
1,150 VA garbage disposer
700 VA attic fan
<u>1,920</u> VA garage door opener
8,970 VA connected load x 75% (demand factor) = 6,728 VA demand load

65. D 240.24(A) pg. 103
404.8(A) pg. 264

66. A 210.52(C)(1) pg. 69

67. C 424.22(B) pg. 292

68. D 210.4(C) pg. 60

69. B 250.94(A)(1)-(6) pg. 125

70. A 550.32(C) pg. 479

71. A 3-phase current formula
I = VA ÷ E x 1.732

$I = \frac{72,000}{208 \times 1.732}$ $I = \frac{72,000}{360.25}$ I = 200 amperes

72. D 700.12(D)(2)(a) pg. 609

73. B 518.4(A) pg. 453

74. C 368.17(B), Exception pg. 224

$\frac{600 \text{ amperes}}{3}$ = 200 amperes Therefore, the length of the 200 ampere busway may be 50 feet.

75. A	410.116(B)	pg. 282
76. D	500.5(D)(2)	pg. 363
77. C	210.63	pg. 70
78. A	502.130(B)(4)	pg. 381
79. A	210.52(A)(2)(1)	pg. 68
80. B	210.52(C)(3)(3)	pg. 69

##

APPENDIX A
State Licensing Offices

Alabama
Electrical Contractors Board
2777 Zelda Road
Montgomery, AL 36106
(344) 420-7232
aecb.state.al.us

Alaska
Division of Occupational Licensing
Construction Contractor Section
P.O. Box 110806
Juneau, AK 99811-0806
(907)465-2550
dced.state.ak.us/occ/

Arizona
Registrar of Contractors
1700 W Washington Street, Suite 105
Phoenix, AZ 85007-2812
(602) 542-1525
azroc.gov

Arkansas
Board of Electrical Examiners
10421 W Markham Street
Little Rock, AR 72205
(501) 682-4549
Fax (501) 682-1765
labor.ar.gov/divisions/Documents/
electrician_app.pdf
(850)487-1395 Fax (850) 488-8748

California
Department of Consumer Affairs
Contractors State License Board
9821 Business Park Drive
Sacramento, CA 95827
(916) 255-3900 (800) 321-2752
cslb.ca.gov/

Colorado
State Electrical Board
1560 Broadway, Suite 110
Denver, CO 80202
(303) 894-7855
dora.state.co.us

Connecticut
Department of Consumer
Protection License Services
165 Capital Avenue, Room 147
Hartford, CT 06106
(860) 713-7240
state.ct.us/dcp

Delaware
Division of Professional Regulation
Board of Electrical Examiners
861 Silver Lake Blvd., Suite 203
Dover, DE 19904
(302) 744-4500
dpr.delaware.gov/boards/electrician/index.shtml

Florida
Dept. of Business and Professional
Regulation
Electrical Contractors' Licensing
1940 North Monroe Street
Tallahassee, FL 32399-0071
myfloridalicense.com/dbpr/

Georgia

State Construction Industry
Licensing Board
Division of Electrical Contractors
237 Coliseum Drive
Macon, GA 31217-3858
(478) 207-2440 Fax (478) 207-1425
xsos.state.ga.us/plb/

Hawaii

Department of Commerce and
Consumer Affairs
Board of Electricians and Plumbers
Division of Professional and Vocational
Licensing
P.O. Box 3469
Honolulu, HI 96801
(808) 586-3000
hawaii.gov/dcca/pvl/boards/electrician

Idaho

Division of Building Safety
Electrical Bureau, Licensing Section
1090 E Watertower
Meridian, ID 83642
(208) 334-3950 Fax (877) 810-2840
dbs.idaho.gov/

Illinois

The State of Illinois does not issue State Contractor's Licenses. Licensing is done on a local level. Look in the telephone directory under "Town of," "City of," or "County of."
Idfpr.com

Indiana

The State of Indiana does not issue State Contractor's Licenses. Licensing is done on a local level. Look in the telephone directory under "Town of," "City of," or "County of."
in.gov/pla

Kansas

The State of Kansas does not issue State Contractor's Licenses. Licensing is done on a local level. Look in the telephone directory under kansas.gov

Kentucky

Department of Housing, Buildings,
Construction
Electrical Licensing
101 Sea Hero Road, Suite 100
Frankfort, KY 40601
(502) 573-2002
dhbc.ky.gov/

Louisiana

Licensing Board of Contractors
2525 Quail Drive
Baton Rouge, LA 70808
(225) 765-2301 (800) 256-1392
1s1bc.louisiana.gov

Maine

Electricians' Examining Board
35 State House Station
Augusta, ME 04333-0035
(207) 624-8603
state.me.us/pfr/olr/

Maryland

Board of Master Electricians
500 N Calvert Street, Room 302
Baltimore, MD 21202
(410) 230-6270
dllr.state.md.us/license/master_elec

Massachusetts

Division of Professional Licensure
Board of State Examiners
Of Electricians
1000 Washington Street, Suite 710
Boston, MA 02118
(617) 727-9931
mass.gov

Iowa
Must be registered with the state. Licensing is done on a local level. Look in the telephone directory under "Town of," "City of," or "County of."
iowaworkforce.org/labor/contractor.htm

Michigan
Department of Labor
Electrical Administrative Board
7150 Harris Dr.
P.O. Box 30254
(517) 241-9320
michigan.gov/lara

Minnesota
Electrical Licensing and Inspection
443 Lafayette Rd N.
St. Paul, MN 55155
(651) 284-5005 Fax (651) 284-5743
dli.mn.gov/main.asp

Mississippi
Contractor Licensing Board
2679 Crane Ridge Dr., Suite C
Jackson, MS 39216
(601) 354-6161
msboc.us

Missouri
The State of Missouri does not issue State Contractor's Licenses. Licensing is done on a local level. Look in the telephone directory under "Town of," "City of," or "County of."
mo.gov/

Montana
State Electrical Board
301 South Park, 4th Floor
P.O. Box 200513
Helena, MT 59620-0513
(406) 841-2309-Fax

Nevada
State Contractors Board
2310 Corporate Circle, Suite 200
Henderson, NV 89074
(702) 486-1100 Lansing, MI 48909
nvcontractorsboard.com/

New Hampshire
Electricians' Licensing Board
Office of the State Fire Marshall
110 Smokey Bear Blvd.
Concord, NH 03301-0646
(603) 223-4289
nh.gov/jtboard/electricians.htm

New Jersey
Board of Examiners of Electrical Contractors
124 Halsey Street, 6th Floor
P.O. Box 45006
Newark, NJ 07101
(973) 504-6401
state.nj.us/lps/ca/electric/

New Mexico
Construction Industries Division
2550 Cerillos Rd., 3rd Floor
Santa Fe, NM 87505
(505) 476-4700
rld.state.nm.us/construction/

New York
The State of New York does not State Contractor's Licenses. Licensing is done on a local level. Look in the telephone directory

Nebraska
State Electrical Division
800 S 13th Street, Suite 100
P.O. Box 95066
Lincoln, NE 68509-5066
(402) 471-3550 Fax (402) 471-4297
electrical.state.ne.us

North Carolina
State Board of Examiners of
Electrical Contractors
3101 Industrial Dr., Suite 206
P.O. Box 18727
Raleigh NC 27619
(919) 733-9042 (800) 392-6102
Fax (800) 691-8399
ncbeec.org

North Dakota
State Electrical Board
1929 N. Washington Street, Suite A-1
Bismarck, ND 58507
(701) 328-9522 Fax (701) 328-9524
ndseb.com

Ohio
Construction Industry Licensing Board
6606 Tussing Road
P.O. Box 4009
Reynoldsburg, OH 43068-9009
(614) 644- 2223 Fax (614) 644-2618
com.ohio.gov/dico/ocilb/

Oklahoma
Occupational Licensing Service
Electrical Division
2401 NW 23rd St., Suite 2F
Oklahoma City, OK 73107-1299
(405) 521-6550
ok.gov/cib

Oregon
Department of Consumer and
Business Services
Building Codes Division-Licensing
1535 Edgewater Street, N.W.
Salem, OR 97304
(503) 378-4133
oregonbcd.org

South Carolina
Contractors Licensing Board
P.O. Box 11329
Columbia, SC 29211
(803) 896-4300
llr.state.sc.us/POL/Contractors/

South Dakota
State Electrical Commission
308 S. Pierre Street
Pierre, SD 57501
(605) 773-3573 (800)233-7765
Fax (605) 773-6213
dol.sd.gov/bdcomm/electric/

Tennessee
Board of Licensing Contractors
500 James Robertson Parkway
4th Floor
Nashville, TN 37243
(615) 741-8307
tn.gov/regboards/contractors/

Texas
Department of Licensing
P.O. Box 12157
Austin, TX 78711
(800) 803-9202 (TX)
Fax (512) 463-9468 (no applications)
license.state.tx.us/electricians/elec.htm

Pennsylvania

The State of Pennsylvania does not Issue State Contractor's Licenses. Licensing is done on a local level. Look in the telephone directory
dli.state.pa.us

Rhode Island

Department of Labor & Training
Division of Professional Regulation
1511 Pontiac Avenue
P.O. Box 20247
Cranston, RI 02920-0943
(401) 462-8000 Fax (401) 462-8872
dlt.ri.gov/

Virginia

Board for Contractors
9960 Maryland Dr., Suite 400
Richmond, VA 23233-1066
(804) 367-8511 Fax (804) 430-1033
dpor.virginia.gov/boards/contractors

Washington

Department of Labor and Industries
Electrical Section
P.O. Box 44000
Olympia, WA 98504-4000
(360) 902-5800
lni.wa.gov/TradesLicensing/
Electrical/default.asp

West Virginia

State Fire Marshal
Electrician's Licensing Section
1207 Quarrier Street, 2nd Floor
Charleston, WV 25301
(304) 558-2191 Fax (304) 558-2537
firemarshal.wv.gov/rldivision/pages/
electricallicensing.aspx

Utah

Division of Occupational Licensing
160 East 300 South
P.O. Box 146741
Salt Lake City, UT 84114-6741
(801) 530-6628
dopl.utah.gov/

Vermont

State Electricians Licensing Board
1311 US Route 302, Suite 600
Barre, VT 05641
(802) 479-7561
firesafety.vermont.gov/boards/electrical

Wisconsin
Safety and Building Division
201 West Washington Avenue
P.O. Box 7970
Madison, WI 53707-7970
(608) 266-1018
dsps.wi.gov/so/sb-homepage.html

Wyoming
Department of Fire Prevention
And Electrical Safety
Herschler Bldg., 122 W. 25th St.,
1-West
Cheyenne, WY 82002
(307) 777-7288 Fax (307) 777-7119
wyofire.state.wy.us/

NOTES

APPENDIX B

NEMA Classifications

NEMA 1 – Enclosures constructed for indoor use to provide a degree of protection to personnel against incidental contact with the enclosed equipment and to provide a degree of protection against falling dirt.

NEMA 2 – Same as NEMA 1 including protection against dripping and light splashing of liquids.

NEMA 3 – Enclosures constructed for either indoor or outdoor use to provide a degree of protection to personnel against incidental contact with the enclosed equipment; to provide a degree of protection against falling dirt, rain, sleet, snow, and windblown dust; and that will be undamaged by the external formation of the ice on the enclosures.

NEMA 3R – Same as NEMA 3 excluding protection against windblown dust.

NEMA 3S – Enclosures constructed for either indoor or outdoor use to provide a degree of protection to personnel against incidental contact with the enclosed equipment; to provide a degree of protection against falling dirt, rain, sleet, snow, and windblown dust; and in which the external mechanism(s) remain operable when ice laden.

NEMA 4 – Enclosures constructed for either indoor or outdoor use to provide a degree of protection to personnel against incidental contact with the enclosed equipment; to provide a degree of protection against falling dirt, rain, sleet, snow, windblown dust, splashing water, and hose-directed water; and that will be undamaged by the external formation of ice on the enclosure.

NEMA 4X – Same as NEMA 4 including protection against corrosion.

NEMA 5 – Enclosures constructed for indoor use to provide a degree of protection to personnel against incidental contact with the enclosed equipment; to provide a degree of protection against falling dirt; against settling airborne dust, lint, fibers, and flyings; and to provide a degree of protection against dripping and light splashing of liquids.

NEMA 6 – Enclosures constructed for either indoor or outdoor use to provide a degree of protection to personnel against incidental contact with the enclosed equipment; to provide a degree of protection against falling dirt; against hose-directed water and the entry of water during occasional temporary submersion at a limited depth; and that will be undamaged by the external formation of ice on the enclosure.

NEMA 6P – Same as NEMA 6 including protection against the entry of water during prolonged submersion at a limited depth.

NEMA 7 – Enclosures are for indoor use in locations classified as Class I, Groups A, B, C, or D, and shall be capable of withstanding the pressures resulting from an internal explosion of specified gases, and contain such an explosion sufficiently that an explosive gas-air mixture existing in the atmosphere surrounding the enclosure will not be ignited. Enclosed heat generating devices shall not cause external surfaces to reach temperatures capable of igniting explosive gas-air mixtures in the surrounding atmosphere. Enclosures shall meet explosion, hydro-static, and temperature design tests.

NEMA 9 – Enclosures are intended for indoor use in locations classified as Class II, Groups E, F, or G, and shall be capable of preventing the entrance of dust. Enclosed heat generating devices shall not cause external surfaces to reach temperatures capable of igniting or discoloring dust on the enclosure or igniting dust-air mixtures in the surrounding atmospheres. Enclosures shall meet dust penetration and temperature design test, an aging of gaskets (if used).

NEMA 12 – Enclosures constructed (without knockouts) for indoor use to provide a degree of protection to personnel against incidental contact with the enclosed equipment; to provide a degree of protection against falling dirt; against circulating dust, lint, fibers, and flyings; and against dripping and light splashing of liquids.

NEMA 12K – Same as NEMA 12 including enclosures constructed with knockouts.

NEMA 13 - Enclosures constructed for indoor use to provide a degree of protection to personnel against incidental contact with the enclosed equipment; to provide a degree of protection against falling dirt; against circulating dust, lint, fibers, and flyings; and against the spraying, splashing, and seepage of water, oil, and non-corrosive coolants.

Hazardous Location Basics

Definitions:

Hazardous location [NEC®-500] – An area where the possibility of explosion and fire is created by the presence of flammable gases, vapors, dusts, fibers or flyings.

Class I [NEC®-500.5(B)] – Those areas in which flammable gases or vapors are or may be present in the air in qualities sufficient to produce explosive or ignitible mixtures.

Class II [NEC®-500.5(C)] – Those areas made hazardous by the presence of combustible dust.

Class III [NEC®-500.5(D)] – Those areas that are hazardous because of the presence of easily ignitable fibers or flyings, but in which such fibers or flyers are not likely to be in suspension in the air in quantities sufficient to produce ignitible mixtures.

Division 1 [NEC®-500.5(B)(1), 500.5(C)(1), 500.5(D)(1)] – Division One in the normal situation, the hazard would be expected to be present in everyday production operations or during frequent repair and maintenance activity.

Division 2 [NEC®- 500.5(B)(2), 500.5(C)(2), 500.5(D)(2)] – Division Two in the abnormal situation, material is expected to be confined within closed containers or closed systems and will be present only through accidental rupture, breakage, or unusual faculty operation.

Groups [NEC®-500.6(A)(1,2,3,4) & 500.6(B)(1,2,3)] – The gases of vapors of Class I locations are broken into four groups by the code. A, B, C, and D. These materials are grouped according to the ignition temperature of the substance, its explosion pressure and other flammable characteristics.

Class II – dust locations – groups E, F, and G. These groups are classified according to the ignition temperature and the conductivity of the hazardous substance.

Seals [NEC®-501.15 & 502.15] – Special fittings that are required either to prevent the passage of hot gasses in the case of an explosion in a Class I area or the passage of combustible dust, fibers, or flyings in a Class II or III area.

Articles 500 through 504 (2011 NEC®) – Explains in detail the requirements for the installation of wiring of electrical equipment in hazardous locations. These articles along with other applicable regulations, local governing inspection authorities, insurance representatives, and qualified engineering/technical assistance should be your guides to the installation of wiring or electrical equipment in any hazardous or potentially hazardous location.

Typical Class I Locations:

- Petroleum refineries, and gasoline storages and dispensing areas.
- Industrial firms that are flammable liquids in dip tanks for parts cleaning or other operations.
- Petrochemicals companies that manufacture chemicals from gas and oil.
- Dry cleaning plants where vapors from cleaning fluids can be present.
- Companies that have spraying areas where they coat products with paint or plastics.
- Aircraft hangars and fuel servicing areas.
- Utility gas plants and operations involving storage and handling of liquefied petroleum gas or natural gas.

Typical Class II Locations:

- Grain elevators, flour and feed mills.
- Plants that manufacture, use, or store magnesium or aluminum powders.
- Plants that have chemical or metallurgical processes of plastics, medicines, and fireworks, etc.
- Producers of starch or candies.
- Spice-grinding plants, sugar plants, and cocoa plants.
- Coal preparation plants and other carbon-handling or processing areas.

Typical Class III Locations:

- Textile mills, cotton gins, cotton seed mills, and flax processing plants.
- Any plant that shapes, pulverizes, or cuts wood and creates sawdust or flyings.

Note: Fibers and flyings are not likely to be suspended in the air, but can collect around machinery or on lighting fixtures and where heat, a spark, or hot metal can ignite them.

Glossary

A

Adjustable-trip circuit breakers: Circuit breakers whose trip setting can be changed by adjusting the ampere rating, trip time characteristics, or both, within a particular range.

Aluminum wire: An electrical conductor composed of aluminum metal.

Ambient temperature: The surrounding temperature present in a specific area.

American Wire Gauge (AWG): Standard used to identify the size of a wire.

Ampacity: The maximum current, in amperes that a conductor can carry continuously, under the conditions of use without exceeding its temperature rating.

Ampere: The unit of current measurement. The amount of current that will flow through a one ohm resistor when one volt is applied.

Appliance: Utilization equipment, installed to perform one or more functions, such as clothes washing, air conditioning, cooking, etc.

Appliance branch circuit: A branch circuit that supplies energy to one or more outlets to which appliances are to be connected.

Arc-Fault Circuit Interrupter (AFCI): A device intended to provide protection from the effects of arc faults by recognizing characteristics unique to arcing and by functioning to de-energize the circuit when an arc fault is detected.

Automatic: Performing a function without the necessity of human intervention.

B

Balanced load: The load of an electrical system, in which two or more branches are balanced and symmetrical with respect to voltage and intensity of current.

Ballast: An electrical circuit component used with discharge lighting luminaires to provide the voltage necessary to strike the mercury arc within the lamp, and then to limit the amount of current that flows through the lamp. (Examples of discharge lighting luminaires are fluorescent and HID lighting fixtures.)

Bare conductor: A conductor with no insulation or covering of any type.

Bonded (Bonding): Connected to establish electrical continuity and conductivity.

Bonding conductor: The conductor that connects the non-current carrying parts of electrical equipment, cable raceways or other enclosures to the approved system ground conductor.

Bonding jumper: A conductor used to assure the required electrical connection between metal parts of an electrical system.

Bonding jumper, System: The connection between the grounded circuit conductor and the supply-side bonding jumper, or the equipment grounding conductor, or both, at a separately derived system.

Box: A metallic or nonmetallic electrical enclosure used to house utilization equipment and devices, the support of luminaires and pulling or terminating conductors.

Branch circuit: That portion of a wiring system beyond the final overcurrent protection device protecting the circuit and the outlet(s).

Branch circuit, Multiwire: A branch circuit that consists of two or more ungrounded conductors that have a voltage between them, and a grounded conductor that has equal voltage between it and each ungrounded conductor of the circuit and that is connected to the neutral or grounded conductor of the system.

Branch-circuit rating: The ampere rating or setting of the overcurrent device protecting the conductors.

Building: A stand-alone structure or a structure which is separated from adjoining structures by fire walls.

Buried cable: A cable laid directly in the ground without being enclosed or protected in an electrical conduit.

Bus: A conductor, or group of conductors, that serve as a common connection for two or more circuits.

Busway: A sheet metal enclosure that contains factory assembled aluminum or copper busbars which are supported on insulators.

C

Cable: One or more insulated or non-insulated wires used to conduct electrical current.

Cable assembly: A flexible assembly containing multiconductors with a protective outer sheath.

Cablebus: An assembly of insulated conductors and terminations in an enclosed, ventilated protective metal housing.

Cable tray system: An assembly of sections and associated fittings which form a rigid structural system used to support cables and raceways.

Carrying capacity: The MAXIMUM current strength, in amperes, that a conductor can safely carry continuously. (See ampacity)

Celsius: A unit of measurement, in degrees, for temperature at which the freezing point is 0° and the boiling point is 100°. It is commonly represented by the letter "C".

Circuit: A complete path over which an electric current can flow.

Circuit breaker: A device which opens and closes circuits by nonautomatic means and opens circuits automatically when a predetermined overcurrent exists.

Circuit voltage: The greatest effective difference of potential between any two conductors in a given circuit.

Circular mil (CM): A measurement of the cross-sectional area of a conductor. The area of one circular mil equals .001 inches in diameter.

Circular mil foot: A unit of conductor size, equal to a portion of the conductor having a cross-sectional area of one circular mil and length of one foot.

Clamp: A device intended to secure raceways, tubing or cables.

Commercial equipment: Equipment intended to be used on commercial, industrial or institutional premises, such as schools, hotels, office buildings, manufacturing facilities, libraries and other public buildings.

Computer: An electronic machine which, by means of stored instructions and information, performs rapid, often complex calculations or compiles, correlates and selects data.

Conductor: A wire that is used to transmit the flow of electrons in an electrical circuit. Copper wire is the most common used today in the electrical industry.

Conduit: A metallic or nonmetallic pipe or tubing used to enclosed conductors.

Connected load: The sum of the rating(s) of the load consuming equipment, connected to an electrical system or any part thereof.

Contactor: An electrically operated switch, usually by a coil or solenoid. The switch contains one or more sets of contacts which controls one or more circuits.

Continuous duty: Operation at a substantially constant load for an indefinitely long time.

Continuous load: A load in which the MAXIMUM current may continue for three hours or more.

Controller: A device, or group of devices, which serves to govern in some predetermined manner the electric power delivered to the apparatus to which it is connected.

Control panel: A panel containing switches and other protective, controlling and measuring devices for electrical equipment, motors, and/or machinery.

Copper: A brownish-red, malleable, ductile, metallic element that is an excellent conductor of electricity and heat. The most common element used for conductors in the electrical industry.

Copper Wire: An electrical conductor composed of copper metal.

Cord: A small cable, very flexible, and substantially insulated to withstand wear. There is no sharp dividing line in respect to size between a cord and a cable, and likewise no sharp dividing line in respect to the character of insulation between a cord and a stranded wire.

Cord-and-plug connected appliance: An appliance to be connected to the power source by means of a supply cord.

Cord-connected unit: A unit intended for connection to the power source by means of a supply cord to prevent vibration or enable the unit to be moved.

Cross-section: A cutting or piece of something cut off at right angles to an axis. The cross-sectional area is 100% of the cross-section.

Current: The flow of electricity in a circuit, measured in amperes. Represented by the letter "I" or "A".

Current transformer (CT): An instrument transformer with a primary winding in series with a current-carrying conductor and secondary winding connected to a meter or device which is actuated by conductor current and current changes.

D

Demand factor: The ratio of the MAXIMUM demand of a system, or part of a system, to the total connected load of a system or the part of the system under consideration. All the loads of a system are usually never used all at the same time due to the many uses of the power.

Device box: A box which houses an electrical device(s), such as receptacles and switches.

Device: Electrical components, such as receptacles, switches and dimmers, that are designed to carry and/or control electric energy as its principle function, but not use electricity.

Disconnecting means: A device, or group of devices, by which the circuit conductors are disconnected from their source of supply.

Double pole: Switch or device connected to both lines of a circuit or controlling both lines of a circuit.

Dry location: A location not normally subject to dampness or wetness. A location classified as dry may be temporarily subject to dampness or wetness, as in the case of a building under construction.

Duty cycle: The time interval occupied by a device on intermittent duty in starting, running, stopping and idling.

Dwelling: A structure that contains eating, living and sleeping space and permanent provisions for cooking and sanitation.

Dwelling unit: A dwelling with one or more rooms used by one or more people for housekeeping.

E

Effectively grounded: Grounded with sufficient low impedance and current-carrying capacity to prevent hazardous voltage build-ups.

Efficiency: The ratio of output power to input power, expressed as a percentage.

Electrical discharge luminaire: A luminaire (lighting fixture) that utilizes a ballast for the operation of the lamp.

Electrical metallic tubing (EMT): A lightweight tubular steel raceway used to enclosed conductors.

Electric circuit: The complete path of an electric current.

Electric power production and distribution network: Power production, distribution, and utilization equipment and facilities, such as electric utility systems that deliver electric power to the connected loads, that are external to and not controlled by an interactive system.

Electric sign: A fixed, stationary, or portable self-contained, electrically illuminated, utilization equipment with words or symbols designed to convey information or attract attention.

Electrode: A conducting substance through which electric current enters or leaves.

Enclosed: Surrounded by a case, housing, fence or walls which will prevent persons from accidentally contacting energized parts.

Enclosure: The case or housing of equipment or other apparatus which provides protection from live or energized parts.

Equipment: A general term including devices, luminaires, appliances, materials, machinery, apparatus, etc. used in conjunction with electrical installations.

Equipment bonding jumper: A conductor that connects two or more parts of the equipment grounding conductor.

Equipment grounding conductor: An electrical conductor that provides a low-impedance path between electrical equipment and enclosures and the system grounded conductor and grounding electrode conductor.

Explosionproof equipment: Equipment enclosed in a case that is capable of withstanding an explosion of a specified gas or vapor that may occur within it and of preventing the ignition of a specified gas or vapor surrounding the enclosure by sparks, flashes, or explosion of the gas or vapor within, and that operated at such an external temperature that a surrounding flammable atmosphere will not be ignited thereby.

F

Fahrenheit: A unit of measurement, in degrees, for temperature at which the freezing point is 32° and the boiling point is 212°. It is commonly represented by the letter "F".

Fault: An electrical defect.

Fault current: Any current that travels an unwanted path, other than the normal operating path of an electrical system.

Feeder: All circuit conductors between the service equipment or the source of a separately derived system and the final branch circuit overcurrent device.

Feeder neutral load: The maximum unbalanced load between any of the ungrounded conductors and the grounded conductor of a feeder.

Fished: A means of installing electrical wiring in existing inaccessible hollow spaces of buildings with a minimum damage to the building finish.

Fixed appliance: An appliance which is fastened in place or otherwise secured at a specific location.

Fixed equipment: Equipment intended to be permanently connected electrically and not easily moved.

Flexible cord: An assembly of two or more insulated conductors, with or without braids, contained within an overall outer covering and used for the connection of equipment to a power source.

Flexible metal conduit (FMC): A raceway consisting of metal strips which are formed into a circular cross-sectional raceway, which is used to enclose conductors.

Fluorescent light: A method of lighting which makes use of ultraviolet energy to activate a fluorescent material coated inside of the bulb's surface.

Full-load amperes (FLA): The amount of current, in amperes, in an electrical circuit when the load is operating in a full-capacity condition.

Full-load current (FLC): The current required by a motor to produce the full-load torque at the motor's rated speed.

Fuse: A protective device with a fusible element that opens the circuit by melting when subjected to excessive current.

G

Galvanizing: The process of coating metals with zinc to prevent corrosion.

Ganged switch box: A box containing more than one switch.

General lighting: Lighting designed to provide a substantially uniform level of illumination throughout an area, exclusive of any provision for special local requirements.

General-purpose branch circuit: A branch circuit that supplies a number of outlets for lighting and appliances.

General-use snap switch: A form of general-use switch constructed so that it can be installed in device and/or outlet boxes.

General-use switch: A switch for use in general distribution and branch circuits. The ampere rated switch is capable of interrupting its rated current at its rated voltage.

General-use receptacle: 125-volt, single-phase, 15-or-20 ampere receptacles connected to a branch-circuit supplying two or more receptacles provided for the purpose of supplying cord-and-plug connected loads. Not provided for specific loads such as small appliances or laundry equipment.

Generator: A device that is used to convert mechanical energy to electrical energy.

Grade: The final level or elevation of the earth at a given location.

Ground: A conducting connection between electrical circuits or equipment and the earth.

Grounded (Grounding): Connected to the earth or a conducting body connected to the earth.

Grounded circuit: A circuit in which one conductor or point (usually the neutral) is intentionally grounded, either solidly or through a grounding device.

Grounded conductor: A conductor that has been intentionally grounded.

Ground-fault: An unintentional connection between an ungrounded conductor and any grounded raceway, box, enclosure, fitting, etc.

Ground-fault circuit interrupter: An electrical device which protects personnel by detecting hazardous ground faults and quickly disconnects power from the circuit.

Grounding: The connection of all exposed non-current carrying metal parts to the earth.

Grounding conductor: A conductor used to connect equipment or the grounded circuit of a wiring system to a grounding electrode or electrodes.

Grounding electrode: A conducting object through which a direct connection to earth is established.

Grounding electrode conductor: The conductor used to connect the system grounded conductor and/or the equipment to a grounding electrode or to a point on the grounding electrode system.

H

Handhole enclosure: An enclosure for use in underground systems, provided with an open or closed bottom, and sized to allow personnel to reach into, but not enter, for the purpose of installing, operating, or maintaining equipment or wiring or both.

Health care facility: A location, either a building or a portion of a building, which contains occupancies such as, hospitals, nursing homes, limited or supervisory care facilities, clinics, medical and dental offices and either ambulatory facilities.

Hermetic refrigerant motor-compressor: A combination of a compressor and motor enclosed in the same housing, having no external shaft or shaft seals, with the motor operating in the refrigerant.

Hickey (fitting): A fitting used to mount a lighting fixture in an outlet box or on a pipe or stud. It has openings through which fixture wires may be brought out of the fixture stem.

HID lamp: A high-intensity discharge lamp.

High-intensity discharge (HID) luminaire: A luminaire (lighting fixture) that generates light from an arc lamp contained within an outer tube.

Horsepower (hp): A unit of power equal to 746 watts that describes the output of electric motors.

Hybrid system: A system comprised of multiple power sources. These power sources may include photovoltaic, wind, micro-hydro generators, engine-driven generators, and others, but do not include electrical production and distribution network systems. Energy storage systems, such as batteries, do not constitute a power source for the purpose of this definition.

I

Identified: Recognized as suitable for the use, purpose, etc.

Illumination: The supplying of light or lighting up a given area. The density of light flux projected on a surface, measured in footcandles (FC).

Impedance: The total opposition to the flow of current in an ac circuit.

Incandescent lamp: A lamp in which the light is produced by a filament of conducting material contained in a vacuum and heated to incandescence by an electric current.

Individual branch circuit: A branch circuit that supplies only one unit of utilization equipment.

Induction: The process by which an electrical conductor becomes electrified when near a charged body and becomes magnetized.

Information Technology Equipment (ITE): Equipment and systems rated 600 volts or less, normally found in offices or other business establishments and similar environments classified as ordinary locations that are used for creation and manipulation of data, voice, video, and similar signals that are not communications equipment as defined in the NEC®.

Instantaneous: A qualifying term used in giving properties and characteristics of apparatus indicating that no delay is purposely introduced in its action. Done in an instant.

Instantaneous-trip circuit breakers: Circuit breakers with no delay between the fault or overload sensing element and the tripping action of the device.

Insulated: Separated from other conducting surfaces by a dielectric substance or air space permanently offering a high resistance to the passage of current and to disruptive discharge through the substance or space.

Insulated conductor: A conductor covered with a material identified as electrical insulation.

Intensity of current: The strength of an electric current. It is the quantity of electricity that flows past any point in a circuit in one second, and is measured by a unit called the ampere. Represented by the letter "I".

Interactive system: A solar photovoltaic system that operates in parallel with and may deliver power to an electrical production and distribution network. For the purpose of this definition, an energy storage subsystem of a solar photovoltaic system, such as a battery, is not another electrical production source.

Intermittent duty: Operation for alternate intervals of (1) load and no load; or (2) load and rest; or (3) load, no load, and rest. A requirement of operation or service consisting of alternate periods of load and rest so apportioned and regulated that the temperature rise at no time exceeds that specified for the particular class of apparatus under consideration.

Intermittent load: A load in which the MAXIMUM current does not continue for three hours.

Interrupt: To stop a process in such a way that it can be resumed.

Interrupting rating: The maximum rating, in amperes, of an overcurrent protective device (OCPD).

Intersystem bonding termination: A device that provides a means for connecting bonding conductors for communications systems to the grounding electrode system.

Inverse-time circuit breakers: Circuit breakers with an intentional delay between the time when the fault or overload is sensed and the time when the circuit breaker operates. The greater the overload the less time the circuit breaker takes to trip. Conversely, the smaller the overload the more time the circuit breaker takes to trip.

Inverter: Equipment that is used to change voltage level or waveform, or both, of electrical energy. Commonly, an inverter [also known as a power conditioning unit (PCU) or power conversion system (PCS)] is a device that changes dc input to an ac output. Inverters may also function as battery chargers that use alternating current from another source and convert it into direct current for charging batteries.

J

Junction box: A box in which splices, taps or terminations are made.

K

kcmil: One thousand circular mils. Conductor sizes from 250 kcmil through 2,000 kcmil are expressed in this manner.

Kilo: A prefix often used with a physical unit to designate a quantity one thousand times as great. Designated by the letter "K".

Kilo-volt amperes (kva): One thousand (1,000) volt amperes.

Kilowatt (kw): One thousand (1,000) watts.

L

Lamp: A light source. Reference is to a light bulb, rather than a lamp.

Lampholders: Devices designed to accommodate a lamp for the purpose of illumination.

Lighting outlet: An outlet intended for the direct connection of a lampholder, a lighting fixture (luminaire) or pendant cord terminating in a lampholder.

Lighting outlets: Outlets that provide power for lighting fixtures (luminaires).

Lighting track: An assembly consisting of an energized track and luminaire units which can be positioned along the track.

Liquidtight flexible metal conduit (LFMC): A flexible metal raceway of circular cross-section with an outer liquidtight, non metallic, sunlight-resistant jacket over an inner helically-wound metal strip.

Liquidtight flexible nonmetallic conduit (LFNC): A flexible nonmetallic raceway of circular cross-section with an outer jacket which is resistant to oil, water, sunlight, corrosion, etc. The inner core varies based on intended use.

Load: The amount of electric power used by any electrical unit or appliance at any given moment.

Location, damp: Partially protected locations under canopies, marquees, roofed open porches and like locations and interior locations subject to moderate degrees of moisture, such as some basements, barns and cold storage warehouses.

Location, dry: A location not normally subject to dampness or wetness. A location classified as dry may be temporarily subject to dampness or wetness, as in the case of a building under construction.

Location, wet: Installations underground or in concrete slabs or masonry, in direct contact with the earth and locations subject to saturation with water or other liquids, such as vehicle washing areas and locations exposed to weather and unprotected.

Locked rotor: The condition when a motor is loaded so heavily that the shaft can not turn.

Locked rotor current: The steady-state current taken from the line with the rotor locked and with rated voltage applied to the motor.

Luminaire: A complete lighting fixture consisting of the lamp or lamps, reflector or other parts to distribute the light, lamp guards and lamp power supply.

M

Main bonding jumper: The connection at the service equipment that bonds together the equipment grounding conductor, the grounded conductor and the grounding electrode conductor.

MAXIMUM: The greatest value in any given group. A value greater than any which precedes or follows it in succession of values.

Metal wireway: A sheet metal raceway with a hinged or removable cover that houses and protects wires and cables laid in place after the wireway has been installed.

Mil: One thousandths of an inch (0.001").

Mobil home: A transportable factory assembled structure or structures constructed on a permanent chassis for use as a dwelling. A mobile home is not constructed on a permanent foundation but is connected to the required utilities. The term "mobile home" does not include manufactured homes.

Module: A complete, environmentally protected unit consisting of solar cells, optics, and other components, exclusive of tracker, designed to generate dc power when exposed to sunlight.

Motor: A device for converting electrical energy into mechanical energy.

Motor branch circuit: The point from the last fuse or circuit breaker in the motor circuit out to the motor.

Motor control center: An assembly of one or more enclosed sections with a common power bus and primarily containing motor control units.

Motor Efficiency: The effectiveness of a motor to convert electrical energy in to mechanical energy. The more efficient a motor is the less current it draws. Conversely, the less efficient a motor is the more current it draws.

Motor starter: An electrically operated switch (contactor) that includes overload protection.

Multiconductor cable: It consists of a number of individually insulated wires, either solid or stranded, which may or may not be grouped together within an outer covering. Sometimes an outer sheath of aluminum or steel is placed over the cable.

Multifamily dwelling: A dwelling with three or more dwelling units.

Multioutlet assembly: A metal raceway with factory-installed conductors and attachment plug receptacles. Usually surface mounted.

Multiwire branch-circuit: A branch circuit with two or more ungrounded conductors having a potential difference between them, and is connected to the neutral or grounded conductor of the system.

N

Nameplate: A plaque giving the manufacturer's name, current rating and voltage of a transformer, generator, motor, appliance, etc.

Neutral: Neither positive nor negative; having zero potential; having electrical potential intermediate between the potentials of other associated parts of the circuit, positive with reference to some parts, negative with reference to others.

Nipple: A short piece of conduit or tubing having a length not exceeding 24 inches.

Noncoincidental loads: Loads that are not on at the same time.

Nonlinear load: A load where the wave shape of the steady-state current does not follow the wave shape of the applied voltage. Examples of nonlinear loads are electronic equipment, such as computers and HID and fluorescent lighting.

Nonmetallic-sheathed cable (NM): A factory assembly of two or more insulated conductors having an outer sheath of moisture-resistant, flame-retardant, non-metallic material.

Non-time delay fuses: Fuses that may detect an overcurrent and open the circuit without any delay.

O

Ohm: The unit of measurement of electrical resistance. One ohm of resistance will allow one ampere of current to flow through a pressure of one volt.

Ohm's Law: A law which describes the mathematical relationship between voltage, current and resistance.

One-family dwelling: A dwelling with one dwelling unit.

Outlet: Any point in the electrical system where current supplies utilization equipment.

Overcurrent: Any current in excess of that for which the conductor or equipment is rated. It may result from overload, short circuit, or ground fault.

Overload: Operation of equipment in excess of normal, full-load rating, or of a conductor in excess of its rated ampacity that, when it persists for a sufficient length of time, would cause damage or dangerous overheating. A fault, such as a short circuit or ground fault, is not an overload.

Overload protection: A device that prevents overloading a circuit or motor such as a fuse or circuit breaker.

P

Panelboard: A single panel or group of assembled panels with buses and overcurrent devices, which may have switches to control light, heat or power circuits.

Parallel conductors: Two or more conductors that are electrically connected at both ends to form a single conductor.

Pendants: Hanging luminaires (lighting fixtures), that use flexible cords to support the lampholder.

Permanently-connected appliance: A hard-wired appliance that is not cord-and-plug connected.

Permanently installed swimming pool: A pool constructed in ground or partially above ground and designed to hold over 42 inches of water and all indoor pools regardless of depth.

Phase: Used in ac terminology, refers basically to time. Usually the phase position is defined by specifying the number of electrical degrees between the phase and the reference position. The number of electrical degrees that two quantities are out of phase is called the phase angle.

Phase conductor: The conductors other than the neutral conductor.

Phase converter: An electrical device that converts single-phase power to three-phase power.

Phase-to-ground voltage: The maximum voltage between any two phases of an electrical distribution system.

Portable appliance: An appliance which is actually moved or can be easily moved from one place to another in normal use.

Power (watts): A basic unit of electrical energy, measured in watts. Power is usually expressed as the letter "P" or "W".

Power (volt- amperes): The apparent power in an ac circuit or electrical system. Represented by the letters "VA".

Power factor: The ratio of the voltage and current, or volt-amperes that do useful work in an ac circuit or equipment, to the total voltage and current, volt-amperes, flowing in the circuit. Power factor is usually expressed as "pf."

Premises wiring: Basically all interior and exterior wiring installed on the load side of the service point or the source of a separately derived system.

Primary: The part of a motor or transformer having windings that are connected to the power supply line.

Primary current: The current in the primary of a transformer.

Primary winding: The coil of a transformer which is energized from a source of alternating voltage and current. The input side.

Pull box: A box used as a point to pull or feed electrical conductors in the raceway system.

R

Rated current: The load, in amperes, that a circuit breaker is intended to carry continuously without opening of the circuit.

Raceway: A metal or nonmetallic channel for enclosing and protecting conductors.

Receptacle outlets: Outlets that provide power for cord-and-plug connected equipment.

Recreational vehicle: A vehicular type unit which is self-propelled or is mounted on or pulled by another vehicle and is primarily designed as temporary living quarters for camping, travel or recreational use.

Resistance: That property of a conductor by which it opposes the flow of an electric current, resulting in the generation of heat in the conducting material. Usually measured in ohms. Resistance is usually represented by the letter "R".

Rigid metal conduit (RMC): A conduit used to enclose conductors, made of metal with a galvanized protective coating.

Rigid nonmetallic conduit (RNC): A conduit made of materials other than metal, usually polyvinyl chloride (PVC).

S

Secondary current: The current induced in the secondary of a transformer or induction coil.

Separately derived system: A premises wiring system whose power is derived from a source of electric energy or equipment other than a service. Examples of separately derived systems are transformers, generators and storage batteries. Such systems have no direct connection from circuit conductors of one system to circuit conductors of another system, other than connections through the earth, metal enclosures, metallic raceways, or equipment grounding conductors.

Series circuit: A circuit supplying energy to a number of loads connected in series. The same current passes through each load in completing its path to the source of supply.

Service: The conductors and equipment for delivering electric energy from the serving utility to the wiring system of the premises served.

Service conductors: The conductors from the service point or other source of power to the service disconnecting means.

Service drop: The overhead service conductors that extend from the last pole of the utility supply system to the service-entrance conductors at the building or structure.

Service-entrance cable (SE): A single or multiconductor assembly with or without an overall covering.

Service-entrance conductors: Conductors that connect the service equipment for the building or structure with the electrical utility supply conductors.

Service equipment: All of the necessary equipment to control the supply of electrical power to a building or a structure.

Service lateral: The underground service conductors that connect the utility's electrical distribution system with the service-entrance conductors.

Service mast: An assembly consisting of a service raceway, guy wires or braces, service head and any fittings necessary for the support of service drop conductors.

Sheath: The final outer protective coating applied to a cable.

Short circuit: The unintentional connection of two ungrounded conductors that have a potential difference between them. The condition that occurs when two ungrounded conductors (hot wires), or an ungrounded and grounded conductor of a circuit, come in contact with each other.

Short circuit protection: Any automatic current-limiting system that enables a power supply to continue operating at a limited current. and without damage, into any output overload including short-circuits.

Show window: Any window used or designed to be used for the display of goods, products, services, or advertising material. Usually visible by the general public from street or floor level.

Single phase: A term applied to a simple alternating current of uniform frequency as distinguished from polyphase currents.

Single-phase circuit: An ac circuit consisting of two or three intentionally interrelated conductors.

Solar cell: The basic photovoltaic device that generates electricity when exposed to light.

Solar photovoltaic system: The total components and subsystems that, in combination, convert solar energy into electric energy suitable for connection to a utilization load.

Spa (hot tub): An indoor or outdoor hydromassage pool or tub that is not designed to have the water discharged after each use.

Special permission: The written approval of the authority having jurisdiction.

Splice: A joint used for connecting conductors together.

Stationary appliance: A cord-connected appliance that is intended to be fastened in place or located in a dedicated space.

Switch: A device, with a current and voltage rating, used to open or close an electrical circuit.

Switchboard: A single panel or group of assembled panels with buses, overcurrent devices and instruments.

T

Temperature rise: The amount of heat that an electrical component produces above the ambient temperature.

Thermal protection: Refers to an electrical device which has inherent protection from overheating. Typically in the form of a bimetal strip which bends when heated to a certain point.

Three-phase circuit: a combination of circuits energized by ac that differ in phase by one third of a cycle, which is 120 degrees.

Three-phase power: A combination of three alternating currents (usually denoted as a, b and c) in a circuit with their voltages displaced 120 degrees or one third of a cycle.

Three-phase transformer: A combination in one unit of three single phase transformers with separate electric circuits, but having certain magnetic circuits in common. There are three magnetic circuits through the core and the fluxes in the various circuits are displaced in phase.

Time delay fuse: Fuses designed to provide a time interval upon detection of an overload, before blowing. This type of fuse is used primarily for overcurrent protection for motors.

Transformer: An electrical device that contains no moving parts, which converts or "transforms" electrical power at one voltage or current to another voltage or current.

Transformer vault: An isolated enclosure either above or below ground, with fire-resistant walls, ceiling and floor, for unattended transformers.

True power: The actual power used in an electrical circuit measured in watts or kilowatts. Represented by the letter "P" or the letter "W".

U

Unfinished basement: The portion of area of a basement which is not intended as a habitable room, but is limited to storage areas, work areas, etc.

Ungrounded: A system, circuit or apparatus without an intentional connection to ground except through potential indicating or measuring devices or other very high impedance devices.

Uninterruptible power supply: A power supply used to provide alternating current power to a load for some period of time in the event of a power failure.

Utilization equipment: Any electrical equipment which uses electrical energy for electronic, mechanical, heating, lighting, or similar purposes.

V

Ventilated: Provided with a means to permit circulation of air sufficient to remove an excess of heat, fumes or vapors.

Volt: The practical unit of electric pressure. The pressure which will produce a current of one ampere against a resistance of one ohm.

Voltage: The greatest root-mean-square (effective) difference of potential between any two conductors or the circuit concerned.

Voltage drop: The drop of pressure in an electric circuit due to the resistance of the conductor. This loss exists in every circuit. It is directly proportional to the length of the conductor, and is inversely proportional to its cross-sectional area.

Voltage, nominal: A nominal value assigned to a circuit or system for the purpose of conveniently designating its voltage class (e.g., 120/240-volts, 480Y/277-volts, 600-volts). The actual voltage at which a circuit operates can vary from the nominal within a range that permits satisfactory operation of equipment.

Voltage-to-ground: The difference of potential between a given conductor and ground.

Volt-ampere: the volt-ampere is the apparent power in an ac circuit. Represented by the letters "VA".

W

Wall mounted oven: An oven for cooking purposes designed for mounting in or on a wall or other surface and consisting of one or more heating elements.

Watt: The practical unit of power, being the amount of energy expended per second by an unvarying current of one ampere under a pressure of one volt.

Weatherproof: So constructed or protected that exposure to the weather will not interfere with successful operation.

Wireway: A metallic or nonmetallic trough with a hinged or removable cover designed to house and protect conductors and cables.

Wye connection: A connection that has one end of each coil connected together and the other end of each coil left open for external connections.

Made in the USA
Las Vegas, NV
22 September 2024

95643636R00181